Library of
Davidson College

ATLANTIC RELATIONS
Beyond the Reagan Era

ATLANTIC RELATIONS

Beyond the Reagan Era

Edited by Stephen Gill

HARVESTER WHEATSHEAF
ST. MARTIN'S PRESS, NEW YORK

First published 1989 by
Harvester Wheatsheaf,
66 Wood Lane End, Hemel Hempstead,
Hertfordshire, HP2 4RG
A division of
Simon & Schuster International Group

First published in the United States of America 1989 by
St. Martin's Press, 175 Fifth Avenue,
New York, NY 10010

© Stephen Gill 1989

All rights reserved. No part of this publication may be
reproduced, stored in a retrieval system, or transmitted,
in any form, or by any means, electronic, mechanical,
photocopying, recording or otherwise, without the
prior permission, in writing, from the publisher.

Printed and bound in Great Britain by
BPCC Wheatons Ltd, Exeter

Library of Congress Cataloging-in-Publication Data

Atlantic relations: beyond the Reagan era/edited by Stephen Gill.
   p. cm.
  Includes index
  ISBN 0–312–03268–4   45.00

  1. World politics—1975–1985.   2. World politics—1985–   3. United States—Foreign relations—1981.   I. Gill, Stephen, 1950–
D849.A835   1989
327′.09′048—dc2   89–30436   CIP

British Library Cataloguing in Publication Data

Gill, Stephen, *1950–*
  Atlantic relations: beyond the Reagan era.
  1. United States.   Foreign relations with Western
  Europe   2. Western Europe.   Foreign relations with
  United States
  I. Title
  327.7304

  ISBN 0–7450–0435–0

---

1 2 3 4 5   93 92 91 90 89

For Jill Kirby

> On three or four evenings a week I still find myself taking that path down to the river and the little wooden bridge still known to some as 'the Bridge of Hesitation'. We called it that because not so long ago, crossing it would have taken you into our pleasure district, and conscience-troubled men – so it was said – were to be seen hovering there, caught between seeking an evening's entertainment and returning home to their wives. But if sometimes I am to be seen on that bridge, leaning thoughtfully against the rail, it is not that I am hesitating. It is simply that I enjoy standing there as the sun sets, surveying my surroundings and the changes taking place around me.
>
> Kazuo Ishiguro, An Artist of the Floating World
(London, Faber and Faber, 1986), p. 99.

CONTENTS

Preface   xi

Acknowledgements   xiv

Contributors   xv

1 Introduction: Some Questions and an Overview of Trends   1
Stephen Gill

Background to the Atlanticist Debate   2
Theorising Change in Atlantic Relations   4
What has Changed?   7

2 American Perceptions and Policies   14
Stephen Gill

Continuities in American Perceptions   16
Three Images of Europe   21
Developments in the 1970s   22
Reaganism and Atlanticism   26
Reagan's Strategic Vision   28
Reaganomics and the World Economy   31
Conclusion and Prospects   35

3 Soviet Perceptions of Atlantic Relations During the Reagan Era   40
Neil Malcolm

Sources   42
Two Soviet Views of International Relations   44
European Integration   49
The Atlantic Balance of Forces   50
Conflicts in Atlantic Relations   51
The Strategic Defense Initiative   53
Perceptions and Policy   55

4 Restructuring the Atlantic Ruling Class in the 1970s and 1980s   62
Kees van der Pijl

Introduction	62
The Trilateral Concept and its Demise	64
The Rise of Neo-liberal Hegemony: New Forms of Enrichment, New Moral Codes	70
International Monetarism and the New Cold War	74
The Neo-liberal Atlantic Unity: West Germany and France	77
Struggle Between Trilateralism and Unilateralism	78
The Resurrection of Trilateralism?	81

5 Western Europe in the Atlantic System of the 1980s: Towards a New Identity?   88
David Allen and Michael Smith

Western Europe in the Atlantic System	88
A First Case Study: East–West Relations	91
East–West Trade	92
Armaments and Arms Control	94
A Second Case Study: Regional Conflicts Outside Europe	98
The Middle East	99
The Persian Gulf	102
The Western Hemisphere	103
Reassessment and Conclusion	105

6 Economic Conflicts and the Transformation of the Atlantic Order: The USA, Europe and the Liberalisation of Agriculture and Services   111
Alan W. Cafruny

Interpreting the Rise and Decline of Atlanticism	112
The Atlantic Relationship	112
The Changing Face of American Power	114
The Decline of American Hegemony	115
The Construction of Transatlantic Hegemony, 1944–60	115
The Decline of Hegemony, 1960–71	116
Minimal Hegemony: 1971 to the Present	118
Europe, the USA and the Liberalisation of Agriculture	120
The USA's Post-War Agricultural Policy: A Global New Deal	121
The Breakdown of the New Deal Settlement	122
The USA, Europe and the GATT	123
The USA, Europe and the Liberalisation of Services	125
American Domestic and International Policy: Telecommunications	126
Conclusion	129
Epilogue	131

7 Transatlantic Economic Co-operation: The Baker Initiatives and Beyond 139
David Law

Introduction	139
Structural Change and the Background to the Initiatives	140
The Baker Initiatives	142
The Fate of the Initiative on Exchange Rates	146
Prospects for Transatlantic Economic Internationalism	149
Conclusions	152
Postscript	153

8 Strategic Aspects of Atlantic Relations in the Reagan Era 156
Steve Smith

The Rise of a Second Cold War	164
The Resurgence of American Power	166
The Decline of Arms Control and the Arms Build-Up	167
The Strategic Defense Initiative	168
American INF in Europe	171
Raising the Nuclear Threshold	173
Conclusion	174

9 The Strategic Defense Initiative and the European Response in High-Technology Research and Development: The Military–civilian Dilemma for Western Europe 179
Michael Lucas

SDI Research Agreements and Contracts	182
SDI and the Technological Revolution	184
European Research and Development: Collaboration and Responses	187
The European Research and Co-ordinating Agency (EUREKA)	187
The European Strategic Programme of Research in Information Technology (ESPRIT)	188
Research in Advanced Communications in Europe (RACE)	189
The Dangers of Militarisation and the Policy Challenge	191

10 Beyond the Western Alliance: The Politics of Post-Atlanticism 196
Bradley S. Klein

Strategy	197
The Western Alliance as a Project	201
The Politics of Post-Atlanticism	207

Index   213

PREFACE

One of the most important political issues of our time concerns the nature and development of Atlantic relations. This issue lies at the heart of our understanding of post-1945 world politics and thereby our concerns over war and peace, economic well-being and indeed, the future of our civilisations. A co-operative and fruitful set of transatlantic and superpower relations is a pre-requisite to a sustained attempt to provide the long-term conditions for the survival of the human species and the planet itself. Since the mid-1980s there have been a number of encouraging signs that the leaders of some of the world's major powers have come to increasingly recognise these global imperatives.

With these wider and more fundamental issues in mind, this collection of essays attempts to place the evolution of Atlantic relations in a long-term context, in order to assess the changes which took place during the decade of the 1980s. This decade began with widespread fears, in Europe, of the policy consequences of the Reagan Presidency, with particular anxieties concerning the new leader of the Western Alliance who seemed committed to intensifying superpower conflict and to denying the USSR legitimate status as a power in world politics. How far were these fears well-founded? What was the geopolitical and economic balance sheet at the end of the Reagan era? What was the legacy for Presidents Bush, Gorbachev and the leaders of the west European nations to ponder as the world contemplated the new decade?

In some respects, the Reagan era seemed to be a return to the 'normal politics' of transatlantic relations: the USA reasserted its leadership of the West, intensified its political conflict with the USSR, re-armed at great expense, and renewed its commitment to its post-war policy of globalism. The Reagan Administration's obsession with Nicaragua stopped short of direct armed intervention although the invasion of Grenada and the so-called 'surgical strike' against Libya served notice that the era of American interventionism in the Third World had not come to an end.

There were worries about the morality and law-abidingness of certain members of the Reagan team, but this was explained by the enormously popular President as the result of an excess of zeal or patriotism.

In the economic sphere, there was growing concern in western Europe and Japan at what was seen as gross macro-economic mismanagement by the Americans, reflected in irresponsible fiscal policies and in enormous American budget and trade deficits. After the stock market crash of October 1987 there was even concern at the overall stability of the American economy, perched precariously on a pyramid of credit and debt. Reaganites brushed these criticisms aside for most of the 1980s, pointing out that after the recession of 1979–82 (the worst since the 1930s), the USA had enjoyed the longest boom in peacetime history. This boom helped carry Vice-President Bush to victory in the Presidential election of 1988, along with the claim that the President's policy of 'peace through strength' had brought the USSR back to the negotiating table on American terms. Although the Soviets had not yet surrendered, the President's agenda had prevailed. Reagan had refused to negotiate away his commitment to the Strategic Defense Initiative. The President triumphantly signed the INF Treaty and talked about a world free of nuclear weapons. Ronald Reagan had constructed the possibility for liberal capitalism's victory against the forces of what he had once called the 'evil empire'.

On the other hand, many analysts perceived the contours of a very different political landscape amid the rhetorical chimeras of Reaganism. Although Reagan's 'supply-side' revolution had apparently brought prosperity to the American economy, it did so by creating ever-widening inequalities and a growth in the numbers of Americans below the poverty line. Moreover, the 'market place magic' at the heart of Reagan's vision, and the policies of global deregulation and tax-cutting which embodied this economic alchemy went with a world economy which had become more integrated and yet more unstable. Economic and technological competition had become more global and more cut-throat. Moreover, whilst the US economy appeared to prosper after 1981, this was much less the case for west European economies, and, indeed, for the debt-laden Third World. Whilst the USA was sucking in capital from around the world to feed its apparently insatiable appetite for weaponry and consumables, many Third World economies faced bankruptcy and negative growth rates.

In addition, many feared that the modernisation of NATO forces, as well as the SDI, was actively destabilising the strategic relationships between East and West, making the world a more dangerous place. The new production and military technologies and structural economic changes, along with other political questions were eroding traditional constituencies of support for the prevailing Atlanticist arrangements. These questions preoccupied not only members of the peace movements and green parties, but also those in the political centre. Some of the broad political and economic concern with these questions was reflected in the passage of the Single European Act in 1987 and the movement towards a fully-integrated single internal market within the Community by 1992, as well as in a wide range of pan-European political, economic and to a lesser extent military initiatives during the 1980s. Some informed journalists, like the *Guardian*'s European Editor, John Palmer, began to speak of 'Europe Without America'. In the view of the majority of contributors to this collection this is too dramatic a proposition, although as an idea it does capture what, even 10 years ago, was probably unspeakable, if not unthinkable, on the part of west European political leaders. Indeed after the political fall-out of the Reykjavik summit of 1986, when President Reagan almost bargained away half of NATO's nuclear arsenal, perhaps the complexities and uncertainties of Europe's future are better captured by the pre-modern metaphor in Paul Valéry's *The Crisis of the Mind:* 'Our Hamlet of Europe . . . is watching millions of ghosts'.

In essence, therefore, it can be suggested that there are two ideal–typical 'stories' of the development of Atlantic relations during the 1980s. The first, and for Reaganites, 'happy' story, is akin to the arguments for liberal capitalism before its triumph: despite problems, the Reagan era points towards a brave new world of global capitalism, led with vigour by the hegemonic power of the USA. Here, Atlantic relations remain stable, and under American leadership, but become one of several regional American concerns, although one of its most important. The second, and more complex, story sees the developments of the 1980s as heralding a more fundamental restructuring of Atlantic relations, with a shift to a qualitatively different type of transatlantic relationship. In this context, some commentators saw western Europe regaining some of its strength relative to the USA in the late 1980s, after fears earlier in the decade of the onset of 'Eurosclerosis', that is atrophied political institutions and moribund economic structures. Europe's renaissance was partly as a result of an apparently rejuvenated capacity for collective action. Moreover, since the prevailing faction within the Soviet leadership of the late 1980s apparently wished a permanent end to the Cold War, western Europe's political independence from Washington would increasingly be put to the test, not only in the late 1980s, but in the 1990s and beyond. These are some of the many themes and questions which animate the contributors to this book, as well as with a concern to probe and to consider the normative and ethical basis of Atlanticism, in the post-Reagan era.

Stephen Gill
December 1988

ACKNOWLEDGEMENTS

I would like to thank, on behalf of myself and the contributors, both the executive committees of the British International Studies Association and of the International Studies Association of the USA. We appreciate their encouragement of this project and their hospitality in allowing us to convene panel sessions and round tables to debate Atlantic relations at conferences and conventions in Reading, England (1986) and Washington DC (1987). They, like us, perceived this to be a topic crucial to an understanding of contemporary global politics. We would also like to thank those who were good enough to attend the conference sessions and who engaged in discussions. We are particularly grateful to those who made trenchant but constructive criticism of our papers, either verbally or in writing.

I should like to express my thanks to the following people who have helped in the production of this collection: Jill Kirby and Angela Shaw for typing; Peter Johns at Harvester Wheatsheaf for editorial assistance; and Liz Newman and her team at Woodhead-Faulkner for sub-editing.

Finally, as editor, I would also like to express my appreciation to the contributors for tolerating my foibles and shortcomings. Whilst they remain responsible for the content of their chapters, I remain accountable for both initiating the enterprise (with the encouragement of both Steve Smith and Michael Smith) and for the shape of the final product.

Stephen Gill

CONTRIBUTORS

David Allen is Senior Lecturer in European Studies at Loughborough University, England. He is the author of a number of essays on the European Community, European foreign policy making and European policy analysis. He has contributed to and edited *European Political Co-operation* (1982) and *European Foreign Policy Making in the Middle East* (1984).

Dr Alan W. Cafruny is Assistant Professor of Government at Hamilton College, New York, USA. He has published a number of essays in the field of international political economy and, with the aid of a German Marshall Fund Fellowship, is writing a book on US–European economic relations. He is the author of *Ruling the Waves: the Political Economy of International Shipping* (1987).

Dr Stephen Gill is Senior Lecturer in Politics, The Polytechnic, Wolverhampton. In 1989–90 he is Hallsworth Fellow in Political Economy at Manchester University, England, and from 1990 he is Associate Professor at York University, Toronto, Canada. His publications include: *The Global Political Economy: Perspectives, Problems and Policies* (co-written with David Law, 1988) and *American Hegemony and the Trilateral Commission* (1989).

Dr Bradley S. Klein is Assistant Professor of Political Science at the College of the Holy Cross, Worcester, Massachusetts, USA and is a Research Affiliate of the Center for International Studies, Harvard University. He has published a number of essays on strategic and international studies and is currently working on a book, *Social Theory and Strategic Studies: the New Politics of Peace, War and Violence*.

David Law is Senior Lecturer in Economics, The Polytechnic, Wolverhampton. He is the author of a number of essays in the field of development studies and political economy, and has a special interest in multinational corporations. David Law is the co-author, with Stephen Gill, of *The Global Political Economy* (1988).

Michael Lucas is a freelance researcher, based in Frankfurt, West Germany. He has published widely in Britain, West Germany and in the USA on questions of arms control, technological developments in weaponry and related areas. He is a member of the World Policy Institute in Washington DC.

Dr Neil Malcolm is Principal Lecturer in Russian and Soviet Studies at The Polytechnic, Wolverhampton, and has contributed to the RIIA Soviet Foreign Policy Research Programme with *Soviet Policy Perspectives on Western Europe* (1989). The author of a number of articles on Soviet policy making and foreign policy, his publications include: *Soviet Political Scientists and American Politics* (1984).

Dr Kees van der Pijl is Professor of International Relations at the University of Amsterdam. His publications include: *The Making of an Atlantic Ruling Class* (1984). The author of a number of published short stories, Kees van der Pijl is now writing a novel as well as working on a history of international relations theory, provisionally titled *Class and World Politics*.

Michael Smith is Reader in International Relations at Coventry Polytechnic, England. He has published widely on European–American relations and US foreign policy. His publications include: *Western Europe and the United States: the Uncertain Alliance* (1984); *The United States, the European Community and Industrial Policies* (editor, 1986); *The European Community, The United States and Japan: Trade Policies and the World Economy* (editor, 1987).

Dr Steve Smith is Senior Lecturer in Politics at the University of East Anglia, England. He has published widely in the fields of international relations theory, foreign policy, arms control and nuclear strategy. He has written the following books: *Foreign Policy Adaptation* (1981); *Politics and Human Nature* (co-editor with Ian Forbes, 1983); *International Relations: British and American Perspectives* (editor, 1985); *Foreign Policy Implementation* (co-editor with Michael Clarke, 1985); *The Cold War: Past and Present* (co-editor with Richard Crockatt, 1987); *British Foreign Policy* (co-editor with Michael Smith and Brian White, 1988).

1 · INTRODUCTION
Some Questions and an
Overview of Trends

Stephen Gill

The idea for this book originated at the 1986 meeting of the British International Studies Association, where the editor organised two panels to discuss the nature and trajectory of Atlanticism in the 1980s and beyond. The sessions provoked a lively debate, and it was decided that essays on this theme might produce a thought-provoking volume. What follows is a brief attempt to provide a context for the debate on Atlanticism, and a sketch of a number of structural trends which may lead to a substantial intensification of what I would call the crisis of Atlanticism which unfolded in the 1970s, and more pointedly, in the 1980s.

There are two basic meanings to the term 'Atlanticism' in this book. The first refers to a relatively cohesive set of relationships between the countries of western Europe and North America (notably the USA) which has developed in a cumulative sense, at least since 1945. This has generated the overall structure of transatlantic economic, military, political and cultural forces. The second refers to Atlanticism as a set of ideas and values which help constitute a set of policies and civilisational concepts (e.g. the 'free world'; the 'West'). As such, our discussion is not solely confined to questions concerning the nature and future of the North Atlantic Treaty Organisation (NATO). With this in mind, let us raise what seems to me to be a number of basic questions concerning Atlanticism:

1. What are the most important aspects of Atlantic relations in the 1980s? What are the primary centripetal and centrifugal forces within Atlantic relations? With respect to changes, which of these are structural (or relatively permanent, long-term) and which are cyclical (or short-term) or conjunctural changes?
2. How do Atlantic relations relate to the wider context of international relations and foreign policy? For example, what is their significance in the global political economy, or in terms of superpower rivalry and geopolitical changes?

3. Is there a crisis of Atlanticism? If so, to what extent is this unprecedented?
4. What issues and forces will shape the evolution of Atlantic relations in the 1990s?

Implicit or explicit in many of the resulting contributions was the view (which I share) that current tensions can be best understood as part of a wider crisis of the post-war, American-centred capitalist world order. In this crisis, there may well be a growing lack of congruence between the basic economic, political and ideological structures on both sides of the Atlantic, as well as a number of unprecedented strategic challenges for the NATO alliance in the 1990s. It might also be noted in passing that a parallel crisis has emerged for a range of communist states, with economic, and to a lesser extent political changes in China and the USSR raising significant questions concerning the nature of communism in the 1990s and beyond. To sum up, the 1980s was a decade of flux and transformation in the basic structure of the East–West and Atlantic relationships.

BACKGROUND TO THE ATLANTICIST DEBATE

The post-war literature on the nature and evolution of Atlantic relations is voluminous, partly because the subject touches directly or indirectly on the concerns of a very wide range of groups, interests, states and social movements. Indeed any post-war history of international relations hinges significantly upon the interpretation of the meaning and evolution of the Atlantic relationship. What follows is of necessity a selective and, to a certain extent, an impressionistic overview of trends.

One major source of European concern during the 1980s was that American perceptions and policies increasingly came to reflect a basic shift in the centre of gravity of the USA's orientations away from the Atlantic towards the Pacific. This is often said to reflect both an internal shift in the distribution of economic and political power in the USA towards the 'sunbelt' states of the south and west, and a global shift in economic and political power towards what Europeans call the East, and what Americans, particularly Californians, call the West. In addition, the Hispanic influx into the USA may serve to increase European anxieties even further, since it threatens to strengthen the USA's western hemisphere links, rather than transatlantic ones.

This shift to the 'West' was widely seen as embracing not just the rising economic and strategic importance of Japan, but also in the longer-term that of China, and the Pacific Basin region. This region is thus seen as becoming the principal centre of economic dynamism in the latter part of this waning century, in sharp contrast to the west European region, which, some have argued, has entered an economic climacteric, and appears unable to reverse its relative decline: the region as a whole is seen as politically disunited, and its socio-economic system beset, to use the fashionable term of the mid-1980s, by 'Euroschlerosis'.

Such pessimistic views are, of course, by no means unprecedented. They can be seen, for example, as being rooted in the traditional debates concerning the decline of the 'Old World'. As Denis de Rougemont notes, the prophets of European decline, such as Spengler, Valéry and Toynbee, all based themselves on the precedent of the fall of the Roman Empire and of the Graeco-Roman world, Toynbee adding that the arrogance of the West's aggression towards the rest of the world was coming to an end in 1945, when the USSR and China began to open a new chapter in modern history as the non-Western peoples rebelled.[1] On the key to European decline, de Rougemont quotes André Siegfried's preface to the French translation of Diez de Corral's *Rape of Europe:*

> Two dates – 1764 and 1914 – marked the beginning and end of the period when Europe dominated the world. This was her optimum. Already benefiting from all the advantages of the machine, she continued to feed her strength on the dynamism she received from her conception of knowledge and the individual. This extraordinary hegemony, however, could not last forever. Her technology could be borrowed from her, and the more readily because she did not keep it to herself . . . What a subject for reflection for a twentieth-century Bossuet – the technological lesson of Europe, transmitted to Asia not by its initiators, but through the intermediary of a barely Europeanised Russia – no doubt a disciple of Europe, but a rebellious one![2]

Such pessimism is the obverse of the view that the USA was a promised land which would be at the vanguard of the development of civilisation. Although not unambiguously so, this view is scattered throughout a range of European writings, such as those of de Tocqueville, Hegel and Goethe. Moreover, for many writers of the nineteenth century and earlier, 'Europe' was more of an idea than a reality. In so far as there was such a thing as European history, it was interpreted in terms of a Promethean ideal, an assemblage of contrasting cultural and political traditions, or as a history of contradictions: for example between the universalism of its Enlightenment culture and its propensity to internecine warfare and nationalist particularism. Hegel referred to Europe as both 'truly the end of History' and as a 'ruined fortress', the simultaneous embodiment of civilisation and violence, the dialectical crossroads of mankind.

Whilst the USA was often seen as a land of hope and bounty, many European writers, including Sorel, de Maistre and Proudhon were none the less severely critical of the development of American society. The USA was viewed as a place of dull conformity and materialism. Indeed, this view became commonplace among European nationalists of right and left in the nineteenth century. Marx's view of the USA was more ambivalent: he saw it simultaneously as a progressive civilisation, the embodiment of an ideal bourgeois republic, but also a potential long-term threat to the development of socialism. In *The Eastern Question,* Marx seemed to believe that the intervention of the USA in Europe would be inevitable, whilst the great adversary of the liberation of Europe from the yoke of tyranny would be Russia, a power which rested between a progressive Europe and the 'Mongol barbarism' of the oriental hordes. His view of Russia was commonplace on the left and in nationalist circles of his time.

Contemporary observers, such as the historian Geoffrey Barraclough, have taken this theme further: that a rising Pacific region would come to succeed the Euro-Atlantic region, despite the extensive influence of the superpowers.[3] Such arguments about a further shift westward suggest that the historical process is coming full circle, with its vanguard now in the East, perhaps to haunt the USSR.

THEORISING CHANGE IN ATLANTIC RELATIONS

It is easy to be bewitched by the above argument. The nature of European hegemony and its offspring, American hegemony, are, in significant respects, qualitatively different to that of their Roman predecessor, partly by virtue of their claim to have had a universal civilisational character. Europeans, in a typically Eurocentric and perhaps racist way, have made arrogant claims to have discovered what they call the modern world and to have developed the universal idea of the 'human race' (although followers of religions other than Christianity, notably Islam, would dispute this). This assertion raises the question whether it is advisable to analyse Atlanticism in the 1980s as part of a cyclical historical process, that is in terms of the rise and fall of nations or regions.

If Western hegemony is qualitatively different to previous hegemonies, is it also the case that the character of the contemporary world is such that we need new concepts and perspectives to explain the historical process? These questions go to the heart of one of the major debates within the study of international relations. Whereas realists and world systems thinkers, following the likes of Spengler and Toynbee, tend to adopt a cyclical theory of historical change, transnational theorists, be they liberals or historical materialists, argue that the post-war global system has a significantly different character from that of its predecessors. This means that whilst historical analogy is useful, new concepts and theories may be needed for contemporary analysis, and some of our contributors indeed attempt this. For example, in this book a major theme concerns the nature and extent of American hegemony within the non-communist world, and the implications for world order and Atlanticism which result from changes (or decline) in such hegemony. The analysis of this question raises the issue of which perspective or school of international study is best able to explain the issues at hand.

Modern neo-realist thinkers, in their search for a parsimonious theory of international politics, have reduced the richness and complexity of the realist tradition of Thucydides, Machiavelli and E. H. Carr. The search for parsimonious explanation has led to the development of theories which tend to separate both economics and politics, and the international and domestic 'levels of analysis'. The neo-realist tradition, of which Kenneth Waltz is an exemplar, has been the dominant discourse in the Western study of international relations at least since the 1950s, particularly because of the influence of its adherents in the USA and because of the pre-eminent influence of American social science in the post-war world.[4] The neo-realist tradition defines hegemony as the dominance of one state over others, that is as a specific case of imperialism. The founding father of the realist tradition, Thucydides, for example, analysed the ancient Greek world in these terms, although as G. E. M. de Sté Croix notes, 'we must be careful, if we ever speak of Thucydides as a believer in *realpolitik* or *machtpolitik*, to make clear that it was something he accepted as a fact of life, which even the best-intentioned men are obliged to take account of because all states practise it, without exception'.[5]

The neo-realist school of study has developed, following the work of Charles Kindleberger, the theory of hegemonic stability.[6] This theory, in essence, suggests that international economic relations are more likely to be characterised by periods of order and plenty if there is a hegemonic power, which acts, rather like Hobbes' *Leviathan* at the domestic level, to provide leadership, discipline, and international 'public goods' in the economic relations between states. Waltz's variant of this theory suggests that international political conflict and war is made less likely by the existence of a dominant power, or by two superpowers, than would be the case in a world of a larger number of great powers vying for hegemony.[7] As such, in a period of hegemonic decline, international relations are likely to be characterised by higher levels of conflict than when hegemony was at its peak. In this view, therefore, the end of American hegemony signals a transition to a more dangerous world. This theory has been criticised by non-American writers as ahistorical, overstating the extent of the USA's relative decline, and not least, as an apology for American imperialism.[8]

Neo-realist writers have been criticised for being too state-centric in their approach to the study of international relations. Their approach focuses heavily on the relationships between governments, and often separates domestic and international levels of analysis. Neo-classical international economics is similarly open to criticism, since it concentrates on the relationships between national economies. By contrast, some writers have favoured a broader socio-political or political economy approach. It is the latter which most of the contributors to this book take up, in an attempt to go beyond neo-realist interpretations of international relations. One aspect of this is that they prefer to define hegemony not simply as a type of power relation between states, but as a specific alignment of social (or civilisational) forces. This means that hegemony involves not only material power, but also the relationship of class and other political forces, the power of ideas, and the role of institutions at both the domestic and international levels. Hegemony, in this view, involves the degree of congruence or fit between these different social forces at the level not only of states and world orders, but also domestically.[9] This also implies that such a perspective will give rise to a rather different interpretation of the nature and evolution of Atlantic relations.

Seen from the latter perspective, the political effects of hegemony are both direct and indirect, the latter partly referring to power being exercised through the modern, global capitalist system, rather than simply by one state over other states. Many of the institutional contours of this system have been shaped by post-war American foreign policy. The success of this policy itself rested upon the expansionist nature of American economic and social forces and their ability to overcome, incorporate and to interact with those of other nations in a historically unprecedented way. This interaction generated the most productive system of accumulation the world has ever known, as well as being accompanied by superpower rivalry, the cold war and the social psychosis of 'bomb culture'. Thus, whilst there may be shifting geographical 'power centres', it may be asserted that the contemporary world is characterised by forms of cultural, economic, and technological integration and interdependence which may well be historically unprecedented, although it is true that the world economy prior to 1914 was, in certain respects, more integrated and perhaps more stable than it had become in the mid-1980s.

From the height of its dominance in the 1940s, the USA sought to construct a world order which would be more congruent with its own political values, its civil society and its major economic forces. Some commentators have identified this process as the internationalisation of the American New Deal political settlement. Post-war west European anxieties with respect to American policy have tended to stem from two contradictory implications of this new form of imperialism, and from the ambiguities of an alliance based upon members separated by the vast geographical space of the Atlantic ocean.

First, western European nations, like many others subjected to American cultural, political, economic and military penetration, have been concerned at their loss of national sovereignty and autonomy. Second, and perhaps perversely, many western European leaders have also been concerned at the implications of a possible retreat from the USA's post-war commitment to a forward military presence in Europe, and a shift away from the axiomatic centrality of western Europe in American foreign policy. These anxieties relate to a central theme in the literature: assessments of the centripetal and centrifugal forces which are at work within the Atlantic alliance and political economy. In this respect, much of the literature concerning the perennial theme of a crisis of Atlanticism, is related to these questions. Consistently, questions have been raised about the 'future' of the relationship. Indeed many writers have viewed, as it were, the 'present crisis', as it appeared to them at different times, as the most grave and threatening in, for example, NATO's short history.[10]

WHAT HAS CHANGED?

What is new about the 1980s, and what does this imply for Atlanticism in the 1990s? The literature of the 1980s contained the same themes of crisis and change as that of the 1960s and 1970s, although some of the diagnoses of the problems which created tensions in the 1980s were in important respects quite different, reflecting new appraisals of a range of economic, military and political forces. What seemed to be new about the 1980s was that the structure of the world political economy had been transformed substantially since the 1950s and 1960s, and important, perhaps unprecedented, problems in the strategic field had arisen.

The 'economic' (and, indeed, political) aspects of the above claim involve the assessment of a changed international political economy, with a new international division of labour bound up with a globalisation of production and exchange; and, especially in the 1980s, more globally integrated and volatile capital and exchange markets. There was also significant international monetary instability. The level of monetary instability was partly related to technical changes concerning the freedom of mobility of capital as markets were liberalised. However, these changes occurred in conditions which were likely to, and did in fact, generate highly undesirable repercussions, for example the large swings in the origins and destinations of capital flows. This was partly because of a pervasive lack of international market confidence in the future, so that market behaviour increasingly came to reflect a short-term outlook. Manifestations of this phenomenon in the late 1980s were statements from American economic policy-makers that the proper horizon for macro-economic policy-making is one year, and that considerations of long-term policy should be subordinated to the political objective of winning elections.[11] The changing global economic structure has also served to intensify transatlantic economic conflicts, for example in services and agricultural trade. These are analysed in Chapter 6.

These developments relate to an ongoing debate on the appropriate steering mechanisms for the contemporary world capitalist economy. On the one hand are the advocates of planned and co-ordinated international capitalism (reflected, for example, in the mainstream of the influential Trilateral Commission) and, on the other, are the high priests of the brave new world of liberal, deregulated global capitalism (heavily represented in the first Reagan administration). At the heart of the debate is the question whether a highly integrated and liberalised world economy can provide any substantial degree of stability. This issue is addressed in Chapters 4 and 7.

Despite such unstable economic conditions, the 1970s and 1980s also witnessed a return to the levels of international economic integration which prevailed prior to World War I, in large part under the aegis of the transnational (or multinational) corporation. This has meant that the links between the Atlantic economies, and also to a lesser extent that of Japan, have been strengthened. As Kees van der Pijl indicates in Chapter 4, such economic changes also brought with them the renewed importance of transatlantic class formations, which have gradually extended at the level of the international bourgeoisies to incorporate Japanese elites.[12]

The above can be seen as part of a cumulative process in which capital and national class structures are becoming more internationally interpenetrated within the advanced capitalist countries. On the other hand, these developments also signalled the sharpening of international economic competition, for example in high-technology and military industries. In this context, some political forces have proposed mercantilist responses, either on a national or, increasingly, a European scale. One reason for this is to enable European companies to have a wider economic and technological platform from which to compete with American and Japanese firms. Others, notably that of the British government under Mrs Thatcher (although most of her Cabinet were more in favour of further European integration), opted for a neo-Gaullist attitude to Europe, based upon the primacy of a global market orientation in concert with the further cultivation of the so-called 'special relationship' with the USA. Soviet writers carefully observed and analysed these tendencies, in part to help generate a new foreign policy for the USSR in the 1990s, one which implied closer co-operation with western Europe as well as the reconstruction of superpower detente (see Chapter 3).

These changes took place against the backdrop of a period characterised by both global economic stagnation and rapid innovation and technological change. Stagnation generated rising unemployment, much of it concentrated in the declining labour-intensive industries of the Atlantic economies, especially in western Europe. This decline was intensified by the strict austerity policies practiced during 1979–82, which provoked the most severe recession experienced since the Great Depression. Such decline helped to promote not only attempts to mitigate these effects by state intervention (and also by co-ordinated European policies), but also a defensive stance by organised labour in a range of countries, in contrast to much of the 1970s when labour was generally on the offensive. At the same time, many observers argued that the vanguard of economic development was characterised by a third wave of technological innovation. Although no clear predictions were possible, it seemed likely that such developments would lead to permanent changes in the world of work and leisure, with significant social and political implications.

At the strategic level, a debate ensued over whether the development of such technologies, for example in the American Strategic Defense Initiative or the pan-European EUREKA programme, would be predominantly 'civilian' or 'military' in character, and whether such development would, or would not help to reduce the long-term problem of unemployment (see Chapter 9). These questions were raised in parallel to debates concerning strategic force modernisation, arms control and disarmament and, in a wider sense, the coherence and political stability of NATO. As Steve Smith points out in Chapter 8, in the early 1980s at least, the USA seemed to have abandoned any serious attempt at arms control. Indeed, the USA seemed intent on re-establishing its nuclear superiority, whilst at the same time NATO experienced considerable difficulty in presenting a convincing case for its policies to the populations of western Europe. American policies and west European responses created a crisis in terms of both the basic operative and publicly avowed concepts of deterrence within NATO, a crisis which seemed likely to intensify in the 1990s, irrespective of Presidents Reagan and Gorbachev's success in obtaining an INF agreement. The Reagan Administration appeared at one stage to have openly rejected any notion of East-West detente, and its bellicose anti-Soviet and interventionist stance of the early 1980s was an important catalyst in promoting the growth of not only the peace movements, but also as Mike Smith and David Allen note in Chapter 5, the development of a distinctive Euro-identity which pointed towards a potentially more autonomous foreign and military policy for Europe during the 1990s. A catalyst for this developing identity was the way President Reagan reversed his previous positions and astounded NATO allies with his proposals to make deep cuts in nuclear weapons at the 1986 American–Soviet Reykjavik summit. The important issue here was not that American proposals were likely to lead to deep cuts, but what they implied for the American political commitment to the defence of western Europe.

A crucial political aspect of politico-strategic developments in Atlanticism, particularly during the 1980s, was that, for probably the first time since the foundation of the alliance, there was a widespread domestic politicisation of the questions of defence and nuclear weapons across a range of member states. This occurred at the same time as a serious divergence of perspectives concerning appropriate strategy towards the

USSR emerged amongst west European and American political leaders. The wider political backdrop to this, particularly in the first half of the 1980s, was the intensification of the so-called second Cold War. A further development during the 1980s was a growth in the pan-European peace movements, elements of which involved not only peace proposals, but also attempts to develop alternative concepts of social organisation to those which have prevailed within Atlantic civilisation. These embryonic alternatives sought to go beyond an Atlantic-centred view of the world and to acknowledge and incorporate a wider global consciousness. Further, they challenged the character of Atlanticism and its association with the post-war political settlements in Europe.

For example, at the cultural level, some elements in the peace coalitions challenged the very idea that the Atlantic nations were civilised. Their arguments were made within a general critique of modernist culture or the western civilisational project, in some cases along some of the lines followed by nineteenth century critics of American materialism. These arguments, for example as reflected in the debates of the Green parties of western Europe, often incorporated wider critiques of militarism and the short-term mentality of scientific materialism, with its disregard for the long-term ecological and social consequences of industrial and post-industrial development. In addition, some of their arguments challenged many of the hegemonic concepts of social organisation, and the associated social values which underpinned post-war Atlanticism. This would suggest, if not the onset of a cultural crisis, then a spreading malaise among many younger and better-educated people concerning the trajectory of Western civilisation during the 1990s. Some of these ideas are reflected in Chapter 10. This cultural malaise includes, although in a quite different way, the rise in possessive individualism and the spreading willingness to preach at the 'yuppie' altar of the god of Mammon: the long-term eco-consciousness of the Greens is in stark contrast to the short-term, market mentality of the new fraternity of young, aggressive entrepreneurs in the world's financial and commercial centres.

This latter mentality has also challenged many of the concepts which helped to constitute post-war social order: honesty, prudence and a tendency among the rich to eschew conspicuous consumption, and at least to behave as if they were law abiding and conscious of a wider social obligation. The leitmotif of this new eldorado was reflected for example, in the outlook of Ivan Boesky, the fallen American financial wizard. Prior to his exposure for multi-million dollar fraud, Boesky apparently announced to a large gathering at the Harvard Business School in the mid-1980s that it was good and noble to be greedy. Boesky's remark was reportedly greeted with tumultuous applause. This culture of greed and individualism is related, in Chapter 4, to a constellation of social forces which van der Pijl labels 'neo-liberalism'. These forces have increasingly challenged the hegemony of the corporate liberal and social democratic perspectives in the Atlantic region during the 1970s and 1980s.

At the same time, and in different ways, the Warsaw Pact nations entered a period of internal structural crisis during the 1970s and 1980s, with Gorbachev's attempted reforms *(perestroika)* of the Soviet planned economy and social liberalisation *(glasnost)* a major response to this. In the Soviet case, President Gorbachev's initiatives can be interpreted in similar ways to those of President Reagan and Prime Minister Thatcher (despite the obvious differences of philosophy and circumstances): they were political offensives aimed at the remobilisation of key elements of their respective economies and societies.

Indeed, Gorbachev adopted Mrs Thatcher's phrase, saying 'there is no alternative' to his policies if the USSR is to meet the challenges of the 1990s. Such remobilisation was a response to the (perceived) relative decline in the status and performance of their respective nations. It reflects an appreciation that the twin forces of economic and technological competition on the one hand, and inter-state rivalry on the other, may be intensifying. These forces may provoke substantial changes in the foreign policy stance of the USSR, at least if the speeches of Secretary Gorbachev are to be believed. These use western concepts such as global interdependence to characterise important aspects of international relations. As Neil Malcolm notes in Chapter 3, Gorbachev's foreign policy thinking, whilst still configured by the demands of *realpolitik,* seems to have taken a quantum leap forward from that of his predecessors. Whether his initiatives will be welcomed and reciprocated in eastern Europe and in the West is one of the key issues which will affect Atlantic and global relations in the coming decade.

In conclusion, underlying this argument is the view that the American-centred transatlantic system, is, in Gramscian terms, undergoing a 'crisis of hegemony', involving, at the political level, a shift away from the post-war transatlantic consensus on East-West relations and from accepted domestic formulas for governing the Atlantic political economies. This crisis involves both elements of decay of the old order and elements of change and innovation. As is noted in Chapter 2, the traditional Atlanticist consensus was widely shared by the forces of the political centre in western Europe and the USA, at least until the early 1970s. It was represented in a mix of welfarism, Keynesianism, fairly benign mercantilism and gradual economic liberalisation, based upon the axioms of social democracy and American corporate liberalism. Whilst these views and the social forces which underpin them still persist, they have been strongly challenged by neo-liberal market-oriented perspectives and transnational forces which reflect the increased importance of internationally-mobile capital.

These changes have been taking place at the same time as a more aggressive reassertion of the power of the American state *vis-à-vis* its allies and the USSR, for example by attempts in the early 1980s to impose an economic blockade against the USSR, thereby injuring west European economic and political interests. These attempts rode roughshod over established procedures of alliance consultation, showing scant regard for alliance consensus. Hence the crisis of Atlanticism of the 1980s should be interpreted as part of a longer-term crisis (or transformation) of American and capitalist hegemony in the global political economy.

On the evidence of the 1980s, it would appear that many of the social forces which will shape Atlanticism in the 1990s are likely to be different from those which prevailed during the period up to the mid-1970s. In the West, the transatlantic corporate liberal/social democratic consensus had, by the mid-1980s, largely collapsed; in the East, the statist, centrally-planned model was in crisis. On both sides of the East-West divide, market forces were becoming more pervasive, and capital (or management in the East) was becoming more powerful relative to labour. The global forces of economic competition and inter-state rivalry suggested that the nature of Atlanticism in the 1990s and beyond would be leaner and harsher than its predecessors. These forces, and others, implied that the decade of the 1990s would probably be a period of significant transition in Atlantic relations, and that the label 'Atlanticist' would, as we approach the end of the century, become increasingly anachronistic.

NOTES

1. Arnold Toynbee, *The World and the West* (London, Oxford University Press, 1953).
2. Cited by Denis de Rougement, *The Idea of Europe*, translated by Norbert Guterman (New York, Meridian Books, 1968, orig. 1966), pp. 417–18.
3. Geoffrey Barraclough, *An Introduction to Contemporary History* (Harmondsworth, Penguin, 1967).
4. Robert O. Keohane (ed.), *Neorealism and Its Critics* (New York, Columbia University Press, 1986).
5. G. E. M. de Sté Croix, *The Origins of the Peloponnesian War* (London, Duckworth, 1972), p. 15. See pp. 22–23 for a quintessential statement of Thucydides' views on international relations.
6. Charles Kindleberger, *The World in Depression, 1929–39* (Berkeley, CA, University of California Press, 1973).
7. Kenneth Waltz, *Theory of International Politics* (Reading, Mass., Addison-Wesley, 1979).
8. See for example, Susan Strange, *Casino Capitalism* (Oxford, Blackwell, 1986); Stephen Gill, *American Hegemony and the Trilateral Commission* (Cambridge, Cambridge University Press, 1989), Chs 4 and 5.
9. Robert Cox, *Production, Power and World Order: Social Forces in the Making of History* (New York, Columbia University Press, 1987).
10. See, for example, Stephen Graubard (ed.), *A New Europe?* (Boston, Beacon Press, 1964); Robert Kleiman, *Atlantic Crisis: American Diplomacy Confronts*

a Resurgent Europe (New York, W. W. Norton, 1964); Henry A. Kissinger, *The Troubled Partnership: A Re-Appraisal of the Atlantic Alliance* (New York, McGraw-Hill for Council on Foreign Relations, 1965); Harold van Buren Cleveland, *The Atlantic Idea and its European Rivals* (New York, McGraw-Hill for Council on Foreign Relations, 1966); John Pinder and Roy Pryce, *Europe After de Gaulle: Towards a United States of Europe* (Harmondsworth, Penguin, 1969); Alastair Buchan, *Europe's Futures, Europe's Choices* (London, Chatto & Windus for International Institute of Strategic Studies, 1969); David P. Calleo, *The Atlantic Fantasy* (Baltimore, Johns Hopkins Press, 1970); Ernest Mandel, *Europe versus America: Contradictions of Imperialism* (London, New Left Books, 1970); Andrew Shonfield, *Europe: Journey to an Unknown Destination* (Harmondsworth, Penguin, 1972); Karl Kaiser, *Europe and the United States: the Future of the Relationship* (Washington DC, Columbia Books for Aspen Institute for Humanistic Studies, 1973); Joseph Godson (ed.), *Transatlantic Crisis: Europe and America in the '70s* (London, Alcove Press, 1974); J. Robert Schaetzel, *The Unhinged Alliance: America and the European Community* (New York, Harper & Row for Council on Foreign Relations, 1975); David S. Landes (ed.), *Western Europe: the Trials of Partnership* (Lexington, Mass., Lexington Books for the Twentieth Century Fund/Critical Choices for Americans, 1977); Alfred Grosser, *The Western Alliance: European–American Relations Since 1945* (New York, Vintage Books, 1982, orig. 1978); Riccardo Parboni, *The Dollar and its Rivals: Recession, Inflation and International Finance*, translated by Jon Rothschild (London, Verso, 1981).

11. Martin Wolf, 'The need to look to the long-term', *Financial Times*, 16 November 1987.
12. Kees van der Pijl, *The Making of an Atlantic Ruling Class* (London, Verso, 1984).

2 · AMERICAN PERCEPTIONS AND POLICIES

Stephen Gill

My argument in this chapter is that changes in American perceptions and policies with respect to Atlanticism are, to a large extent, products of changing appraisals of the USA's place in the international system, and the development of strategic approaches to deal with the transition from a situation of unchallenged dominance within the capitalist world in the 1940s, to a position of perceived relative decline. These changes reflect, and are bound up with, the fact that the USA is now more integrated into the world economy. The Reagan years represented a concerted attempt to reverse such relative decline, and to reassert American hegemony, in both the military and the economic spheres, over its allies in Europe. The wider context for these developments was a crisis in Atlantic relations and of capitalist hegemony at the global level.

The 1970s fractured the consensus on Atlantic relations which had generally held in the USA since the 1950s. From this point, with the exception of a short interlude during the early part of the Carter Administration, American hegemony would show its more coercive face towards its European (and Japanese) allies. In Gramscian terms, American hegemony was entering a phase of 'decadence'. At the same time, during the 1970s and 1980s, there was a progressive transnationalisation of the world economy, with banking and other forms of internationally-mobile capital gaining increasing primacy within the world economy. These changes were also linked to the rise of a neo-liberal economic strategy which challenged the Keynesian corporate liberalism which prevailed in the USA and, in a more social democratic form, in western Europe, since the 1950s. Thus a double transformation was emerging, the latter part corresponding to a rising hegemony of transnational capital in general, and of financial capital in particular. In the American case, by the mid-1980s, its previously relatively self-sufficient economy had become significantly internationalised, and therefore increasingly interwoven with the global political economy. These developments had a dual effect on the conditions under which American economic policy was made: on the one hand they constrained the USA's freedom of manoeuvre; on the other hand, in the particular conditions of the 1980s, they served to re-emphasise American economic centrality within the world economy. At the same time, President Reagan's strategy of Pentagon capitalism and massive military build up reasserted American primacy within the global security structures relative to its key allies.

The bedrock of current American perceptions about the international system and Atlantic relations was formed in the 1950s and 1960s. To the extent that these perceptions have changed, it is because American leaders sought to make sense, in different ways, of what they saw as a significant relative erosion in American military and economic power, and a changed relationship between the previously highly self-sufficient American economy, and the world economy.

Reaganism can be related to the recrudescence of some of the ideas of the 1950s, as well as a particular, and even unconscious appreciation of the short-run implications of new conditions. Thus Reaganism at one level appears to be an anachronistic perspective, a relic from a previous era. On the other hand, it is a specific response to the challenges of the 1980s and beyond. This apparently anomalous development has taken place in a political culture which is now more ambivalent concerning the status and importance of Europe for the USA. The Reaganite period was one when the USA sought to remobilise its global power and reassert its international dominance. The most obvious manifestation of this was through gigantic military expenditures. It was also reflected in statements concerning winnable nuclear war and others which revived the concepts of roll-back of the Cold War days of the 1950s. James Rosenau and Ole Holsti relate Reaganism to a cluster of ideas which they characterise as 'Cold War Internationalism' (CWI).[1] These views were in sharp contrast with prevailing sentiment in contemporary Europe, which welcomed detente and the lessening of Cold War tensions.

In contrast to certain elements within the Reagan coalition, there was, during the 1980s, relatively consistent support for NATO and the current Atlanticist arrangements from many of the liberal elements of the foreign policy establishment, as well as from a majority of public opinion. During the 1980s, public opinion was committed to the defence of Europe, a commitment which was even higher amongst foreign policy elites. The level of support for European defence increased gradually from the 1960s, according to well-informed observers.[2] Strongly Atlanticist views were also accompanied by a sizeable majority of public opinion which was against any form of protracted intervention by American forces in other contexts, such as for example might have been countenanced to oust the Sandinistas in Nicaragua. Reaganite positions were thus not fully representative of elite nor of mass opinion.

CONTINUITIES IN AMERICAN PERCEPTIONS

The traditional bastions of 'Atlanticist' thought and opinion are to be found in the liberal flanks of both major political parties, in much of Ivy League corporate America, particularly in Wall Street and New York City, and in prestigious, blue-chip internationalist associations and policy planning groups, such as the New York Council on Foreign Relations, the Committee on Economic Development and the Atlantic Council of the United States. Many of the personnel and programmes of the major liberal foundations, such as the Ford and Rockefeller foundations, the Carnegie Endowment for International Peace and the German Marshall Fund, have a strong Atlanticist thrust. Prominent Atlanticists are also numerous in liberal think-tanks such as the Brookings Institution. In the Federal government, there is a strong Atlanticist faction in the State Department, as well as to a somewhat lesser extent in the Pentagon and the Treasury. The perspectives of this flank of the establishment are frequently expressed in the journals *Foreign Affairs* and *Foreign Policy*. Rosenau and Holsti link this to a tendency called 'Post-Cold War Internationalism' (Post-CWI), a view which sees the international system as essentially multipolar, configured by economic interdependence, a system in which the USSR is militarily powerful but economically weak. The USSR is seen as inherently a defensive power.

Atlanticists of both sides of the ocean have traditionally met in not only the quasi-official Atlantic Institute (headquartered in Paris), but also in the highly secret Bilderberg meetings, which observers have suggested has acted as a private counterpart to NATO, since Bilderberg's foundation in the mid-1950s. The more recently-formed private Trilateral Commission (TC), launched in 1973 by David Rockefeller, is also strongly Atlanticist, but in a rather unique way, since it seeks to consolidate the Atlantic axis within the context of the triangular North American–Japanese–west European relationships. Many of the European members of the TC are both Atlanticists and advocates of a closer political union for Europe, reflecting two of the strands in traditional Atlanticist thought in the USA as well as in Europe.

Reagan's right-wing world view is, in its quintessential form, more associated with the 'nouveaux riches' of American civil society, represented in the concept of sunbelt capitalism. This perspective is more stridently anti-communist, anti-statist, anti-union and more individualist than the corporate liberalism of the mainstream establishment view. Moreover this viewpoint is less 'internationalist' in the sense of repudiating organisations such as the United Nations and being suspicious of the activities of the World Bank. In addition, through its espousal of a military-industrial strategy for the revitalisation of American capitalism, its basic perspective is a realist-mercantilist one, seeing the interests of American producers as being in conflict with those of its overseas competitors.

The institutes which correspond to this perspective include the Hoover Institution at Stanford University in California, (some theorists in) the Center for Strategic and International Studies, Georgetown University and the Heritage Foundation in Washington DC. Reaganites see the world in bipolar terms, with the key form of interdependence being military. In contrast to the liberal internationalists, the CWI perspective portrays a militarily aggressive USSR, a power that must be contained and even undermined by re-establishing the USA's military superiority and eventually 'peace through strength'. This commitment was embodied, for example, in many of the writings in *Commentary* magazine and in the wide-based Coalition for Peace through Strength, the successor to the 1970s Committee on the Present Danger.

Its view towards the allies is less pragmatic and more coercive, seeking to reassert American prerogatives within alliance policies. This coalition of forces was strongly linked to the geopolitical perspectives and material interests of the USA's military–industrial complex. Increasingly, also, the leadership of the American labour movement in the AFL-CIO and conservatives in the Democratic Party tended to move towards this perspective.

Our two perspectives should not, however, be seen as mutually exclusive and competing, but also overlapping. Rosenau and Holsti suggest that the 'mind-set' of each was rooted in a 'politics of contraction', that is a set of political responses to a perceived erosion in the USA's international power. This perceived erosion created a fundamental political crisis in the USA in the 1970s and 1980s. The Reagan Administration provided one response to this problem, and not necessarily one which the majority of the establishment, or the European allies fully endorsed. The prevailing view, at least until the 1970s, was that associated with the liberal internationalists, who were, of course, also Atlanticists. Let us now discuss the foundations of this perspective to prepare the ground for a further discussion of Reaganism and the developing crisis of Atlanticism.

Post-war American elite attitudes towards western Europe were fundamentally shaped by the experience of World War II, and in particular by the assessment of liberal internationalists of the major economic forces which had helped cause the war.

Following the views of Cordell Hull, the disintegration of the world economy during the inter-war years into rival mercantilist blocs was seen as significantly contributing to a zero-sum and unstable condition in international relations. Post-war plans were made to try to break down these blocs (e.g. through decolonisation and the destruction of the British imperial preference system) and to create an integrated world economy based upon liberal principles, to eliminate inter-bloc rivalry and thus create the political conditions for post-war economic growth. In addition, the monetary instability of the inter-war years was also seen as contributing to the short-term, beggar-thy-neighbour outlook which came to prevail in economic relations.

In consequence, international economic institutions, and a liquidity system based around the dollar, were engineered to try to create long-term, more stable economic conditions for capitalist growth. At the political level, the USA endeavoured to reconstruct the political systems of the defeated Axis powers so that they might move towards more liberal democratic politics. The militarisation of the alliance between the USA and its former allies and adversaries was consummated in the establishment of NATO. The catalyst for the further militarisation of the transatlantic relationship was the onset of the Cold War. This led to the development of the bipolar security structure which had the effect of consolidating the blocs under the leadership of each superpower.[3]

At this stage, the key differences between the USA and its west European allies were more or less submerged in a widely-based consensus on the need to consolidate the political centre in the West as a bulwark against Soviet expansionism, as a means of remobilising west European capitalism, and to assist the growth and spread of American companies overseas. This consensus reflected a convergence of basic Atlantic interests in four categories:

1. Defence of individual nations against the Soviet military threat and potential military threats from each other (for example, French fears of a resurgent Germany).
2. Economic growth and monetary stability (underwritten by American aid and investment in an institutionalised international economic system based upon a dollar standard).
3. Security in the North Atlantic area and in adjacent regions, notably the Baltic, the Mediterranean and Middle East, the latter guaranteeing Western access to cheap energy supplies deemed essential for industrial growth.
4. The preservation and extension of the liberal democratic system, and the containment of communism both at home and abroad.

Each of these basic interests allowed the west European countries to accept the new American imperial system.

The consensus was also expressed in the notions of the mixed economy, the welfare state, social democracy, and an anti-communism based upon the view of the USSR as an oppressive, totalitarian power. The introduction of Fordist methods of accumulation (mass consumption and mass production) took place in the context of a class compromise, reflected in the phrase 'the end of ideology'. Charles Maier has used the phrase 'the politics of productivity' to stress that economic well-being and a concern for productive efficiency dominated the consciousness and action of the Western working classes and their social democratic leaders in this period.

This consolidated the political centre, as did the willingness of politicians from other parties to support the welfare state and corporatist modes of economic and social decision-making.[4] Such a domestic consensus underpinned the willingness of the previously mercantilist and imperialist European states to accept not only American military leadership, but also a more open international economy, and allow an 'open door' with respect to foreign direct investment.[5]

This enabled many American corporations to gain a significant foothold in Europe, as well as helping to generate economic recovery. In this context, and in an alliance structure which would reduce the likelihood of a resurgent Germany again threatening continental peace, the USA was able to consolidate a dynamic hegemony, but one in which a wide range of interests and aspirations were given significant weight. It is worthwhile noting, however, that although the positions which Americans took on these questions were, as Calleo has put it, 'notable for their disregard of the cost to other nations of their loss of self-determination', the USA made numerous concessions to allow some self-determination.[6]

The relative stability of the Atlantic alliance persisted through the 1950s and 1960s as its members united politically under American leadership. To this extent, American hegemony took a generally consensual, Gramscian form, although both the UK and France felt humiliated by Suez. Under General de Gaulle, France provoked the first significant political challenge to such hegemony, fracturing some aspects of the earlier consensus which had been shaken by the events of 1956.

At the level of ideas, the consensus was linked to what Calleo called the 'Atlanticist ideology' which typified the liberal parts of the USA's foreign policy establishment during World War II and through the 1950s and 1960s. For Calleo, this ideology allowed the USA to construct a 'masquerade' of multilateralism in the post-war international economic institutions which disguised its monetary hegemony based upon a dollar standard. This ideology, popular in American corporate and academic circles, mixed 'classical economics, world federalism and American imperialism', and had as its basic tenet:

> integration for the world's developed capitalist economies. To the classical economic arguments for free trade and free capital movements, the Atlanticist ideology adds the integrating role of the international corporation. Impelled by transnational interests and institutions, the developed capitalist countries are alleged to move toward a single cosmopolitan economy. The steady worldwide integration of markets and production continues (it is said) to enmesh regional economies in a web of mutual interests so intimate that withdrawal becomes more and more costly and improbable.[7]

The implications of this American perspective, when combined with a call for a forward-based American military presence in Europe and elsewhere, would inevitably mean that the USA would be at the apex of a transatlantic hierarchy, despite its fairly consistent public support for west European political unity.

This vision of a hegemonic system was, as Calleo elsewhere points out, a shift away in American thinking from an earlier 'two pillars' of Atlanticism concept.[8] This latter concept was embodied in the writings of George Kennan, who had envisaged containment in primarily economic terms, and had assumed, when writing his famous 'X' article in *Foreign Affairs* in 1947, that the western European countries would, at some point, be able to defend themselves from Soviet aggression.[9]

It was the strategy of across-the-board military containment with an implicit military Keynesianism represented in NSC 68, a top-secret review of Soviet intentions conducted in 1950, which symbolised the movement away from Kennan's vision in the American leadership. NSC 68 suggested that the USSR would triumph over the allies if the USA did not respond rapidly. It called for defence programmes which would triple the Pentagon budget, much of which would be focused on Europe. NSC 68, or at least the political response to it in the USA, guaranteed a militarised and hegemonic transatlantic relationship. (NSC 68 was never officially adopted by the Truman Administration, but apparently had a strong impact on the views of the establishment, and indirectly on public opinion.) Thus geopolitical, ideological and economic aspects of American strategy were fused.

The Cold War went through three phases, periodised by Alan Wolfe as 1948–52; 1952–57 (years of retrenchment reflecting the essentially defensive stance of the Eisenhower Administration, notwithstanding the bellicose rhetoric of John Foster Dulles); and 1957–1963 (an early period of consolidation, followed by the more activist and more confrontational stance of President Kennedy). This was followed by an uneven period of Cold War and detente during the 1960s, then detente proper from 1968 to around 1978. The next phase was a mixture of Euro-Soviet detente and US-Soviet hostility (1978–85).[10] Since 1985 there has emerged the contours of a new detente between the superpowers.

Kennan's view of the two pillars of Atlanticism indirectly reflected a strong strain of isolationism relative to Europe: at some point western Europe would be rebuilt and the USA could withdraw its military forces. Indeed, the widely publicised arguments about 'no first use' of nuclear weapons made in the 1980s by Kennan, Gerard Smith, Robert McNamara and McGeorge Bundy, should be interpreted in a similar context to right- and left-wing demands for reduction or withdrawal of the USA's military forces based in Europe. These representations of Mansfieldism reflect a powerful isolationist tradition in American political thought. The new forms of isolationism reflected the view that the economic integration of western Europe produced a relative equality in economic capacity, and Europeans were now able to pay for their own defences. However, as Rosenau and Holsti have argued, there is still nothing like a substantial minority in favour of this perspective in the USA. The Cold War Internationalists and the Post-CWI perspective were still vying for hegemony within the foreign policy elite during the 1980s. Since the latter half of the Carter Administration, the synthesis between these views as represented in policy toward the USSR tended to shift rightward, at least until the mid-1980s.[11]

THREE IMAGES OF EUROPE

Catherine McArdle Kelleher suggests that within competing views of the transatlantic relationship, three images of Europe predominated in the USA during the 1950s and 1960s, and aspects of these can be seen in American reactions to its allies in the 1980s.[12] These images can be also seen as rationalisations for American policies, as well as reflecting a pervasive belief that the USA has a *droit du seigneur* over the actions of its allies.

The first and dominant image was of Europe as the prize in the struggle between the superpowers. It was the central battleground in the ideological war for freedom and democracy. A second 'missionary-interventionist' image reflected the strains of Manifest Destiny. American leaders came to see the USA as the 'best European'. In this view, the USA had a mission to unify and consolidate western Europe and, as Kelleher puts it, to make sure it 'worked'. By the mid-1960s, the litmus test of American policy was the degree to which it promoted the unity of NATO:

> By the mid-1960s the common elite image of 'doing it right' had become focused on the unity of NATO. The health of the Alliance and the loyalty of members became surrogate tests for how well Europe's interwar problems of stability and co-operation had been resolved. Also, NATO became the framework for the co-ordination of Western interests, the symbol for Americans of the new Europe they had helped construct . . . [For conservatives] . . . the NATO framework attained the symbolic status virtually of man's last best hope. Thus Senator Mansfield's successive resolutions on American troop withdrawals . . . struck at the core of the West. The primary problem . . . was . . . the weakness that they revealed in Western political resolve, and the unravelling of the basic Atlantic political bargain to ensure European stability.[13]

A third cluster of images focused on how many Americans saw Europe attempting to preserve its old imperialism in the 1950s, and later failing to appreciate fully both the 'Soviet threat' and challenges to long-term

Western interests in other regions. It might be noted that this latter view ignored the long west European tradition of viewing the USSR as an oppressor of progress and enlightenment. Put simply, west European states were seen as self-seeking and ungrateful for American support. This view had roots in the traditional American moralist and isolationist views of the Old World as corrupt, decadent, riven by power politics and lacking principle in foreign policy. Thus the fairly high degree of allied co-operation over Korea was contrasted unfairly by Americans with the relative lack of such co-operation over Vietnam.[14]

This strand of American thinking, or rationalisation, was reflected in President Carter's attempt to impose collective allied sanctions on Iran after the 1978 revolution, and on the USSR after the 1979 Soviet invasion of Afghanistan; President Reagan's call for sanctions after the declaration of martial law in Poland; in Reagan's attempts to used extraterritorial imposition of American law to force west European countries to pull out of the Siberian pipeline deal in 1982; and Reagan's criticisms of the allies for their refusal to rally behind Washington's fight against state-sponsored 'international terrorism' in 1985 and 1986.

DEVELOPMENTS IN THE 1970s

The 1970s was a period when American perceptions about the world, Europe and the appropriate model of foreign policy seemed to change. This was symbolised in a more active policy of detente, as well as the elaboration of a politics of economic rivalry with western Europe. Until the early 1970s the USA fairly consistently supported European unification. Thereafter, the perception of western European countries as economic rivals began to figure more prominently in the minds of many American leaders, as well as organised labour. This reflected anxieties about the loss of American competitiveness and slowing relative productivity growth, fears which persisted into the Reagan years.

Preoccupied by Vietnam, and in the context of a geopolitical perspective of *realpolitik* rather than of corporate liberal internationalism, the Nixon-Kissinger foreign policy began to attack traditional Atlanticist concepts, appearing to downgrade the importance of the Atlantic alliance whilst undermining one of its key rationales by engaging in a policy of super-power detente. American policies took a more directly unilateralist, and some would say aggressively nationalist-mercantilist course, apparently abdicating America's post-war role as the 'benevolent custodian' of the international economy.

Henry Kissinger's new Atlantic Charter of 1973–74, coming as it did in the wake of an assault on western European economic interests in 1971 (when the USA effectively devalued the dollar and placed a tariff surcharge of 10 per cent on imports, including those of west European firms) was not enough to reassure the USA's allies that there had not been a basic shift in the USA's commitment and leadership of the alliance. Kees van der Pijl argued that these measures marked the end of Atlantic integration under American hegemony, although this claim was perhaps premature given the attempts of the Reagan Administration to reassert American supremacy.[15]

Internationalist and Atlanticist elements on both sides of the Atlantic (and in Japan) reacted strongly against what Fred Bergsten called the 'xenophobia' of President Nixon's Secretary of Treasury, Texan John Connally, and Nixon's New Economic Policy. This reaction was a crucial catalyst in the formation of the influential Trilateral Commission, and the later establishment of the seven-power summits as a defence against American unilateralism. The backdrop to Nixon's moves was a significant deterioration in the USA's balance of payments, and pressure on the fixed exchange rate regime as a result of the now much more integrated and volatile world economy. Nixon's shocks provided a new impetus towards greater European unity. The fact that these measures seemed to be aimed more at Japan than at western Europe provided little consolation to European interests. Moreover, in the late 1960s, France and West Germany, under President Pompidou and Chancellor Brandt had begun to construct a political detente with the East whilst attempting to forge a closer European, rather than Atlantic, unity. Kees van der Pijl summarises the significance of these developments:

> Common to the yet disparate strategic initiatives undertaken in 1969–71 was their departure from the conceptual basis on which bourgeois hegemony in Europe had so far been based: American supremacy, Atlantic integration and the Cold War, as well as a passive attitude towards American neo-colonialist penetration in the formerly European periphery.[16]

Part of the reason for these departures was a change of American orientation towards a more directly nationalist perspective: the Administration seemed prepared to risk Atlantic unity in order to reassert its prerogatives in the shaping of Western policy. The October War of 1973 provided the USA with an opportunity to force its allies to bend to its will, whilst the massive increase in the real price of oil as well as the economic dislocations caused by the Arab embargo (itself made possible by the willingness of the oil companies to co-operate in implementing the measures) severely hit their much more vulnerable economies.

This, in the context of the dollar devaluation and Nixon's import surcharges, provided the Administration with yet another means to gain a competitive advantage for its domestic producers, windfall profits for its oil companies (the largest in their history), and emphasised the geopolitical advantage of the more self-sufficient American economy. The USA, in contrast to the west European countries and the phenomenally vulnerable Japan, had massive domestic oil reserves and its oil majors, in conjunction with Shell-BP, had effective (if indirect) control over the distribution of international oil supplies.

The heretofore dominant Cold War liberal Atlanticism of the foreign policy establishment was therefore brushed aside by the much more uncompromising mercantilist policies of the Nixon Administration. As has been noted, this was partly a response to a pervasive sense of the USA's relative decline, and to the perception of an economically strong western Europe. Expressed in the Nixon doctrine, which was, as David Calleo put it, a strategy of 'hegemony on the cheap', the USA attempted to shift the imperial burden towards its allies and surrogates in the Third World, notably Iran, a policy which would have disastrous repercussions for American power in the Middle East.

The concept of detente had become widely discredited in the USA by the time Jimmy Carter was elected in 1976, reflected in the fact that President Ford banned its use for his re-election platform in the Presidential election. Thus although the Carter Administration, replete with Trilateralists (that is, ex-members of the Trilateral Commission) in all key positions, came into power with the restoration of allied relations as the centrepiece of its foreign policy strategy, it was quickly outflanked by the right, and by the remobilisation of the military-industrial complex, symbolised by the growing influence of the Committee on the Present Danger. Carter rapidly shifted towards a more confrontationist position towards the USSR. These moves alarmed the allies. This was particularly the case for West Germany, which at this stage had developed a strong economic and political stake in its detente with the East.

American–German relations were not helped by Chancellor Helmut Schmidt's open contempt for Carter, but larger differences had served to create a deterioration in the Washington-Bonn axis. For example, the Carter Administration's nuclear non-proliferation policies were strongly opposed by West Germany: the Carter Administration tried to prevent a lucrative sale of German nuclear technology to Brazil on grounds unacceptable to Bonn. The Carter human rights policy ran into difficulties in Moscow and in Bonn. The West Germans believed that it would serve to undermine their carefully cultivated *ostpolitik*. The scale of these tensions, and the willingness of the Germans to challenge American leadership, reflected the growing economic power of the Federal Republic, and its new political confidence and assertiveness. Many members of the American establishment also perceived these developments as further evidence of the weakening of American hegemony.

The Carter Administration's international economic policy makers had to grapple with a record trade deficit in 1977–78, which was caused, so it was thought, by an overvalued dollar. The Administration was also concerned at the slowing of world economic growth, and fears of a challenge from the left in Europe, as shown by the rise of Eurocommunism. This challenge was widely interpreted within the Administration as resulting from the lacklustre economic performance of the west European region. The Administration's response, despite its avowed commitment to Trilateral consultation, was to try to force Japan and West Germany to expand, to appreciate their currencies, and thus to bring down the value of the dollar. The allies met these initiatives with the argument that Washington was trying to impose its own economic priorities on them.[17] Nonetheless, as Bergsten observed:

> Just as that effort began to succeed in mid-1978, however, the needed decline of the dollar accelerated and – prompted by an acceleration of US inflation and growing lack of overall confidence in Administration policies – turned into a "free fall" which overshot on the downside. The authorities were forced to work out a co-operative defense of the dollar and adopt more restrictive domestic policies, particularly monetary policy after October 1979, as urged by other countries.[18]

Bergsten was referring, somewhat euphemistically, to the famous 'Volcker shift' of 1979 when measures taken by the Federal Reserve precipitated a deep, worldwide recession, which had, perversely, a more severe impact on the American economy than on those of most other allied countries. This forced up real interest rates to unprecedented levels in the USA and worldwide (at one point these levels broke the usury laws of certain American states), and helped to create the international monetary conditions for the Third World debt crisis of the 1980s.

Domestically, these policies accelerated the decline of the 'rustbelt' industries and, because of a flood of bankruptcies and a rising tide of unemployment, put organised labour on the defensive. These changes reflected the triumph of neo-liberal monetarist economic strategy over the previous Keynesian consensus. This is not to say that Keynesianism was dead (the USA continued to spend freely on the military and in social programmes). It merely suggests that a new emphasis had emerged, with a stress on the virtues of the market mechanism and an attempt to reduce the role of the state in the economy.

After the Senate's refusal to ratify the SALT II Treaty, and the 1979 Soviet intervention in Afghanistan, superpower hostility intensified, placing the west European–east European detente in jeopardy. Despite the dispute over the neutron bomb, and the failure of SALT II ratification, the American commitment to NATO remained strong, reflected in the 1979 decisions to place Cruise and Pershing II missiles in Europe at the request of the West German government (to respond to Soviet installation of SS20s), and in the broad allied commitment to raise military outlays by 3 per cent per annum over a five-year period. However, superpower detente had evaporated: Carter imposed an embargo on grain exports to the USSR (later quickly revoked by Reagan, since it hit American agricultural producers who had become dependent on the Soviet market), and organised a boycott of the Moscow Olympics (to which the USSR replied with a boycott of the 1984 Los Angeles games).

REAGANISM AND ATLANTICISM

In the wake of the 444-day Iranian hostage crisis, which permeated the last phase of the Carter Administration and was crucial in Reagan's electoral triumph, a more assertive, aggressive, and revanchist mood was developing in American circles. Much of this was directed at the west European nations because of their reluctance to participate fully in sanctions against the USSR and Iran. The Reagan Administration, in contrast to its predecessors, also began to focus more of its attention on developing its bilateral relations with Japan.

Reaganism can be interpreted as partly returning to a series of traditional axioms about the international system, in a broad offensive to reassert American ideological, political, economic and military dominance. In this offensive, the interests of the west European allies were seen as very much as secondary to American prerogatives, reflecting what Mike Smith has identified as a 'secular decline' in the attention to, and support for, Atlanticism within the Reagan constituency.[19]

The dominant perspective within the Reagan Administration, and increasingly within the American elite, was a more pragmatic and instrumental Atlanticism, based much more clearly on the assertion of American prerogatives. Nonetheless, the platforms of both the Republicans and Democrats in 1984 stressed the importance and indivisibility of the Atlantic Alliance. This commitment partly reflected American public opinion. Theodore Sorenson has reviewed over 400 opinion polls conducted between the mid-1970s and mid-1980s, pointing out that:

> NATO and the members of the Atlantic Alliance have enjoyed a majority of support along the American political and ideological spectrum, rising over the last decade . . . never falling into serious disfavour even during the Vietnam War years of disenchantment. American opinion polls did not even support the Reagan sanctions on European contracts for the Soviet gas pipeline . . . [However] Most Americans . . . state now that they do not want to see US nuclear weapons used even in response to Soviet tanks conquering Europe . . . [but] do support a posture of nuclear retaliation for a Soviet first strike.[20]

Sorenson's findings give scant support to the argument that, broadly defined, American commitment to Atlanticism was substantially on the wane during the 1970s and 1980s. In so far as a 'secular decline' occurred, it was restricted to specific constituencies.

What was probably most significant about the perspectives of the Reagan Administration – in contrast to Carter's – was the degree to which they reflected a great deal of confidence in American power. Reagan clearly repudiated the thesis that the decline of American hegemony was inevitable, and that the world system had entered a post-hegemonic period. Nor did Reagan accept the contention that the USA would have to share power increasingly with its major allies in a multipolar world, a major argument of the Trilateralists.[21]

To sum up, Reagan questioned or repudiated some of the central tenets of not only the Trilateralists, but also of his Republican predecessors in the Nixon–Ford Administrations. For the Reaganites, the USA still wielded massive international power, and was willing and able to use it. It was essential, therefore, to correct the public's misperceptions on this issue: Americans had to be convinced once again of American primacy. In this regard, central to Reaganite strategy in the first half of the 1980s was the ability of the President to renew American nationalism through an appeal to traditional values.

At the popular level, Reaganism harnessed the growing dissatisfaction with Carter's leadership and sought to reverse what Carter called the 'crisis of confidence' in American society which had developed during the 1970s. In order to advance his programme with the public, Reagan drew selectively on the ideological resources available to him in the American political culture, taking foreign policy 'back to the people'. For example, Reagan rekindled the pervasive manicheanism in American political culture and the myths of vigilantism in order to justify his 'get tough' approach to the Russians and to 'rogue' regimes like that of Libya. Likewise, the popular appeal of the Strategic Defense Initiative (SDI), or 'Star Wars', can be related to important strands in the American political culture: the manichean idea of good, God-fearing Americans versus evil, atheistic Russians; the search for a separate, isolated but impregnable USA, with a 'superior' nuclear weapons system to that of the Soviets. Reagan's supporters on the right, such as Norman Podhoretz, have called this the 'war of ideology' in which Reagan, 'the Great Communicator', was the spearhead.

Reagan saw himself leading the USA into a new crusade for freedom and democracy. Irving Kristol and other right-wing hardliners like Jeane Kirkpatrick echoed Reagan's views when they argued (with more than a trace of hyperbole) that Carter's policies shrank into what they called a 'self-loathing isolationism' which stressed human rights, arms control (or appeasement), a defensive policy towards the USSR, and 'American subordination to international organisations' *(sic)*. This meant that the USA was not prepared to try to win the 'basic conflict' with the USSR.[22] Reagan intensified Carter's military build up, reasserted American leadership within NATO, and attempted to coerce allies into complying with

American policies on East-West trade and technology transfer to stop what one senior Reagan official, Assistant Secretary of Defense (1981–87) Richard Perle, referred to as the 'technological haemorrhage to the East'.

REAGAN'S STRATEGIC VISION

Reagan strategy was a right-wing synthesis of different strands of thinking about how to promote American national interests. Reagan's instinctive approach was to see Europe as a political battleground between East and West, but nuances were added in response to allied complaints. Relations with western Europe were redefined in terms of the new 'tough-minded consensus' on foreign policy. This policy ratified the priority given to short-run American economic interests typical of the Nixon years, but also embarked on a long-term goal of renewing American military and economic leadership on a global basis. In this context, whilst expecting the west European countries to follow its lead, the Reagan Administration intensified its economic, and most obviously, technological rivalry with Europe, symbolised by the SDI, as well as in the increasingly acrimonious debates over trade in agriculture and services (see Chapters 6 and 9).

Reagan's policies towards communist regimes, despite the President's impressive (and to many Europeans terrifying) rhetoric, were relatively consistent. Reagan was initially harsh and confrontationist towards the USSR and more pragmatic towards China. The pursuit of increased American military power and strategic superiority, in particular through the SDI, was the centrepiece of the strategy. This, of course, provoked the USSR, and threatened west European–Soviet detente. This reflected a fundamental divergence between European and American perspectives and basic evaluations of East–West relations.

The backdrop to Reagan's politico–military perspective was the post-detente debate over the appropriate policy towards the USSR. A concensus had arisen in American political circles on the need for a return to the strategy of containment. Dimitri Simes has distinguished three variants within the neo-containment consensus, each of which corresponded to certain aspects of Reagan policies, namely 'ideological containment', 'realist containment' and 'containment without confrontation'.[23] Like Irving Kristol (who argued that NATO was dead), the editor of *Commentary*, Norman Podhoretz, and other neo-conservatives, advocated a virtually indiscriminate ideological form of containment, confronting communism on a world-wide basis, partly through a propaganda offensive directed at eastern Europe. In pursuit of this there were extra funds for the United States Information Agency, which was placed under the leadership of Reagan's friend Charles Wick. In addition there was a substantial increase in the budget of the Central Intelligence Agency (which rose, for example, at 25 per cent per annum between 1981-1984). There was a renewed stress on covert action.[24]

Robert Tucker, notorious for his proposals for military intervention in the Persian Gulf in the mid-1970s, advocated a more modest, 'realist' form of containment. The view focused on the so-called 'vital areas' of western Europe, the Far East, the Persian Gulf, and mineral-rich South Africa. In Tucker's view, containment needed to be more selective and geared to resisting the geopolitical momentum of the USSR, rather than communism on a global basis. Tucker's perspective seemed to form the bedrock of the Administration's approach, although its emphasis on a military build up might be seen as misguided from a realist perspective, particularly if it were to detract from the economic revitalisation of the USA's domestic base.[25]

In this context, attempts to contain the USSR led the USA to pressurise the west Europeans and Japan to curtail their trade with eastern Europe by extending the COCOM list of embargoed items after it failed to stop the Siberian pipeline deal. This was similar to American actions in the 1950s, although, in the 1980s, these restrictions badly hit western Europe, and particularly German exporters, rather than American companies, which had relatively little trade of this kind. In purely economic terms, the USA was denying substantial economic benefits to its west European allies at a time when their economies were stagnating. In political terms these policies were aimed at undercutting European detente. Their main purpose was to put economic pressure on the USSR in the same way as the pipeline embargo was in part an attempt to deny it access to foreign exchange and credits.

The Reagan administration justified its actions by claiming that the allies put 'profits above principle', as well as arguing that European regionalism was an obstacle to Atlantic unity. In effect, Reagan's vision sought to combine a large measure of freedom of manoeuvre for the USA with the subordination or incorporation of its allies. An example of this was the Reagan administration's offer of participation in the SDI. As Michael Lucas and Steve Smith point out in Chapters 8 and 9, west European leaders were concerned that SDI would lead to a drain on European technological capabilities under conditions where the Pentagon would exercise direct control over their use.

In addition, the longer-term strategic dilemma was that SDI might decouple the USA from west European defence, partly by encouraging a 'fortress America', neo-isolationist attitude to develop. At any event, a likely outcome of the SDI might be a renewal of the arms race, a development which would be welcomed by right-wing elements in the Reagan coalition who believed that this would weaken the Soviet economy and provoke an internal crisis of the Soviet system. Given these fears, Reagan shifted tactics, under allied pressure, to stress the 'research' aspects of the Initiative. On the other hand, as Mike Smith and David

Allen argue in Chapter 5, Reagan's security policies appeared to push west European leaders more actively to consider creating an autonomous defence capacity, although the old divide between 'Atlanticists' and 'Europeans' was still evident in the debates. This question was linked to the debate on the 'Europeanisation' of NATO (advocated by Henry Kissinger) and calls for a reduction in the American troop presence in Europe unless western European governments paid more for the provision of NATO defences (a position associated with the influential senator, Sam Nunn).

In the Third World, neo-containment was far from indiscriminate, with direct military intervention only taking place in 1983 in Grenada (without any consultation with the UK before the US Marines landed) and in 1986 in Libya (in this case only the UK provided the USA with a forward base from which to launch the attack). The Administration preferred to use proxy forces, such as the Nicaraguan Contras and the Afghan 'freedom fighters'. Although it tested the limits of the so-called 'Vietnam syndrome' in Grenada, the American public was, and still is, generally strongly opposed to the use of American troops for Third World interventions, notably in Nicaragua.

It should be pointed out here that the concepts of liberty espoused by many of the proxy forces sponsored by the USA have often been at considerable variance with the ideology that the Reagan Administration was seeking to promote. This type of inconsistency, as well as the ambivalence towards west European interests in general, and the so-called 'special relationship' between the USA and the UK in particular, was vividly illustrated in the Reagan Administration's response to the 1981 Falklands/Malvinas War. The Administration vacillated between support for a major ally, the UK, and an Argentinian military junta which had carried out its notorious 'dirty war' against domestic centrist and leftist forces within Argentina. Right-wing advocates of the USA's hemispheric interests (such as United Nations Ambassador Jeane Kirkpatrick) backed the Argentinian junta against the UK. The short-lived tenure of General Alexander Haig (an Atlanticist who backed the UK and allied unity) as Secretary of State further reflected the initial weakening of the Atlanticist perspective within the Administration.

A third variant of the strategy of neo-containment, 'containment without confrontation', was represented in the writings of Robert Legvold. By 1985, after the rise to prominence of Secretary of State George Shultz (who replaced Haig), the Administration, although in a sometimes contradictory manner, moved gradually, but by no means consistently, in the direction of this perspective. Legvold, representing the moderate and liberal flanks of the foreign policy establishment, favoured a mixed strategy of containment and detente. This position advocated the pursuit of arms control and trade agreements to help 'moderate Soviet behaviour'.

This more pragmatic view had been reflected in Reagan's initial refusal to reimpose a grain embargo on the USSR, and his later willingness to hold summits with Gorbachev, starting in Geneva in 1985. The pragmatists' view became more prominent after 1985, by which time the Administration seemed satisfied that it had regained the military initiative from the USSR, and that the USSR had been 'forced back' to the negotiating table, in part because of its fears over SDI.[26]

Whilst many members of the public, as well as leaders in the USA and western Europe, have been concerned at Reagan's obsession with defeating the Sandinistas in Nicaragua, and at the wider implications of controversial incidents like the 1986 Tripoli bombing and the 1987 Irangate arms-for-hostages scandal, these deflect attention from the most important part of Reagan's foreign policy, that is the biggest peacetime build up of American military forces in history.

This was the policy of 'peace through strength' which formed the fulcrum of neo-containment. The economic cost of this strategy was enormous federal budget deficits (leaving aside the opportunity costs of using the resources for other purposes), which had worldwide economic repercussions. It is to these aspects of Reaganism that we now turn. To conclude this section, however, it may be observed that the attempt by the USA to reconstruct its relative military power in the late 1970s and 1980s may prove to have been based upon a two-fold illusion: that of regaining its nuclear supremacy *vis-à-vis* the USSR, and that the USA could somehow re-create the capacity to impose military solutions in a world characterised by a massive diffusion of military capacities. By undertaking direct negotiations with Gorbachev (three summits between 1985 and 1987), and actively discussing a 50 per cent cut in strategic arsenals, Reagan seemed willing to recognise that the quest for nuclear supremacy was an impossible dream.

REAGANOMICS AND THE WORLD ECONOMY

Despite questions concerning the military utility of Reagan's arms build up, it is possible to argue with more confidence that Reagan's economic policies had very profound and far-reaching effects, and intensified a worldwide shift towards an economic structure which had become more liberal and more congruent with the interests of the vanguard, transnational forces within American capitalism. (This is not to argue that these effects were necessarily consciously planned.)

The military build up was the key link between the Reagan foreign policy and his international economic policy, since this helped to produce record budget deficits. In the long term, these deficits may well prove to be the Achilles' heel of Reaganomics. Since the economic contradictions of this policy struck virtually every reputable economist in the USA, the question remains: was there a rationale to Reagan's economic strategy? So far the only plausible answer to this question has been given by Henry Nau, who was responsible for international economic strategy as a National Security Council staff member during the first Reagan Administration.

Initially, Reagan's economic policies gave almost total priority to domestic revitalisation, with allied, and indeed other international interests very much as secondary considerations. The exchange in *Foreign Policy* between Nau (advocating the Reagan perspective) and Fred Bergsten (advocating the perspective of the liberal internationalists and Atlanticists) during 1985–86 was instructive for the way it brought to light the different assumptions and perspectives held by each camp.[27] Bergsten criticised the Reagan policies for repudiating the interests of allies and effectively undercutting the longer-term interests of the USA, by recklessly allowing deficits to rise and for stoking the forces which would press for restrictive and protectionist policies in the future. As his starting point, Bergsten stressed the rapid internationalisation of the American political economy, and the constraints of tightening interdependence.

Nau stated in reply that the Reagan Adminstration rejected the central thesis of the 'internationalists', namely that many of America's economic troubles in the 1970s were caused by the relative decline in American economic power, or by increasing economic interdependence. Instead, Nau argued:

> Contrary to those who stress declining hegemony, the domesticists believe that the American role in the world economy was not significantly different in 1970 than it was from the mid- to late 1950s . . . More likely, US domestic policies after the late 1960s squandered US economic power and in the process damaged the world economy . . . Twice during the 1970s the United States tried unsuccessfully to achieve international consensus on economic issues through diplomatic bargaining. But both times America squandered its diplomatic bargaining power by pursuing inflationary domestic economic policies that weakened its power in the marketplace. In the 1980s, domesticists urged for a reversal of this approach: an assertive use of US economic power in the marketplace . . . [which] . . . exploited effectively remains much greater than its power at the bargaining table – a fact which frequently irritates US allies.[28]

Although, as Nau pointed out, neither the President nor key officials were fully conscious of the premises of 'domesticism', they nevertheless underpinned the first Reagan Administration's international economic policy. Put at its simplest, Reagan's mixture of supply-side economics and tax cuts, anti-inflationary policies, deregulation, and Pentagon capitalism, all helped to revitalise the American economy and to reassert its international economic dominance, despite the threat of spiralling budget deficits. The USA was thus able to export both its 'market place magic' and what Nau called 'disinflation' to the rest of the world. This was followed by the

Reagan boom which, by initially sucking in imports and capital, helped to boost the world economy, and helped to mitigate the recession its policies had earlier contributed to in western Europe. The obverse of this was the continuation of very high interest rates which meant, in the context of the 1980s, many less-developed countries became mired in a debt crisis, a crisis which also threatened the solvency of a number of (predominantly American) transnational banks.

After the 1979–82 recession, the USA was able to expand through deficit spending, whilst the other capitalist states were constrained from doing so by international market forces. As I have argued elsewhere with David Law, this reflected the relatively greater set of international pressures and constraints on other states which resulted from the increased mobility of international capital as well as better integrated exchange and capital markets.[29] These market pressures brought a (deflationary and more liberal) convergence in the economic policies of the major allies without the USA needing to use diplomatic leverage to achieve its desired result. The same was true in many other countries, in concert with the imposition of harsh 'IMF medicine'. This enabled the USA to forge a new consensus largely on its own terms.[30] Nau's analysis indicated an awareness of the USA's capacity to mobilise the structural 'power of markets'.[31] The major agents in this process were those companies which were most mobile and resourceful: large-scale international banks and transnational corporations, many of which were American-owned.

American policies, of course, produced political contradictions for an administration committed to the liberalisation of markets: the very high real rates of interest sucked in not only huge amounts of capital (about one-third of world savings was financing the American budget deficit in the mid-1980s), but also, partly by virtue of the strong dollar until 1985–86, massive increases in imports, generating enormous trade deficits.

In response to these contradictions, and in part to alleviate the effects of the debt crisis, there was a shift in the economic strategy of the Administration, represented in the so-called Baker Initiatives of September 1985 (see Chapters 4 and 7 for details). This shift, towards a more comprehensive multilateral approach, involving attempts to co-ordinate macro-economic strategy with other key nations, and a shift away from global austerity policies, paralleled the shifts in strategy towards the USSR: now Reaganism was closer to the mainstream establishment view.

Even though the international value of the dollar against the major currencies fell by well over one-third between 1985 and 1988, the trade deficit remained at record levels, whilst other types of foreign investment in the American economy rose rapidly, particularly from Japan and western Europe. This intensified protectionist sentiment in Congress, which increasingly called for more restrictive trade policies, as well as help for American exporters. This took legal form in the wide-ranging 1988

Trade Act. In October 1987, there was a devastating collapse of stock market values on Wall Street, a collapse which immediately spread to other stock markets, as a new crisis of confidence in American economic policies developed. This crisis largely took the form that Fred Bergsten had been predicting for the previous two years. The developments of the 1980s, however, had the perverse effect of reasserting American centrality within the world economy, and the international impact of US policies underlined the fact that American economic dominance was far from at an end.

Whilst internationally mobile capital loomed larger both worldwide and in the American economy (international transactions were, by 1986, about 25 per cent of American GNP and continued to rise as a proportion of the total in 1987), organised labour was on the defensive, as recession hit hard, especially in the early 1980s. Even amid the Reagan boom of 1982–86, significant sections of organised labour in the USA were taking real pay cuts. This is of course exactly what the Administration wanted, since it was a sign of more 'liberalised' labour markets. Union membership worldwide continued to decline through the 1980s, and strikes decreased in most of the Atlantic economies, as well as in Japan. One effect of the weakening of organised labour in many countries was to marginalise its representatives and perspectives from the construction of the Atlanticist agenda for the 1990s.

Whilst there was a secular decline in the power of organised labour since the early 1970s, in a liberal and globally-integrated structure of capitalism large scale internationally-mobile capital became more powerful, despite a rise in certain forms of protectionism. In this context, many globally-oriented American transnational corporations, particularly in the energy, finance and high technology fields, have prospered (sometimes in alliance or in consortia with Japanese and European companies).

Whilst there was no great consistency in the Reagan Administration's international economic approach, its major orientation was to promote the conditions which would favour large-scale capital relative to smaller scale capital, at the same time as it sought to improve market access overseas for American firms. Thus its avowed economic liberalism (which was mainly applied in areas where giant American companies had a competitive advantage, as well as, of course, in labour markets) was coupled to an aggressive technological and military-industrial mercantilism, with the Pentagon reverting to its role of the early post-war years as a major agent promoting high-technology industrial development. In addition, Reaganism represented a further stage in the collapse of the 'corporate liberal consensus' of the post-war years which provided a crucial politico-economic foundation for Atlanticism. Whereas social democracy was still strong (although weakened) in western Europe, it had been substantially undermined by neo-liberal tendencies akin to those represented in Reagan economic policies.

CONCLUSION AND PROSPECTS

The Reagan era revealed that in its quest to reassert its economic and military dominance, the USA was prepared to risk much of the element of consensus within the Atlantic alliance. For example, despite the public relations claims of the allies, the signing of the INF treaty at the Washington superpower summit in December 1987 was a major setback for alliance solidarity, particularly since the original intention of the Pershing II and Cruise missiles was not to militarily counter Soviet forces *per se,* but to serve the psychological purpose of coupling American strategic nuclear forces more closely to the defence of western Europe, thereby strengthening the alliance's political cohesion. The examples of SDI, nuclear force modernisation, new nuclear war-fighting doctrines (all discussed by Steve Smith and Michael Lucas in Chapters 8 and 9) and a tendency towards American economic unilateralism were all evidence of a willingness to undermine Atlantic cohesion in order to reassert American dominance.

On the other hand, there was a lessening of superpower tensions in the latter half of the 1980s, partly reflected in the USA's efforts to reopen a political dialogue with the USSR at the leadership level and to reduce the growth in its military expenditures. The latter was significant for Atlantic relations, since reduced military expenditures would help to correct the structural imbalance in its Federal budget deficit, which most west European leaders wished to see reduced.

Following market pressures on the government after the 1987 stock market crash and the 1987–88 collapse in the value of the dollar, Presidential-Congressional budget negotiations took on a new urgency. Indeed, such market and political pressures on the Reagan Administration and its successor, the Bush Administration, may prove to be more significant in cutting the American military build up than any agreements signed by the leaders of the two superpowers.

Thus, on the surface at least, there were signs in the latter stages of the Reagan Administration that there were efforts which might serve to restore some of the consensus within allied relations. In this context, despite much talk of Mrs Thatcher's unique relationship with the American President, the efforts of allied leaders in this regard appear to have been rather vestigial. More important have been Reagan's personal desire to be seen in the history books as an architect of peace, and the domestic and international market pressures coming to bear on the American government.

In conclusion, for a range of reasons, the prevailing viewpoint in the Reagan Administration had partly shifted towards post-Cold War Internationalism, with pragmatists in control of the major foreign-policy making positions.

Nonetheless, it should be emphasised that whereas the USA was once heavily preoccupied with the Atlantic axis, in the 1980s a number of key American policies became simultaneously more globalist and unilateralist in character. Also, a tendency towards bilateralism was reinforced, notably with respect to US–Canadian and US–Japanese relations. The latter was partly reflected in the increased importance given to the Pacific basin. In this context, it would appear logical that during the 1990s the USA will attempt to integrate Japan ever more closely into its attempts at policy co-ordination with the major west European nations. In the longer term, this may serve to redefine the meaning of the Atlantic alliance in unprecedented ways. It is Japan which has become the USA's principal ally. This need not necessarily be seen just in terms of the Pacific versus the Atlantic in American foreign policy. Internationalist interests in the USA, notably many members of the Trilateral Commission, have favoured stronger links between western Europe and Japan. From this viewpoint, the issue or problem is how to move from Atlanticism to a fully-fledged Trilateralism.[32]

At a deeper level, however, my argument suggests that the hegemonic form of the post-war settlement between the Atlantic nations has changed, and was being reconstituted by a range of structural forces, as well as by the policies of the USA. What is in the process of emerging, and may perhaps become more clearly manifest in the 1990s, is a basic lack of congruence between the social forces which predominate on each side of the Atlantic. This is a sign of a crisis in Atlantic hegemony from a Gramscian point of view. Whereas for most of the post-war era Atlanticist arrangements were underpinned by an apparently durable domestic concensus, this is no longer the case. There is, at best, despite the convergence of economic policies which occurred in the 1980s, only a minimal concensus on approaches towards the role of the state in economic life, the relationship between the national and world economies, and between the major capitalist and communist states.

In the new conjucture, if it is acknowledged that the forces of internationally mobile capital are more prominent and this is reflected in American (and other states') policies, then the adverse trends for labour and social democracy are likely to continue, particularly given the anti-union climate fostered by neo-liberal politicians (see Chapter 4 on this issue). In so far as these trends continue, attempts to recast Atlanticism in the 1990s in terms of the old forms of Keynesianism and corporate liberalism are likely to fail.

A new, and probably less domestically acceptable, Atlanticist concensus may emerge in the 1990s, assuming that west European governments are able politically to navigate the long-term effects of relative economic decline and persistently high levels of unemployment. The rise of Japan and the newly-industrialising countries, and the structural change away from an international (that is, of separate national economies interacting) to a global economy (a world that is integrated and interdependent) means that the old forms of Euro-Atlanticism, at least in the political and economic spheres, are also likely to perish, whilst long-term doubts concerning the military aspects of Atlanticism have now moved into the open.

An obvious conclusion, therefore, is that, in the 1990s, any prevailing concept of Atlanticism, to be acceptable on both sides of the ocean, will not possess the hegemonic quality of those which prevailed until the late 1960s: the former Atlanticist concepts implied a degree of class compromise and welfarist politics of inclusion, and were developed amid propitious economic conditions. In Gramscian terms, these concepts, and the political consensus which was forged around them, were at the heart of an international historic bloc of forces in the Atlantic area.[33] Notwithstanding military questions, the political and economic form of a new Atlanticist consensus, if one is possible, will be less social democratic, more possessively individualist, and more 'liberal' in an economic sense. Its forms of state interventionism will be premised on support for the 'winners' at the expense of the 'losers' of society.

If this occurs, what we may witness, despite Ralf Dahrendorf's arguments to the contrary, may be a new stage in the 'Americanisation' of Europe, as well as a further redefinition of the place of the Atlantic axis in the world political economy.[34] Notwithstanding the Single European Act of 1987, the other major alternative, a form of Euro-mercantilism coupled to the development of a relatively autonomous west European defence capability, seems less likely, especially given the divisions within the ranks of the European Community (EC) members in the face of the twin problems of unemployment (the average level of which was 11 per cent in 1987) and deindustrialisation on the one hand, and the economic and technological challenge from the USA and Japan on the other.[35] Above and beyond this, any Euro-mercantilist strategy would need to be forged in the context of a *global political economy,* that is one where the forces of production and exchange operate at the global level. This would mean that even if a single integrated European market were achieved by 1992, it would not be built within protectionist walls.

NOTES

1. J. N. Rosenau and O. R. Holsti, 'US Leadership in a Shrinking World: The Breakdown of Consensuses and the Emergence of Conflicting Belief Systems', *World Politics* (1983), vol. 35, pp. 368–92.

2. See, for example, J. Godson (ed.) *Challenges to the Western Alliance* (London, Times Books for the Center for Strategic and International Studies, Georgetown University, 1984), part 4, 'Public Opinion and NATO', especially pp. 100–10 which contain essays by J. E. Reilly and N. Podhoretz. A more recent survey is T. C. Sorenson, 'A Changing America' in A. J. Pierre (ed.) *A Widening Atlantic? Domestic Change and Foreign Policy* (New York, Council on Foreign Relations, 1986), pp. 57–107.
3. The post-war struggles between the UK and the USA over imperial preference and economic spheres of interest are discussed in R. Gardner, *Sterling-Dollar Diplomacy in Current Perspective: the Origins and Prospects of Our International Economic Order* (New York, Columbia University Press, 1980). On the role of the New York Council on Foreign Relations and the plans to create a 'Grand Area' for American and world capitalism, see L. Shoup and W. Minter, *Imperial Brains Trust* (New York, Monthly Review Press, 1977). On the argument that the Cold War became in effect a system which helped each of the superpowers unify its respective sphere of influence, see M. Cox, 'The Cold War and Stalinism in an Age of Capitalist Decline', *Critique* (1986), No. 17, pp. 17–82.
4. On Fordism see A. Gramsci, 'Americanism and Fordism', in Q. Hoare and G. Nowell Smith (eds) *Selections from The Prison Notebooks of Antonio Gramsci* (New York, International Publishers, 1971), pp. 277–320; Kees van der Pijl, *The Making of an Atlantic Ruling Class* (London, Verso, 1984), pp. 90–100. See also C. S. Maier, 'The Politics of Productivity', *International Organisation* (1977) vol. 31, pp. 607–34.
5. J. G. Ruggie, 'International Regimes, Transactions and Change: Embedded Liberalism in the Post-War Order', *International Organisation* (1982), vol. 36, pp. 379–415.
6. D. Calleo, 'American Foreign Policy and American European Studies: An Imperial Bias?', in W. Hanreider (ed.) *The United States and Western Europe: Political, Economic and Strategic Perspectives* (Cambridge, Mass., Winthrop, 1974), p. 69.
7. *Ibid.*, p. 67.
8. D. Calleo, 'Early American Views of NATO: then and now', in L. Freedman (ed.) *The Troubled Alliance* (London, Heineman, 1983), pp. 7–27; see especially pp. 8–14.
9. George F. Kennan ('X'), 'The Sources of Soviet Conduct' *Foreign Affairs*, July 1947, reprinted in H. Fish Armstrong (ed.) *Fifty Years of Foreign Affairs* (New York, Council on Foreign Relations, 1972), pp. 188–205.
10. A. Wolfe, *The Rise and Fall of the Soviet Threat: Domestic Sources of the Cold War Consensus* (Washington DC, Institute for Policy Studies, 1979).
11. Rosenau and Holsti suggest that business and military leaders were more likely to adopt CWI perspectives, whilst educators and media leaders were more likely to be post-CWI. Labour leaders were most likely to be isolationist. Aspects of each approach were to be found at each level in the US foreign-policy making process. See Rosenau and Holsti, *op. cit.*, pp. 382–3.
12. C. M. Kelleher, 'America Looks at Europe' in Freedman (ed.), *op. cit.*, pp. 44–66.
13. *Ibid.*, pp. 49–50.
14. *Ibid.*, pp. 50–51.
15. Van der Pijl, *op. cit.*, p. 257.
16. *Ibid.*, p. 251.
17. For a critique of President Carter's policies, see S. Hoffman, 'Old Wine, Old

Bottles: American Foreign Policy and the Politics of Nostalgia', *Millennium* (1980), vol. 9, pp. 91–107.
18. C. F. Bergsten, 'America's Unilateralism', in C. F. Bergsten, E. Davignon and I. Miyazaki (eds) *Conditions for Partnership in International Economic Management* (New York, Trilateral Commission, 1986), p. 7.
19. M. Smith, *The Reagan Administration and Western Europe: The Shifting Domestic Foundations of Policy Making* (American Politics Group of the Political Studies Association, Occasional Paper, 1985).
20. Sorenson, *op. cit.*, p. 74.
21. Cf. the arguments of the bulk of US Trilateralists, reflected in, for example, R. O. Keohane, *After Hegemony: Cooperation and Discord in the World Political Economy* (Princeton, NJ, Princeton University Press, 1984).
22. Cited in S. Blumenthal, 'New Conservative Journal Aims to Alter US Foreign Policy', *International Herald Tribune,* 17 October 1985.
23. D. K. Simes, 'Disciplining Soviet Power', *Foreign Policy* (1981), no. 43, pp. 33–53; see also T. L. Hughes, 'The Crack Up', *Foreign Policy* (1980), no. 40, pp. 33–60; and R. Legvold, 'Containment Without Confrontation', *Foreign Policy* (1980), no. 40, pp. 74–98.
24. L. Bushkoff, 'The CIA Rides Again', *Times Higher Educational Supplement,* 9 January 1985.
25. R. Tucker, *The Purposes of American Power: An Essay on National Security* (New York, Praeger/Lehrman Institute, 1981).
26. C. Weinberger, 'US Defense Strategy', *Foreign Affairs* (1986), vol. 65, pp. 675–98.
27. H. R. Nau, 'Where Reaganomics Works', *Foreign Policy* (1984–85), no. 57, pp. 14–36; C. F. Bergsten, 'The Problem?' and H. R. Nau, 'Or the Solution?' both in *Foreign Policy* (1985), no. 59, pp. 132–53. Bergsten renewed his attack in Bergsten *et al.*, 'Conditions for Partnership in International Economic Management', *op cit.* See also A. S. Stoga, 'If America Won't Lead', *Foreign Policy* (1986), no. 64, pp. 79–97; E. Wellenstein, 'Euro-American Turbulence – The Trade Issue', *Government and Opposition* (1986), vol. 21, pp. 387–95.
28. H. R. Nau, 'Where Reaganomics Works', pp. 20–2.
29. S. Gill and D. Law, *The Global Political Economy: Perspectives, Problems and Policies* (Hemel Hempstead and Baltimore, Harvester Wheatsheaf/Johns Hopkins University Press, 1988), especially Chs 7, 10, 11.
30. H. R. Nau, 'Where Reaganomics Works', pp. 24–7.
31. S. Gill, 'Global Hegemony and the Structural Power of Capital', paper given to the 83rd Convention of the *American Political Science Association,* Chicago, 3-6 September 1987.
32. See S. Gill, *American Hegemony and the Trilateral Commission* (Cambridge, Cambridge University Press, 1989).
33. On the concept and application of the idea of the transnational historic bloc, see R. W. Cox, 'Gramsci, Hegemony and International Relations: An Essay in Method', *Millennium* (1983), vol. 12, pp. 162–75; S. Gill, 'Hegemony, Consensus and Trilateralism', *Review of International Studies* (1986), vol. 12, pp. 205–21; S. Gill, 'American Hegemony: its Limits and Prospects in the Reagan Era', *Millennium* (1986), vol. 15, pp. 311–38.
34. R. Dahrendorf, 'The Europeanisation of Europe', in A. J. Pierre (ed.), *op. cit.,* pp. 5–56.
35. On the Euro-Mercantilist strategy, see J. Palmer, *Europe Without America?* (Oxford, Oxford University Press, 1987).

3 · SOVIET PERCEPTIONS OF ATLANTIC RELATIONS DURING THE REAGAN ERA

Neil Malcolm

By the first half of the 1980s it was difficult for anyone involved in the administration or discussion of foreign affairs in the USSR to deny the pressing need for a thorough revision of existing policies. Failures abroad had rendered the country more friendless and isolated than it had been for decades, and had interacted with domestic economic problems to generate a situation where, as the new Soviet leader Gorbachev expressed it, if the USSR had been a capitalist enterprise it would be facing bankruptcy. Hard lessons had been learned in fields such as foreign trade and relations with the Third World, but the hardest of all had been in relations with the USA. The collapse of superpower detente had been accompanied by the emergence of militant anti-Sovietism in Washington, an anti-Sovietism whose spokesmen not only denied the legitimacy of the Soviet system, but also undertook to promote policies which threatened its continued existence in quite concrete ways, for example by accelerating and broadening the arms race, by subverting its client regimes, and by enforcing trade embargoes on vital categories of goods.

To facilitate a new start, Gorbachev initiated a large-scale restructuring and restaffing of the Soviet foreign policy apparatus, designed to enhance central control and coherence. In the process, officials who in the past had been involved in forwarding detente, and specialists who had had the job of justifying detente, appeared to gain in influence at the expense of the military and of party hard-liners. The Communist Party of the Soviet Union (CPSU) International Department, the ageing heir to the Comintern, metamorphosed into a foreign policy co-ordinating centre headed by Anatoly Dobrynin, the ex-Ambassador to Washington. The Foreign Ministry was thoroughly shaken up: in the 15 months following Shevardnadze's takeover from Gromyko, one in three ambassadors were replaced, several new departments were set up, and the team of deputy and first deputy ministers was reshuffled.[1]

The kind of 'new thinking' which was expected of the new men would clearly entail not only changes in the USSR's attitude to the West in general (exemplified in the emergence of notions such as those of security and economic interdependence), but also changes in the geographical focus of diplomatic activity, a shift away from superpower bipolarism to some form of multipolarism.[2] As it was stated at the 27th Congress of the CPSU: 'In world politics one cannot confine oneself to relations with any single, even a very important, country. As we know from experience, this only fosters the arrogance of strength.'[3] The relative tenacity of European detente and the antagonism being aroused in allied governments by the assertiveness and what some regarded as the adventurism of the first Reagan Administration made it inevitable that Moscow would throw itself into cultivating western Europe.

Quite apart from their shared desire to lower the temperature of confrontation, both sides were conscious, as the gas pipeline affair in 1982 demonstrated, of the persuasive economic arguments for persisting with East-West European trade and technological co-operation. On the Soviet side, the goals of responding to the American challenge in military technology, of achieving world levels of competitiveness in industrial goods and of satisfying domestic demand for sophisticated consumer goods could not conceivably be met in the period envisaged without access to Western technologies in a number of key areas. 'Restructuring' *(perestroika)* could not succeed without re-equipment. On the Western side, sharpening competition from Far Eastern producers and other newly industrialised countries, large-scale unused production capacity and unemployment increased the attractiveness of large, stable markets in the Soviet bloc, and of the cheap energy supplies potentially embodied in the USSR's gas reserves.[4]

Diplomatic pressure has been applied simultaneously on the military, political and economic fronts, and it has slowly begun to give results. While it was former leader Andropov who first offered to cut the numbers of Soviet intermediate-range nuclear missiles (1982) and then warheads (1983) to match the size of the British and French forces, it was Gorbachev who launched the train of concessions which led the way to an Intermediate Nuclear Forces (INF) agreement in 1987: delinking from strategic and space weapons talks (1985, 1987), offers of talks on cuts in conventional forces (1986), global elimination of Soviet INF (1987), and inclusion of shorter-range missiles in the deal (1987). 1985 was also the starting point for a new emphasis on 'Europe' (from the Atlantic to the Urals) in Soviet rhetoric. In Paris in October of that year, the General Secretary made explicit a shift in policy towards the 'political entity' represented by the European Community (EC), a shift which opened the way for individual east European countries to sign co-operation agreements with Brussels, and which led to active negotiations for the long-delayed mutual recognition of the EC and the Council for Mutual Economic Assistance (CMEA).

Special West German interests in detente were encouraged by easing the path to foreign capital investment in the USSR, and by comments about the possibility of 'overcoming Europe's division into opposing groups in a more or less foreseeable future'.[5]

How much of a change in Soviet foreign policy strategy does this all imply? If it was true, as Reagan charged in his interview with *The Times* in April 1985, and as Gorbachev repeatedly denied, that the USSR was striving to exploit transatlantic differences of opinion, what returns did it hope to gain from the tactic, and how far was Moscow prepared to push it? Was it really hoping to 'split the alliance', or was it merely searching for new points of leverage on American policy? We cannot answer such questions at all convincingly without reference to Soviet perceptions.

SOURCES

Anyone turning to the Political Report delivered to the 27th Congress of the CPSU in 1986 to find evidence of how the Soviet elite perceives current trends in relations between the Western powers would find it difficult to draw any clear-cut conclusions. The document in question announces that 'capitalism now has to cope with an unprecedented interlacement and mutual exacerbation' of all its internal conflicts. There are 'new outbreaks of inter-imperialist contradictions' of an 'especially acute and bitter' kind. Relations between 'the three main centres of imperialism – the USA, western Europe and Japan – abound in visible and concealed contradictions'. But that is only one side of the picture. Later on we read that there is a growing tendency to interdependence, that the three imperialist centres do manage at times to co-ordinate their policies, and that the existing network of economic, strategic and other interests which joins them 'can hardly be expected to break up in the conditions that prevail in the present-day world'. How is this 'contradictory' state of affairs likely to develop in future? 'The clash of centrifugal and centripetal tendencies will, no doubt, continue as a result of changes in the correlation of forces in the imperialist system.'[6] No doubt.

The vagueness and impenetrability of Party statements of this kind are most obviously rooted in the range of conflicting political demands which are made on them. A certain amount of continuity with previous statements must be maintained, potential domestic political opponents must be placated or outmanoeuvred, the shifting priorities of Party and state diplomacy must be observed. There is also the fact that they are compromise documents: they emerge from smoke-filled rooms inhabited by committees, working parties and advisory commissions. It is not just a matter of consulting interested sections of the apparatus. As Soviet social science has flourished, and as the numerical and political weight of institutions such as the Institute of the World Economy and International Relations and the USA Institute has grown, so the number of rival drafts to be considered has tended to increase.

Because of the restrictions placed on public debate over policy in the USSR, the work of academic specialists tends to carry a heavy political charge. Instead of openly advocating particular policies, however, they are obliged to take an indirect route, describing reality in such a way that certain preferred lines of action seem unavoidable. When, sometimes after years of patient work and intrigue, new images of the world and new concepts finally receive the sanction of inclusion in official documents, this can give clues about changes in the climate of top-level discussion. But this evidence, as the example cited above demonstrates, is often blurred and contradictory. An easier way is to look at what is being published by individual authors in the specialised books and journals. Despite their important role in providing rationalisations for Party policy and new forms of words for Party documents on foreign affairs, most specialists probably exert very little direct influence on policy. It is fair to suppose, however, that the way the boundaries of debate and lines of argument move in the expert community can give an indication of the changing climate of opinion among policy makers. This supposition is strengthened by what has become known about the political and social connections of certain research institute directors and other prestigious academic figures.[7]

A few preliminary remarks are required about the style of analysis used by Soviet writers on foreign affairs. It is common in the West for new conceptions in international relations to be presented polemically, as part of a challenge to existing models. Soviet social science, although it describes the world in terms of struggles and contradictions, cannot allow itself the same luxury. Its practitioners describe its growth rather in organic terms, as a process of development, ramification and refinement. Blank areas are filled in, adaptations are made to cope with new phenomena, but there is little explicit challenge to the accumulated body of work, apart from the occasional exposing of 'mistakes'. Change is cautious, in particularly sensitive areas almost surreptitious, and innovative authors are forced into allusiveness and ambiguity. The change in the intellectual climate under Gorbachev may improve matters, but for the moment it is rare to find the kind of original analytical work which is produced by Western writers in the Marxist tradition.[8]

When it comes to writing about 'inter-imperialist relations', matters are made worse by the complexity of the subject matter, and in particular by the difficulty of unravelling the interwoven tendencies to conflict and co-operation in international affairs. Soviet authors habitually cite Lenin's encapsulation of the rival positions of fellow socialist theoreticians of the early decades of the century in a dialectical formula: 'Two trends exist, one which makes an alliance of all imperialists inevitable; the other, which places the imperialists in opposition to each other.'[9] The two contradictory principles, it is understood, are always interconnected, and operate as two aspects of the same process. At one time the centrifugal trend may predominate, at another the centripetal trend. Robert Sodaro remarks, in evident frustration, in his study of Soviet writing about the NATO alliance, that authors invariably balance evidence of the predominant trend with countervailing evidence of contrary tendencies in such a way that it is difficult to determine where they stand.[10] But one should not be put off so easily. Given a degree of familiarity with the debates, and with the evasive techniques of Soviet authors, it is possible to detect consistent patterns of disagreement between different groups of foreign affairs experts. These may in turn give faint, but nonetheless valuable clues about tendencies in the thinking which lies behind Soviet foreign policy.

TWO SOVIET VIEWS OF INTERNATIONAL RELATIONS

The introductory chapter of Vladimir Lukin's recent book, *Power Centres: Conceptions and Reality,* provides good examples of the device of 'creative debunking' employed by Soviet social scientists. This involves criticising the shortcomings of 'bourgeois' theorising while simultaneously popularising it to their own public. It is often accompanied, as we shall see, by quiet appropriation of the more assimilable new ideas for domestic use. Lukin begins by summarising the development of 'multipolarity' thinking in the West, acknowledging the reality of the events (the decline in post-war bipolarity) which stimulated it, but addressing to it two serious criticisms. The first of these is an obligatory one for Soviet authors – it is directed at the realist assumption of a Hobbesian condition of war of all against all amongst states. On the contrary, maintains Lukin, elements of 'international society' are coming into being before our eyes. The former anarchy is yielding to a new type of international relations, most obviously between the socialist states (that is, when the leaders of socialist states do not 'neglect the basic principles of their regimes'). Among the developing states, too, Raymond Aron's 'anarchy-oligarchy' formula is really no longer applicable, in view of the selfless solidarity displayed in their struggles, in the United Nations and elsewhere, and in alliance with the socialist world, to limit the activities of transnational corporations (TNCs) and establish a New World Economic Order.

Lukin's second criticism concerns the application of a 'power-centre' model to advanced capitalist states. Lenin's two tendencies are illustrated in the 1980s, he writes, by an abrupt sharpening of competition between the leading centres of imperialism, accompanied by the rise of protectionism, and increasingly energetic attempts to defend national economic interests, but *also* by 'an unprecedented level of internationalisation of the world capitalist economy', an extension of the scale of activity of the TNCs, and an increasingly marked evening-out of levels of economic development and productive efficiency in the main capitalist countries.[11]

It is an effect of this contradiction in reality, suggests Lukin, that rival groups of politicians and international relations theorists in the West sponsor rival, one-sided doctrines which absolutise one or other of the two tendencies. He summarises the critique of Kissingerian realism offered by Brezinski and other American theorists of interdependence, stressing the latter's anti-Soviet and technicist features, but acknowledging its points of coincidence with the Leninist tradition.

Having paid his dues to orthodoxy and balance, Lukin is now free to develop his own Marxist-Leninist theory of power centres. International relations, he argues, is essentially a superstructural phenomenon in relation to the fundamental class/systemic conflict of the age. It therefore enjoys relative autonomy. The underlying process of socialist advance works itself out in a series of offensives and retreats, and is accompanied by 'a variety of dramatic and complicated collisions which appear at first sight to be lateral in relation to the main tendency'.[12] One of these 'lateral' tendencies is the substantial increase in the number of states which have pretensions to a global or regional special role. The 'typological similarities' of these 'power centres' are in a sense superficial ones: they do not reflect fundamental socio-economic distinctions, but 'refer to a particular kind of great power foreign policy aspiration and to the more or less consistent attempts to put this aspiration into practice' by certain groups on the basis of their perception of national circumstances (size, location), resources (population, raw materials) and capabilities (military, economic, cultural, etc.). Large states do not necessarily strive to become power centres, Lukin explains. This depends on the environment and on the balance of power between ruling groups. Those groups associated with transnational capital will characteristically adopt a more internationalist perspective, those linked to nationally-based capital or (especially in developing countries) to the state bureaucracy are more likely to embrace power-centre doctrines.[13]

According to Lukin, three factors have been at work in recent decades to strengthen the hand of power-centrist elements. These are the evening-out of economic potentials among the USA and its allies, the maturing of Third World nationalism into 'state nationalism', and the limiting of the USA's freedom of action by the growth of Soviet power. The picture which emerges from his book as a whole is one of gradual decline of internationalism among Western ruling elites, stimulated by, and contributing to the decline in American hegemony. In the USA the previous easy harmony between the national interest and the general interest of the capitalist system has vanished. Efforts made in the alliance cause are more and more perceived as sacrifices, and chauvinist currents gather strength, culminating in the early 1970s in the avowedly nationalist doctrine and practice of the Nixon Administration. In the following decade Lukin sees the perennial two tendencies at work in the conflict between the 'multilateralist' Haig and the 'unilateralist' Weinberger. Haig's eventual defeat underscores for him how much the 'power-centre orientation' has gained in weight in American politics since the 1960s.[14]

The post-war history of western Europe, in Lukin's account, reflects a complicated interplay of Atlanticist, Europeanist and Gaullist tendencies, in which the initial Atlanticist cast of European supranationalism was eroded by economic rivalries, by President de Gaulle's breaking of taboos and by American provocations. He considers, however, that by the 1980s the 'European rear' is at last catching up with the Gaullist vanguard. Of course the west European power centre is still in the process of formation. It is weakened by national rivalries which contradict regional-centripetal trends and by the persistence of Atlanticist attitudes among powerful elites. It is undermined by the activities of TNCs and by the efforts of the Reagan Administration to reassert leadership in the alliance. Nevertheless, concludes Lukin, 'the objective tendencies and subjective motivations which work to consolidate the west European "power centre" are long-lasting and increasing in number'.[15]

This line of argument is given general support by a number of other writers who focus on international *economic* processes. 'The logic of inter-imperialist rivalry,' writes one of them, 'prompts small and medium-sized capitalist countries to combine their efforts to confront the superior force of their rivals.'[16] Another hypothesis is that various factors generate processes of economic integration on a regional rather than on a global basis. Such processes are analogous to the formation of crystals in a saturated solution: while new 'crystals' are still relatively amorphous and subject to bombardment by 'active molecules' (for example American TNCs), the gradual integration of production and developing supra-national state-institutional features lend them more and more stability and coherence.[17] However Soviet commentators on the world economy are on the whole less committed to such a view. They tend to share a more consistently 'centripetal' perspective.

The idea of the relative autonomy and activism of the capitalist state was a key weapon in the long struggle of Soviet social scientists to free themselves from Stalinist dogma about the state as an 'instrument' of the finance oligarchy and to develop their own disciplines of politics and international relations.[18] It was also important to economists, who used it to elaborate Lenin's concept of 'state monopoly capitalism' in such a way as to stress the important planning and co-ordinating role of the state. Arguments broke out over this issue as early as the mid-1940s, when Eugen Varga put forward the idea that state-sponsored economic regulation and social reform were capable of rejuvenating capitalism and in particular enhancing its potential for technological advance. Although this view was suppressed during the Cold War years, it re-emerged during the following decade, with powerful backing from highly-placed officials who were in favour of expanding trade and other links with the West. Ever since then prominent academics at the Institute of the World Economy and International Relations (IMEMO) have tended to make the case for wider contacts between the Soviet bloc and the rest of the world economy by emphasising the organised and dynamic features of the Western economies, and their tendency to interact more and more intensively as the 'scientific and technological revolution' gathers pace.[19]

Whereas for Lukin the growing power of the socialist camp encourages polycentrism by lessening the scope for the USA to exercise military blackmail over its allies, for most of this second group of writers this challenge is seen to act as a stimulus to co-operation and planned change. Indeed, the whole face of the world economy is considered to have been transformed. Because of this and because of the imperatives of technological advance, there have emerged certain principles which are common to the operation of both socialist and capitalist world economic subsystems – the law of increasing international socialisation of production, of the increasing integration of national economies into the world economy and the growing necessity for planned management of the productive forces on an international basis.[20]

A number of authors writing in this tradition maintain that, despite the undoubted difficulties involved, state monopoly capitalism is in the process of transforming itself into inter-state monopoly capitalism, with the help of 'an emergent system of inter-state regulation' at the global level. A key part is supposedly played here by the activities of the Organisation for Economic Cooperation and Development (OECD) and by the regular international summits of the seven leading Western powers. Although most of the goals proclaimed at such meetings have tended to be frustrated by 'still powerful centrifugal tendencies', and in particular by American efforts to extract unilateral advantages from international agreements, solid progress has been made in the 1970s and 1980s in a number of areas, notably the fight against high energy costs and inflation.[21]

In a commentary on Lester Thurow's predictions in 1985 of a possible breakdown in the world economy, one Soviet economist chided him for his loss of faith in the future of international Keynesianism. He pointed to the 1985 and 1986 summit agreements on currency regulation and to the decision to set up a strengthened committee of finance ministers to advise the Group of Seven: 'Is this not a step towards the creation of that "international manager" in the field of foreign economic links which Thurow calls for?' There are still antagonisms and contradictions present in the capitalist world, he went on, but they have changed substantially in form, and they can no longer be analysed 'using the measuring rods which were devised in the first half of this century'.[22]

There is a great deal of coverage given in the Soviet press to the progress of international co-operation in research and development, made inevitable by escalating costs. The fact that hitherto rather exclusive large corporations such as IBM and ATT have begun to disperse not just production but also product development facilities on a worldwide scale, frequently in collaboration with local interests, is seen as particularly significant. It is judged to be a 'progressive' phenomenon, in so far as it facilitates scientific and technological advance and promotes the international socialisation of production. Like international economic regulation, it contributes, in the view of the writers concerned, to a situation in the 1980s where centripetal forces in world capitalism 'have the upper hand' and 'have begun to acquire primary significance'.[23]

It is clear that the interests of Soviet elite groups in breaking down barriers with the outside world and the interests of Soviet diplomacy in cultivating 'moderate' world opinion coincide to encourage the publicising of more analyses which stress the continuing possibilities for international political and economic co-operation. This is used to underpin Soviet campaigning in favour of such causes as the New International Economic Order, a negotiated settlement of the conflict in Central America, global collaboration to protect the environment, and so on, in a tone which harmonises well with American liberal and west European centrist and social democratic rhetoric.

A number of political scientists in the USSR reinforce the picture of tendencies to economic integration by drawing attention to what they consider to be trends to cosmopolitanism among Western ruling elites. In the late 1970s a great deal of interest was aroused by the activities of organisations such as the Trilateral Commission and the Bilderberg group, which tended to be regarded if anything with exaggerated respect. Although in the 1980s 'trilateral' values were acknowledged to be in retreat, their underlying strength, linked as it was understood to be to the growth and power of the transnational corporations, was still acknowledged by a number of writers. In regard to the USA's NATO allies this strength was seen to be expressed in 'the power of inertia of "Atlanticism" within whose framework the policy of west European integration initially emerged and which still governs the thinking of influential political forces in these countries'.[24]

How are these two broad perspectives reflected in Soviet analyses of the development of relations between western Europe and the USA in the 1980s? We shall look in turn at perceptions of progress towards European integration, of the balance of forces between the west European and American 'power centres', of the nature of current conflicts between them, and of transatlantic disagreements over high technology/defence issues.

EUROPEAN INTEGRATION

In view of what has already been said, the generally supportive tone of Soviet specialist writing on the subject of west European integration should perhaps not come as a surprise. After all, progress in this direction supports both the 'centrifugal' thesis, on a global level, and the 'centripetal' thesis, on a regional one. In the current international political situation, what is more, west European solidarity has acquired a new respectability for Soviet authors, since it is seen to exert a moderating influence on American anti-Sovietism.

One of the most authoritative accounts of European integration, published by a leading IMEMO scholar, demonstrates how easily the subject yields to treatment in the centripetal tradition. It is a particularly striking expression, the author writes, of the worldwide tendency to internationalisation of the production process, which is generating an active state and inter-state regulatory framework. It is the depth of institutionalisation which accompanies it which makes the EC phenomenon so significant. Subject to the same global pressures to interdependence as others, the west European states have managed through their self-regulatory efforts to consolidate their forces and establish a power centre which is able to challenge the USA and Japan, and react in a co-ordinated and constructive way to East-West and global problems.

In a more recent article, the same writer remarks that European integration is now 'a big factor' in international affairs. Particular progress has been made in the field of political and military co-operation, and the fiascos of the past have given way to solid achievements.[25] Contrary to the impression given by Adomeit in his summary of Soviet writing at the time, institutional innovations of the 1970s designed to facilitate policy co-ordination in the EC have been taken very seriously by a number of writers. Even the largely unimplemented Tindemans report was described in one account as an important blueprint for future development in the direction of political integration.[26]

Less sanguine estimates of progress towards unity are of course available, but even they can be expressed in extremely *communautaire* language. In several articles, Yury Shishkov returns to the 'need' for the west European countries to co-ordinate their efforts more decisively. This means finally breaking with the Luxemburg compromise and accepting the principle of majority voting on major issues. In this respect the outcome of the European Council session of December 1985 was a great disappointment, in that it made no fundamental changes to the decision-making system. The EC has reached a crossroads. It must choose, he writes, 'either to find the strength to make a leap forward towards closer and more binding co-ordination of policies among the member states, or to languish in the present state of endless squabbles and petty arguments that disarm it in the face of the advance of its American and Japanese rivals'.[27]

In the early 1980s, Viktor Lukin reported on active discussion in 'west European ruling circles' directed at enhancing the political autonomy of their power centre by adding a military dimension. Although these discussions did not, in his opinion, imply a breaking out from the NATO framework, they did provide evidence that the process of west European military co-operation had finally emerged from the embryonic stage: discussion of the issues had become much more frequent and widespread, the taboo on questioning American leadership had lost its hold, and top-level consultation procedures (at least between France and West Germany) had become institutionalised.[28]

Most Soviet commentators would be more restrained in their conclusions. The general view is that the USA is perfectly willing to encourage a strengthening of the European pillar of NATO, particularly if it results in some shifting of the expenditure burden and a greater militarisation of the west European economies. In view of the close defence ties between Great Britain and West Germany on the one hand and the USA on the other, prospects for the emergence of a European nuclear force or a dramatic enlargement of the functions of the West European Union (WEU) have been discounted since the 1970s. Further European defence collaboration is foreseen, but on an unambitious scale, through the European Programme Group, or on a bilateral basis, for example in the framework of the Franco-German Elysée treaty of 1963.[29] (See Chapter 5 for more details.)

THE ATLANTIC BALANCE OF FORCES

Looking at recent Soviet estimates of the relative weight of the USA and western Europe, it is not difficult to see a conflict between convictions (or wishful thinking, or politically-motivated assertions) about the long-term trend to a relative increase in west European power, and more concrete assessments of the current situation and short- and medium-term trends, which are far less favourable. Western Europe's relative weakness is especially difficult to ignore in respect of its science-technology-production capacity. The latter is understood by Soviet authors, and particularly IMEMO authors, to be the basis of international competitiveness.

Writers engaged in making a case for the strong emergence of a west European power centre are likely to focus on the improvements which took place during the three decades between 1950 and 1980, in the west European share of world trade, foreign currency reserves, overseas investment and industrial production. They point out that nine of the top 30 non-oil TNCs are in European hands and that competitive pressures are forcing the USA into a balance of payments deficit.[30] But in general the evaluation of western Europe's competitive prospects has followed that of the Western commentators on whose writings Soviet authors heavily rely, and has accordingly become more and more gloomy throughout the 1980s, thus falsifying Lukin's prognosis in 1983 that in view of the long-term tendency to evening-out of economic growth rates in the West, 'a US comeback does not seem possible in the near future'.[31] The USA, it is acknowledged, emerged more rapidly and more strongly from the 1979–82 recession. It maintained its substantial worldwide lead in research and development expenditure, particularly in the most important high-technology industries. Its grip on key sections of European industry has been strengthened through well-placed TNC takeovers, investments and agreements. Speculation is no longer aroused by Atlantic economic rivalry, but by the vitality of the Pacific zone. If there is a real threat to the USA's technological-industrial leadership, conclude Soviet economists, then it comes from Japan and the newly-industrialised countries of the East, not from its NATO allies.[32]

Opinions differ, it is true, about how justified the new 'Europessimism' is. Some suggest that it is being deliberately fostered by certain American circles with the aim of reconciling the Europeans to their new role as museum curators, and that misleading assumptions have been used in estimating relative industrial performance. For example, west European industrialists deliberately decided not to manufacture micro-processors themselves, but to concentrate instead on finding applications for them in a variety of industrial sectors. This means that technological advances are more widely dispersed and show up less well in crudely devised statistics. Some point to the strengths represented by an accumulation of skilled industrial labour, by the stock of scientific know-how, and by established competitiveness in areas such as chemicals. Others place their faith in the EC Framework Programmes in high technology, and in the European Research Co-ordinating Agency (EUREKA) project. But there appears to be a growing agreement that a combination of political weakness and American spoiling makes a competitive recovery unlikely for the time being.[33]

CONFLICTS IN ATLANTIC RELATIONS

In an era when war has become too destructive and too politically dangerous, wrote Yury Shishkov in May 1986, inter-imperialist rivalry plays itself out in less overt but nonetheless desperate conflicts. In its current battle against relative decline, the USA has had recourse, he elaborates, to a variety of 'weapons', some strategic, some tactical, and it has used them with a remarkable degree of ruthlessness and effectiveness.[34] This is a theme which is congenial to those writers who prefer to emphasise centrifugal elements and contradictions in the world capitalist system, but they acknowledge that the USA has owed many of its recent successes to the skilful exploitation of (an unequal) interdependence.

The first strategic weapon is the new Cold War. In the Soviet view, American foreign policy activism since the late 1970s has been aimed primarily against the socialist countries and the developing world, but it has also struck against other Western states. A climate of East-West tension is an appropriate device to strengthen bloc discipline at a time when Atlanticist elites and values have lost ground in governing circles, especially in the USA itself. Since west European inferiority to and dependence on the USA is most marked in the strategic area, the USA can maximise leverage by creating a situation where military factors acquire greater salience. What is more, Soviet commentators point out, stepping up the arms race and forcing it into new technological areas galvanises advanced sectors of the American economy, accentuating relative west European backwardness and subordination (for example as junior partners in Strategic Defense Initiative research). When the allies can be pushed into expanding their own military budgets, their (weaker and less arms-oriented) economies feel the strain sooner, and valuable additional orders for the necessary equipment flow to American defence contractors. A policy of embargoes, sanctions and arm-twisting frustrates the natural development of mutually-advantageous East-West European commercial, scientific and technological links, keeping the allies dependent on American-controlled oil supplies rather than on natural gas from the USSR.

The second strategic weapon is the economic one. High interest rates, Soviet writers comment, have sucked in west European capital on an unprecedented scale. Because of this and the more direct effect of high interest rates, the allies' recovery from recession has been relatively slow and halting, and investment in high-technology research and development ('the nerve of inter-imperialist rivalry') has been crippled. The unnaturally high dollar drove up raw materials and energy costs, which disproportionately affected the USA's less resource-rich competitors.

The main offensive is supported, in the Soviet version, by a series of tactical drives on the economic front. Non-tariff import restrictions multiply, tax concessions and subsidies are lavished on the high-technology sectors and merger restrictions relaxed, export insurance and credit schemes are extended, limitations are placed on the sharing of technology abroad, while every effort is made to impose 'free trade' policies on prospective importers around the world.

The USA, it is explained, is able to get away with these self-serving policies because it still enjoys sufficient economic advantages over its rivals to be able to enforce its will – a large home market, a world currency, leadership in *all* the key production-relevant areas of science and technology, ownership of numerous large, well-established and influential transnational corporations with strong positions in the west European economy – and also because of its political and military trump cards. If there are signs of reluctance to go along with its military projects, then economic pressure can be applied. Veiled threats of strategic withdrawal are effective in imposing discipline in the diplomatic sphere. There are isolated acts of European resistance – over the gas pipeline issue, over Central America, over SDI in the initial stages, but it is in general short-lived, and rapidly declines into posturing and foot-dragging. The Americans, it is concluded, have tended to get their way.[35]

Clearly this kind of Soviet analysis of day-to-day conflicts in the Western alliance, even when it is printed in the specialist press, is constructed partly with an eye to its propaganda value, whether for Soviet or foreign publics. Soviet observers are no doubt aware that the high dollar also *helped* the Europeans by making their exports more competitive on the American market. They presumably do not really believe that the budget deficit was intentionally created principally in order to impose high interest rates on the world economy – one of them is even punctilious enough to admit it. Furthermore, large swathes of this material represent more or less straightforward translation and summary from Western news magazines, economic surveys and government reports. Nevertheless, there is enough evidence to demonstrate that Soviet assessments of the prospects for western Europe have become considerably more pessimistic over the past half-decade. Although it is not normally spelt out, it is clear that the bulk of Soviet analysts see American hegemony as being successfully reasserted by different (less consensual) means in the mid-1980s rather than falling away, certainly in respect of Atlantic relations. An impression of European helplessness in the face of determined American manipulation emerges particularly clearly from Soviet accounts of the arguments surrounding the SDI and EUREKA projects.

THE STRATEGIC DEFENSE INITIATIVE

West European misgivings about the Strategic Defense Initiative were promptly and eagerly reported in the Soviet press, reflecting hopes that they might exert a restraining effect on the US Administration. As more and more European governments, private corporations and academic institutions took the lure of Star Wars research contracts, Soviet commentators continued to amplify the objections which still emerged from defence experts, opposition parties and particularly from France and the smaller NATO countries.[36]

In 1986 the IMEMO journal took the unusual step of publishing two articles in successive issues devoted to precisely the same topic, namely the politics of the EUREKA venture. As part of the reaction to SDI this enterprise is seen as an important test case for west European political coherence in the face of pressures from across the Atlantic. It is likely that the pieces in question represent spin-off from an officially-sponsored research project. Although there are slight differences in the sources used (in one case mainly French, in the other mainly German) and the conclusions reached about the project's likely future, both authors share a broadly common view of events. It is confirmed by a piece published around the same time on the European Defence Initiative.

It was characteristically enough the French, the reports run, who reacted first to the dangers of deepening technological dependence and of vulnerability to political pressure implicit in the preference of certain influential circles in western Europe for a policy of accepting the existing American-Japanese lead in the most advanced industrial sectors, and relying on imports and licences to provide the necessary hardware and know-how. They pointed out that the situation could only be remedied by improving west European co-ordination in research and development. Such is the prevalence of narrow technological nationalism that European firms are more likely if anything to collaborate with American and Japanese concerns than with each other. Existing EC programmes for co-operation in information technology, biotechnology, communications and so on are reasonably successful, but not adequate to the task.

EUREKA was proposed by the French government as a civilian response to the challenge of SDI, which the US Administration intended partly as a device to reinforce its technological dominance. But ever since the concept emerged in the autumn of 1985, write the Soviet authors, it has encountered obstacle after obstacle, most of them placed in its path by the West German and British governments. They are afraid to reject it outright, which would appear 'un-European', but are doing their best to neuter it, by cutting funding to the bone, and by manipulating the programme in such a way as to make it complementary to SDI rather than competitive with it. The 'Atlanticist circles' which dominate the West German Christian Democratic Union (CDU) do not simply want to avoid antagonising the USA. They are reluctant to become locked into large-scale technological co-operation with France, whom they perceive as a weaker partner, with little to offer except possibly in the military sphere. For this reason they offer official encouragement to German firms to conclude bilateral deals either with non-European partners, or in any case outside the EUREKA framework. This harmonises with the efforts being made by the US Administration, continues the Soviet analysis, to undermine west European resistance to SDI, by distributing research contracts to influential west European corporations and by encouraging its TNCs and numerous transatlantic commercial and political contacts to spread a mood of scepticism about EUREKA.

Because of these setbacks, report the Soviet researchers, there is now talk of the need for a military locomotive to drive the programme. The boundaries are starting to be blurred between EUREKA and the European Defence Initiative scheme promoted by West German defence interests and by 'aggressive NATO circles' in the USA since the early years of the decade. France is now evidently willing to envisage a more militarised EUREKA if this will strengthen Europeanist tendencies in the West German leadership and tempt the Germans to participate more wholeheartedly. Thus, in the end, west European technology policy will have been manoeuvred to face in the direction favoured by the Reagan Administration in the first place: the European contribution to the NATO defence effort will be enhanced, anti-American overtones will be eliminated, and endorsement will be granted to the perverse logic of SDI.[37]

PERCEPTIONS AND POLICY

Do the discussions reviewed above provide any help in thinking about the kinds of alternatives being considered by Soviet foreign policy makers? In particular, do they strengthen the supposition occasionally voiced in the West, that the USSR's foreign policy establishment is divided between those who regard bilateral relations with the USA as the overriding priority and those who favour a more multilateral or possibly even a 'Europe first' approach?[38] What do they tell us about official Soviet attitudes to moves in the direction of greater west European unity?

It must be said first of all that the tone of much of the material which is permitted to appear in the Soviet specialist press in the 1980s casts doubt on Adam Ulam's opinion that 'preventing European unity must remain the cardinal objective of the Kremlin',[39] and undermines the view put forward by Moreton and Segal, that the USSR would not welcome a more assertive western Europe, 'even if it were in the cause of greater moderation in policy towards Moscow'.[40] Indeed, it justifies the speculations of other experts that Soviet policy could take on a more decisively Europeanist colouring given favourable circumstances: a new leadership with a more open mind about European security,[41] an upsurge of anti-American feeling in western Europe,[42] American intransigence combined with continuing hunger for Western technology and know-how.[43]

It is not just a matter of divining policy implications from the general tenor of a body of superficially dispassionate academic analysis. There are more explicit contributions, often made by official figures exploiting the greater freedom of discussion permitted in a scholarly context.

Thus the senior Foreign Ministry official with responsibility for European affairs, the man who controlled the Soviet side of the Helsinki negotiations, Anatoly Kovalev, elaborated in the Moscow journal *International Affairs* in 1985 on the 'European dimension' of the USSR's foreign policy. The west European states, he argued, have shown the capacity to stick to an independent line in East-West relations, despite persistent American pressure, and have succeeded in maintaining wide-ranging co-operation with the socialist countries. They have made constructive contributions to the process preceding and following the signing of the Helsinki documents. They form part of a network of pan-European collaboration and interdependence which displays an irresistible tendency to grow and deepen. They take a more mature view of the world than their transatlantic allies, one characterised by pragmatism, tolerance and a sense of reality. Ostensibly a commentary on a (rather short) section of the 27th Party Congress Report devoted to policy towards Europe, this article undoubtedly bears a close resemblance to the kind of Foreign Ministry memoranda which contributed to the drafting of the Congress documents in the first place.[44] Various Soviet authors point out the possibilities for wider east-west European collaboration (in trade and technology exchange, co-operation in the exploration of space, etc.) and refer in an optimistic way to the readiness of west European countries to exploit them, or as the head of the sector for US-west European relations at the USA Institute expresses it, to allow 'the All-European principle' to override 'the Atlantic principle'.[45]

Aleksandr Yakovlev, the ex-director of IMEMO, and who has subsequently become a new member of the Politburo, has already been cited as an adherent of the centrifugal view of international relations. Jerry Hough's suppositions about his 'Europeanist' foreign policy preferences are further strengthened by his repeatedly and forthrightly expressed views concerning the USA. Yakovlev stresses the inexorable decline of America's power and the consistently reactionary nature of its political leadership (against the background of which Nixon's detente policy is best seen as a short-lived aberration, and Reaganite aggressiveness as a predictable and durable phenomenon).[46]

In the light of all this and of the turning towards Europe in practice described at the beginning of this contribution, it makes sense to assume the existence, then, of a 'Europeanist' tendency among some Soviet foreign policy makers and advisors. But it would be unwise to rush to conclusions about its strength and likely outcome, especially in view of the fact that men of similar standing to Yakovlev and Kovalev who hold rather different views about foreign policy priorities are known to remain in influential positions. It is noticeable that some of the writers most emphatic about the favourable prospects for west European self-assertion and unity have shared some of the apprehensions about German militarism normally voiced by more bilaterally-minded commentators.[47] There is a consistent note of concern about the possible repercussions of greater west European defence collaboration, which it is feared would be driven by American pressure (always seen as overwhelming in the military sphere), or by German ambitions, in a direction threatening to the USSR. Nor is there any sympathy for French-sponsored visions of European 'neo-colonial' activism in Africa.

In view of the kind of analysis of Atlantic relations which has been appearing in the Soviet specialist press, it is clear that opponents of an out-and-out readjustment away from US-Soviet bilateralism (as opposed to judicious shifts of emphasis) would have a number of well-documented arguments at their disposal:

1. The future is one of global interdependence and co-operation. Even if it is threatened in one or two areas by the Japanese, the USA is the world leader in science and technology and is likely to remain so.
2. Western Europe, by comparison, lags behind in industrial dynamism and efficiency, and shows little sign of being able to counteract an increasing tendency to fall behind in high technology sectors.
3. Western European elites are as likely to be narrowly nationalist, or Atlanticist, in their orientation as they are to be 'European'. This makes it difficult for western Europe to exercise a substantial degree of autonomy from the USA and to follow its own distinctive line in international affairs.

It seems to make sense to interpret Soviet cultivation of western Europe as part of a wider strategy of diversifying links in foreign policy. This strategy is a natural diplomatic reaction to American hostility, and it can be seen in action in the Far East, the Middle East, Latin and Central America. There is no reason to suppose that the Russians have revised the view, which they clearly held to at the end of the 1960s, that no serious departure in east-west European relations is feasible without the close involvement of the USA. The nature of Western reactions to Reykjavik and to the 1987 proposals to remove intermediate-range missiles from Europe can only have strengthened that conviction.

When Hans Dietrich Genscher (a man perceived in Moscow as a bulwark of Europeanism in the West German government) arrived in the USSR in July 1986 he was welcomed by Shevardnadze in the warmest of terms. But the Soviet Foreign Minister denied any intention to break up the North Atlantic alliance: 'We are of the opinion that, given all the alliances that have taken shape, it is essential to strengthen those threads whose severance is fraught with the danger of severance of the world fabric.' For his part, Gorbachev declared that 'disrupting the existing political and territorial set-up in Europe would result only in chaos and the worsening of the situation'.[48] Although the diplomatic motivations for adopting this kind of posture are obvious enough, that does not necessarily mean that it does not simultaneously express a genuine Soviet attachment to predictability and stability in European affairs. Those Western commentators are surely correct who argue that the Soviet leaders cultivate the USA's allies not in order to fragment NATO, but in order to tug on the 'threads' of alliance consultation in order to modify the behaviour of the USA. Certainly there is nothing substantial in Soviet specialist writing to contradict this impression.

NOTES

1. A. Brown, 'Soviet Political Developments and Prospects', *World Policy Journal*, Winter 1986–87, pp. 68–74; C. Glickham, *New Directions for Soviet Foreign Policy* (Radio Liberty Research Bulletin Supplement 2/86, 1986); N. Malcolm, 'Soviet Policy Making in the Middle East', in P. Shearman and P. Williams (eds), *The Superpowers, Central America and the Middle East* (London, Pergamon-Brasseys, 1988).
2. J. Hough, 'Soviet Perspectives on European Security', *International Journal*, vol.40 (1984–85), pp. 20–41.
3. M. Gorbachev, 'Political Report of the CPSU Central Committee to the 27th Congress of the Communist Party of the Soviet Union', *Moscow News*, 1986, no. 9, supplement, p. 16.
4. J. Stern, *Soviet Oil and Gas Exports to the West* (Aldershot, Gower, 1987); P. Odell, 'Gorbachev's New Economic Strategy; the Role of Gas Exports to Western Europe', *The World Today*, July 1987.
5. M. Gorbachev in *Pravda*, 2 October 1985. *Cf.* 'Mikhail Gorbachev receives Hans Dietrich Genscher', *Soviet News*, 23 July 1986.
6. M. Gorbachev, 'Political Report', pp. 5–6.
7. F. Griffiths, *Images, Politics and Learning in Soviet Behavior towards the United States* (Columbia University, Doctoral dissertation, 1972); M. Schwartz, *Soviet Perceptions of the United States* (Berkeley, University of California, 1978); N. Malcolm, *Soviet Political Scientists and American Politics* (London, Macmillan, 1984).
8. For example, K. van der Pijl's contribution to this volume.
9. V. I. Lenin, *Collected Works*, vol. 27 (Moscow, Progress, 1965), p. 369; M. K. Bunkina, *USA versus Western Europe: New Trends* (Moscow, Progress, 1979), p. 11.
10. R. J. Sodaro, 'Soviet Studies of the Western Alliance', in H. J. Ellison (ed.), *Soviet Policy towards Western Europe* (Seattle, University of Washington, 1983), p. 241.
11. V. P. Lukin, *'Tsentry sily'. Kontseptsii i real'nost'* (Moscow, Mezhdunarodnye otnosheniya, 1983); *Cf.* G. Morozov, 'Mirovoe soobshchestvo i sud'by mira', *Mirovaya ekonomika i mezhdunarodnye otnosheniya*, 1984, no. 10, pp. 3–15. The passage by Raymond Aron being referred to is from his *Progress and Disillusion: The Dialectics of Modern Society* (New York, Praeger, 1968), p. 160.
12. Lukin, *'Tsentry sily'*, p. 15.
13. Lukin, *'Tsentry sily'*, pp. 21–2.
14. Lukin, *'Tsentry sily'*, pp. 50–6.

15. Lukin, 'Tsentry sily', p. 95; also A. N. Yakovlev, 'Imperializm: sopernichestvo i protivorechiya. Voprosy teorii', *Pravda*, 23 March 1984; Yu. Shiryaev, 'The World Economy in the Context of the Technological Revolution', *Social Sciences*, 1986, no. 1, pp. 72–84; G. A. Vorontsov, 'SShA – Zapadnaya Evropa: obshchnost' i protivorechiya na novom etape', *SShA: ekonomika, politika, ideologiya*, 1984, no. 4, pp. 3–13.
16. Yu. Shishkov, 'Interimperialist Rivalry Escalates', *International Affairs* (Moscow), 1986, no. 5, p. 30.
17. A. Borodaevsky, 'Internationalisation and Economic Integration in the Capitalist World', *Social Sciences*, 1985, no. 2, pp. 90–1.
18. W. Zimmermann, *Soviet Perspectives on International Relations* (Princeton, NJ, Princeton University Press, 1969); Griffiths, *Images, Politics and Learning in Soviet Behavior towards the United States;* Malcolm, *Soviet Political Scientists and American Politics.*
19. B. Parrott, *Politics and Technology in the Soviet Union* (London, MIT Press, 1983), pp. 82–8, 133, 140, 195, 201, 237, 245, 267–8; Griffiths, *Images, Politics and Learning in Soviet Behavior towards the United States;* H. Adomeit, 'Soviet Perceptions of Western European Integration: Ideological Distortion or Realistic Assessment?', *Millenium*, 8 (1979), pp. 1–29; E. P. Hoffmann, R. F. Laird, *'The Scientific-Technological Revolution' and Soviet Foreign Policy* (Oxford, Pergamon, 1982).
20. A. Shapiro, 'Eshche raz k voprosu o teorii vsemirnogo khozyaistva', *Mirovaya ekonomika i mezhdunarodnye otnosheniya*, 1985, no. 3, p. 97; also M. K. Bunkina, N. Petrov, 'Vsemirnoe khozyaistvo – ekonomicheskii fundament mirnogo sosushchestvovaniya', *Mirovaya ekonomika i mezhdunarodnye otnosheniya*, 1986, no. 9, p. 53; A. Bykova and N. Shmelev, 'Konkurentsiya i kooperatsiya na mirovykh rynkakh "vysokoi tekhnologii"', *Mirovaya ekonomika i mezhdunarodnye otnosheniya*, 1986, no. 9, p. 69.
21. N. Shmelev, 'Interstate Regulation of the World Capitalist Economy: New Tendencies', *International Affairs* (Moscow), 1985, no. 9; A. Shapiro, 'Protivorechiya mezhdunarodnogo gosudarstvenno-monopolisticheskogo regulirovaniya ekonomiki', *SShA: ekonomika, politika, ideologiya*, 1985, no. 3; M. Maksimova, 'Kapitalisticheskaya integratsiya i mirovoe razvitie', *Mirovaya ekonomika i mezhdunarodnye otnosheniya*, 1978, nos 3, 4; E. Kirichenko, 'On Certain Specific Features of Inter-Imperialist Rivalry', *International Affairs* (Moscow), 1985, no. 6.
22. Ya. Pevzner, 'Novye podkhody k analizu mezhdunarodnykh ekonomicheskikh svyazei kapitalizma', *Mirovaya ekonomika i mezhdunarodnye otnosheniya*, 1986, no. 10, pp. 101–2; L. Thurow, 'A Time to Dismantle the World Economy', *The Economist*, 9 November 1985; reprinted in translation in *Mirovaya ekonomika i mezhdunarodnye otnosheniya*, 1986, no. 10, pp. 97–114.
23. Bykova and Shmelev, 'Konkurentsiya i kooperatsiya na mirovykh rynkakh "vysokoi tekhnologii"', p. 69; Shapiro, 'Protivorechiya mezhdunarodnogo gosudarstvenno-monopolisticheskogo regulirovaniya ekonomiki'; T. Parkhalina, 'NATO – za fasadom "atlanticheskogo edinstva"', *Mirovaya ekonomika i mezhdunarodnye otnosheniya*, 1986, no. 7, pp. 104–11; Bunkina, *USA versus Western Europe: New Trends* (Moscow, Progress, 1979), p. 15.
24. V. Kniazhinsky, *West European Integration: Its Policies and International Relations* (Moscow, Progress, 1984), p. 285; Malcolm, *Soviet Political Scientists and American Politics*, pp. 35–7, 44.
25. Maksimova, 'Kapitalisticheskaya integratsiya i mirovoe razvitie'; Maksimova, 'Evropeiskoe soobshchestvo – real'nost' nashego vremeni', *Mirovaya ekonomika*

i mezhdunarodnye otnosheniya, 1986, no. 8, pp. 137–8.
26. Adomeit, 'Soviet Perceptions of Western European Integration: Ideological Distortion or Realistic Assessment?'; Lukin, *'Tsentry sily'*, pp. 73–7, 92–3; Yu. Levin, 'EES v razvivayushchemsya mire', *Mirovaya ekonomika i mezhdunarodnye otnosheniya*, 1986, no. 8, pp. 68–80; Parkhalina, 'NATO – za fasadom "atlanticheskogo edinstva"'.
27. Yu. Shishkov, 'The EEC in a Vicious Circle of Problems', *International Affairs* (Moscow), 1985, no. 10, pp. 64–73; Yu. Shishkov, 'Evropeiskoe soobshchestvo na perelomnom etape', *Mirovaya ekonomika i mezhdunarodnye otnosheniya*, 1986, no. 6, pp. 40–53; Yu. Shishkov, 'Za tochnost' nauchnoi terminologii', *Mirovaya ekonomika i mezhdunarodnye otnosheniya*, 1986, no. 9, pp. 133–5.
28. Lukin, *'Tsentry sily'*, pp. 84–9.
29. Kirichenko, 'On Certain Specific Features of Inter-Imperialist Rivalry'; V. Beletsky, 'What Lies Behind the European Defence Initiative Project?', *International Affairs* (Moscow), 1986, no. 6, pp. 49–55; D. Mel'nikov, 'Zapadnoevropeiskii tsentr: aspekt politicheskii', *Mirovaya ekonomika i mezhdunarodnye otnosheniya*, 1978, no. 5, pp. 19–29; V. Lavrenev, 'O nekotorykh aspektakh vozmozhnogo rasshireniya EES', *Mirovaya ekonomika i mezhdunarodnye otnosheniya*, 1978, no. 6, p. 53–63; Adomeit, 'Soviet Perceptions of Western European Integration: Ideological Distortion or Realistic Assessment?'.
30. Lukin, *'Tsentry sily'*, pp. 67–9; Yakovlev, 'Imperializm: sopernichestvo i protivorechiya. Voprosy teorii'; A. Vtorov and Yu. Karelov, 'The Dynamic European Policy of the USSR', *International Affairs* (Moscow), 1986, no. 6, pp. 97–106; G. Arbatov, 'When the Pinch Comes on President Reagan's Statement', *Soviet News*, 26 November 1986 (reprinted from *Pravda*, 21 November 1986).
31. Lukin, *'Tsentry sily'*, p. 69.
32. Bykova and Shmelev, 'Konkurentsiya i kooperatsiya na mirovykh rynkakh "vysokoi tekhnologii"'; Kirichenko, 'On Certain Specific Features of Inter-Imperialist Rivalry'; R. I. Zimenkov and A. B. Parkansky, 'Popytka ottesnit' konkurentov', *SShA: ekonomika, politika, ideologiya*, 1985, no. 10, pp. 15–25; Levin, 'EES v razvivayushchemsya mire'; A. Kudryavtsev, 'Istoki, real'nosti, perspektivy "tekhnologicheskoi Evropy"', *Mirovaya ekonomika i mezhdunarodnye otnosheniya*, 1986, no. 10, pp. 26–40; I. Ponomareva and N. Smirnova, 'SShA-Zapadnaya Evropa: rozn' ekonomicheskikh interesov', *Mirovaya ekonomika i mezhdunarodnye otnosheniya*, 1986, no. 8, pp. 131–6; Beletsky, 'What Lies behind the "European Defence Initiative" Project?'; A. Bogdanov, *The USA, Western Europe, Japan. A Triangle of Rivalry* (Moscow, Progress, 1985), pp. 56–7.
33. Yu. Yudanov, '"Evrika" – problemy sozdaniya zapadnoevropeiskogo tekhnologicheskogo obshchestva', *Mirovaya ekonomika i mezhdunarodnye otnosheniya*, 1986, no. 9, pp. 93–100; Kudryavtsev, 'Istoki, real'nosti, perspektivy "tekhnologicheskoi Evropy"'; Bykova and Shmelev, 'Konkurentsiya i kooperatsiya na mirovykh rynkakh "vysokoi tekhnologii"'.
34. Shishkov, 'Interimperialist Rivalry Escalates'.
35. Kniazhinsky, *West European Integration: Its Policies and International Relations*, pp. 323–43; Yakovlev, 'Imperializm: sopernichestvo i protivorechiya. Voprosy teorii'; Kirichenko, 'On Certain Specific Features of Inter-Imperialist Rivalry', pp. 82–6, 106; Zimenkov and Parkansky, 'Popytka ottesnit' konkurentov', pp. 21–5; Beletsky, 'What Lies Behind the "European Defence

Initiative" Project?'; Vorontsov, 'SShA – Zapadnaya Evropa: obshchnost' i protivorechiya na novom etape', pp. 8–12; Yu. P. Davydov, 'Soedinennye Shtaty i obshcheevropeiskii protsess', *SShA: ekonomika, politika, ideologiya*, 1985, no. 8, pp. 51–3; Yu. Shishkov, 'The EEC in a Vicious Circle of Problems', *International Affairs* (Moscow), 1985, no. 10, pp. 64–73; Shishkov, 'Interimperialist Rivalry Escalates'.
36. For an eloquent example see A. Bovin, 'Western Europe: "Strategic Concerns"', *International Affairs* (Moscow), 1985, no. 12.
37. Kudryavtsev, 'Istoki, real'nosti, perspektivy "tekhnologicheskoi Evropy"'; Yudanov, '"Evrika" – problemy sozdaniya zapadnoevropeiskogo tekhnologicheskogo obshchestva'; Beletsky, 'What Lies Behind the European Defence Initiative Project?'.
38. S. Bialer and J. Afferica, 'Reagan and Russia', *Foreign Affairs*, 61 (1982/83), p. 256; Hough, 'Soviet Perspectives on European Security', pp. 39–40.
39. A. Ulam, 'Europe in Soviet Eyes', *Problems of Communism*, May–June, 1983, p. 30.
40. E. Moreton and G. Segal, 'Introduction', in E. Moreton and G. Segal (eds), *Soviet Strategy Towards Western Europe* (London, Allen and Unwin, 1984), p. 8.
41. K. Dawisha, 'Soviet Ideology and Western Europe', in E. Moreton and G. Segal (eds), *Soviet Strategy Towards Western Europe*, p. 37.
42. K. Pridham, 'The Soviet View of Current Disagreements between the United States and Western Europe', *International Affairs* (London), 59 (1983), pp. 27–8.
43. Hough, 'Soviet Perspectives on European Security'.
44. A. Vtorov and Yu. Karelov, 'The Dynamic European Policy of the USSR', *International Affairs* (Moscow), 1986, no. 6 (see Hough, 'Soviet Perspectives on European Security', p. 25, for tentative identification of Vtorov as Kovalev). Kovalev was promoted in 1986 to be one of two First Deputy Foreign Ministers of the USSR.
45. Yu. Karelov, 'USSR – Western Europe: Guidelines of Co-operation', *International Affairs* (Moscow), 1985, no. 11, pp. 23–8; Davydov, 'Soedinennye Shtaty i obshcheevropeiskii protsess', pp. 53–4.
46. A. N. Yakovlev, 'Istoki ugrozy i obshchestvennoe mnenie', *Mirovaya ekonomika i mezhdunarodnye otnosheniya*, 1985, no. 3, pp. 3–4, 15; A. N. Yakovlev, 'Mezhimperialisticheskie protivorechiya – sovremennyi kontekst', *Kommunist*, no. 17 (November, 1986), pp. 13–14; Yakovlev, 'Imperializm: sopernichestvo i protivorechiya. Voprosy teorii'.
47. For example, Lukin, *'Tsentry sily'*; Kniazhinsky, *West European Integration: Its Policies and International Relations;* for the latter, Hough, 'Soviet Perspectives on European Security'.
48. E. Shevardnadze, 'Eduard Shevardnadze's Speech at Reception for Hans Dietrich Genscher', *Soviet News*, 23 July 1986; M. Gorbachev, 'Mikhail Gorbachev Receives Hans Dietrich Genscher', *Soviet News*, 23 July 1986; for an example of Soviet writing about Genscher and his role as a bulwark of 'Europeanism' in the West German government, see Yudanov, '"Evrika" – problemy sozdaniya zapadnoevropeiskogo tekhnologicheskogo obshchestva', p. 99.

4 · RESTRUCTURING THE ATLANTIC RULING CLASS IN THE 1970s AND 1980s

Kees van der Pijl

INTRODUCTION

This chapter analyses the class aspects of changes in Atlantic relations in the context of a shift away from the primacy of the Atlantic economy in world politics. Before 1971, the dominant bourgeois/imperialist interests (in Lenin's sense of the terms) were heavily focused on the Atlantic. Since then, the Atlantic has become only one of several subsets of global class alignments and circuits of capital (flows of capital, goods and services). At the same time there has been an internationalisation of money capital, reflected, for example, in the stupendous growth of the Eurocurrency markets. In this context, there has been a movement away from the embedded pattern of transatlantic class relations, forged around the concept and compromises of *corporate liberalism* (see Figure 4.1). Each pattern is, in effect, an ideal-type which refers to the configuration of domestic and international social forces which comes to represent a prevailing mode of political and economic relations. Each is based on different groupings of material forces: the first is mainly drawn from the interests of productive capital; the second from those of money capital.[1]

Each of these concepts is associated with historically specific 'strategic projects' launched by different fractions of international capital, that is by the metropolitan 'bourgeoisie'. These are attempts, at the level of international relations, to synthesise and advance ruling class interests under changing, often turbulent economic and political conditions. The aims of these are summarised in Figure 4.1. Each is associated with a particular pattern within Atlantic relations. Insofar as the object of each is broadly perceived to be legitimate by various groups and class fractions they can be described as *hegemonic projects*, which simultaneously serve to constitute particular international strategies in capitalism.

Let us now outline the basis for each of our ideal-typical concepts. The concrete mix between each of these depends on the political struggle between different class fractions (e.g. bankers vs industrialists) and

Pattern	Purpose
(i) Trilateral 1975–9 (corporate liberalism) *Basis:* productive forces	to deal with disintegration of the Atlantic order; loss of stature of the West in the face of a rise, and increasing cohesion, in global anti-capitalist forces
(ii) Unilateral 1979–84 (neoliberalism) *Basis:* money-capital; *rentier* interests	to deal with fading of the boundary line between capitalism and socialism in Europe and Third World; to meet the competitive challenges through a reassertion of both state power and freer markets, especially capital markets
(iii) Attempts 1984–8 to resurrect a Trilateral format	to deal with centrifugal tendencies and critical imbalances in the capitalist world, notably those caused by the internationalisation of money capital

Figure 4.1 Patterns of Atlantic relations 1975–88.

between different classes (labour and capital). This means that ruling-class hegemony, insofar as it exists, is constructed within a complex international force field, and takes different forms in each country. This essay seeks to make sense of the general nature of these interactions within Atlantic relations. It is assumed that the salience of each concept depends in considerable part on the material forces which support it. The strength of these forces can be gauged from the analysis of the share of profits accruing to each, in the overall profit-distribution process.

The *money-capital* concept, associated with banking and *rentier interests,* is the vantage point of capital as self-expanding value, as a world system of *relations* of production. Its pre-eminence is tied to phases of restructuring of capital, when political liberalism and economic laissez-faire combine to redirect money capital into new areas of investment. In this sense, it presents capital as a concentrated social force both economically (tied to the necessity of money capital as liquidity) and socially (in that it leads the way to a new configuration of classes).

The role of the state in this perspective is a minimal one, confined to managing residual conflict not solved by the basically harmonious and self-regulating social relations of capitalism, that is, it is akin to that of the 'nightwatchman state'.

The productive-capital concept, on the other hand, is associated with manufacturing and state control over market forces. This is the perspective of *productive forces,* which, of course, includes some fractions of labour as well as capital. If raised to the systematic level, such planning may move society towards 'existing socialism'. In capitalism, it may legitimise corporatism, cartelisation, state intervention and, politically, the entire spectrum of alternatives to liberalism, from conservatism to social democracy.

State and society in this perspective form an organic whole. In other words, the role of the state is a much more comprehensive and interventionist one; it is a role associated with Keynesian planning in post-war Atlantic political economies.

To recapitulate, therefore, the money-capital concept is closely associated with what I have labelled 'unilateralism': the productive-capital concept with many of the early advocates of trilateralism. Trilateralism was, in effect, a partial synthesis of the two, given the prominence of manufacturing companies and associated labour within the ranks of those who advocated this perspective. Following Hilferding, I refer to integrated corporations with both financial and manufacturing interests as *finance capital*.

THE TRILATERAL CONCEPT AND ITS DEMISE

Trilateralism was a specific reaction to the Nixon Administration's departure from Atlantic multilateralism in 1971. More broadly, however, it sought to develop a long-term strategy to deal with newly emerged challenges to the post-war capitalist order. Nixon's unilateral dollar and trade measures of August 1971 mobilised a counter-offensive from the temporarily weakened east coast Atlanticists, their west European counterparts, and a freshly co-opted Japanese constituency. These forces regrouped in 1972, in the shape of the Trilateral Commission (TC) formed at the initiative of David Rockefeller.[2] The TC was aimed at restoring cohesion and unity of purpose to an emerging Atlantic–Pacific ruling class. Only when the crisis of the capitalist order became acute in 1974–75, did trilateralism become a viable option for reorganising world capitalism.[3] The oil shock of 1973 was dealt with in the spirit of Nixon's unilateralism.[4] In the course of 1974, a new set of Western leaders emerged and in December, freshly installed presidents Giscard and Ford agreed not only on the energy issue but also on a trilateral summit eventually held in November 1975 at Rambouillet.

The material basis of the rise to prominence of the trilateral concept was the limited, if highly inflationary, industrial recovery from the 1974–75 crisis. The causes of its demise by 1978–79 were: the failure to stop the creeping 'social-democratisation' of international relations pursued under the slogan of a New International Economic Order; and the growth of an international credit economy undermining expansionary policies (and domestic class compromises) in the trilateral partner states, symbolised by the Eurocurrency markets.

The Atlantic economy had consisted of national economies geared to domestic, demand-led industrial growth, between which the fraction of international finance capital (dominated by American multinationals) could shift freely once non-convertibility and capital controls were removed. This had meant that circuits of money capital were manipulated nationally, to even out national or international business cycles. However, the internationalisation of capital and the liberalisation of both the dollar from gold and money capital from national controls (between 1967 and 1971), unified the circuit of money capital at the world level, in off-shore markets. This meant that the macro-economic policies of all states were subjected to new international conditions and constraints. Therefore, under stagflationary conditions all states (except the reserve-currency nation, the USA) had to apply deflation simultaneously.[5] These monetary conditions emerged at a point where significant transformations in the 'real' economy and in production relations were in train.

With post-war patterns of industrial growth and consumption in crisis, the emphasis of industrial expansion gravitated from domestic mass consumption to equipping runaway industry. As Alain Lipietz has shown, exports were becoming more important from 1965 on, and inter-state rivalry would beset any co-ordinated growth strategy, as advocated by the trilateralists, right from the start.[6] This in turn put the domestic capital-labour compromise, the linchpin of post-war Atlantic productive relations, under pressure. Markets and production locations increasingly failed to coincide. Wage levels were mainly judged according to the criterion of international competitiveness.

Predictably in 1976-77, industrial expansion was both highly uneven and accompanied by competitive devaluations aimed at improving the export positions of the Atlantic countries. The resulting inflation fuelled a growth in the international circuit of money capital (this doubled in size between 1976 and 1979).[7] This was boosted by a second oil price hike. The effect was to shift profit related incomes towards money capital interests (and to the oil companies).

This trend is reflected in Table 4.1, with the exception of Italy. This shift was part of a wider process of class restructuring within the ranks of capital. Table 4.1. suggests, nonetheless, a relative loss in the social stature of the productive-capital concept and a corresponding rise in the relevance of the alternative, money-capital concept of control (here, monetarism). This was part of the economic background to the demise of the co-ordinated trilateral approach. Therefore, the disintegration of trilateral class alignment in both the USA and Europe by 1979 cannot be fully understood if we limit ourselves to Atlantic relations. Money capital assumed the role of the liquidator of post-war corporate liberalism. With the latter's demise came the end of the first instalment of trilateralism. This strategy was too deeply committed to multilateral industrial expansion, based on domestic corporatism. However, the prominence of money capital was part of a *global* restructuring of capital. On the political plane,

Table 4.1 Percentage of money-capital in the profit-distribution process, 1975–79

	1975	1976	1977	1978	1979
United States	48.5	45.8	45.7	48.2	50.6
West Germany	30.9	29.1	29.7	29.6	31.0
United Kingdom	52.8	48.8	38.1	35.7	41.0
France	53.2	54.7	53.2	54.0	54.8
Netherlands	34.2	33.8	31.9	34.4	37.7
Italy	71.8	68.9	71.4	71.3	67.4

Source: OECD, *National Accounts 1972–84,* Paris 1986, Vol. II, country tables (current receipts of financial institutions as a percentage of current receipts of financial and non-financial corporations and quasi-corporations). Figures for Belgium are not available in this form.

this involved an offensive aimed at destroying the emerging network of raw-material-for-equipment agreements linking western Europe with associated Third World countries, OPEC, and the USSR. These threatened, ultimately, to make the internationalisation of capital subject to United Nations jurisdiction.[8]

From the 1973 *coup d'état* in Chile onwards, an aggressive approach emerged, inspired by the pure money-capital point of view. This was committed to the destruction of working-class power, Third World claims for a New International Economic Order and detente. This perspective proposed that neo-liberalism was the way out of the contradictions of Keynesian class compromise on the national and the international levels.[9] This developed along two vectors.

First, the spread of *monetarism*. Following its 'experimental' adoption in Chile, monetarism became part of a wider and more global process of class formation and elite realignment. This process combined apparent economic feasibility (given world-wide inflationary trends, the need to defend national currencies under conditions of monetary uncertainty, etc.) with active political intervention. The latter was associated with identifiable personalities and policy planning bodies, which operated both informally and through governmental and international institutions. Important in reinforcing the credibility of the monetarist approach was the Mont Pèlèrin Society, founded in 1947 by the orthodox liberal economist, F. A. von Hayek. Milton Friedman is its most prominent contemporary luminary. Through associated national bodies who shared members with it (in the USA for instance, the Shadow Open Market Committee and the Heritage Foundation), the Mont Pèlèrin Society played a key international role in moving monetarism to the centre of the political debate.[10]

Secondly, the neo-liberal concept projected a transition away from the welfare, social compromise state towards the night-watchman state of classical liberalism. In this transition, political violence began to appear, often alongside a new emphasis on the state's police powers. This served to obscure the state's relative withdrawal from the sphere of social welfare. Mass repression in Chile, death squad terrorism against the Left in neighbouring Argentina, and Red Brigade and Fascist terrorism accompanying the crystallation of the Historic Compromise in Italy, in this sense, were part of the same process. Of the behind-the-scenes attempts actually to co-ordinate that process, the Argentinian–Italian connection established by Lucio Gelli, the Grand Master of the masonic lodge, *Propaganda Due* (P2), was the most prominent to be exposed publicly.[11]

In western Europe, rising competition in international markets and the need to escape International Monetary Fund (IMF) and international bank pressures to adopt severe deflationary policies led to the initial adoption of neo-liberal economic policies, albeit of a milder form than in Latin America. In the UK, a monetarist strategy was outlined by the Labour Chancellor of the Exchequer, Denis Healey, in his letter of intent to the IMF in 1976. The Thatcher government, taking office in 1979, reinforced this monetarist policy considerably, with the result that there was a shift to greater money-capital profits and *rentier* incomes. 'For the first time in seven years, British companies (were) given the right to pay unlimited dividend to their shareholders.'[12] Thatcher's Trade Minister and protégé, Cecil Parkinson, told Chilean journalists that monetarism had to be applied in the specific political circumstances which prevailed in the UK.[13]

In Italy, however, terrorism scored a macabre victory for the neo-liberal counterrevolution in 1978. The Red Brigades, operating freely amidst the apparent paralysis of the security forces, killed the Christian Democratic architect of the Historic Compromise, Aldo Moro. This not only terminated further discussions with the Communist Party but also dealt a blow to the Mediterraneanist wing of the ruling class bloc. It also reinforced the Atlantic fraction spearheaded by the small Republican Party. The question decided by the Moro assassination was whether Italy would manage its balance of payments crisis by continuing the agreed PCI-CD compromise (and by making direct deals with certain oil-producing countries) or whether the strategy would be based on outside financing of its deficit and alignment with wider monetarist and emerging Cold War trends. The formation of the Cossiga government that took office in August 1979 and the defeat of the trade unions at FIAT in 1980 marked a triumph for the neo-liberal tendency. However, re-orientation to the Atlantic fold was not complete, highlighted in late 1986 by the re-purchase of Libya's share in FIAT under American pressure.[14] Craxi's modernised Socialist Party sought to capitalise on the process of neo-liberal class formation. After 1982, a new Christian Democratic party leadership also set out to win a modern industrial, tertiary-sector-employed constituency that would support a moderate version of Thatcherism. Its strategy succeeded when, after an interlude under Craxi, Giovanni Goria, monetarist finance minister since 1982, became Prime Minister for the CD.[15]

In France, Prime Minister Barre's austerity policy succeeded, at great social cost, in transforming a 20 billion francs trade deficit in 1976 into a 2.5 billion surplus in 1978. In August 1978, a government seminar led by Giscard characterised the turn to deflation as 'an economic war of movement for which the rules will be: the offensive with rapid occupation of terrain and the organisation of orderly withdrawals'.[16] The economic transition was accompanied by the marginalisation of the corporate liberal fraction in the Gaullist party, symbolised by Chalban-Delmas and represented in the Cabinet by Robert Boulin. In 1979, the right-wing Gaullist Jacques Chirac sought to destabilise the Giscard-Barre combination. At this time, reports were leaked to the press concerning a gift of diamonds to Giscard by Emperor Bokassa, but also concerning a real estate scandal involving Boulin, then Minister of Labour. Boulin committed suicide, but from subsequent press reports and an open letter left behind by the deceased, it transpired that the Gaullists, in mid-December, decided to expose Boulin when it became known that he was being considered to succeed Barre as Prime Minister.[17] Eventually, the internecine struggle within the Right led to a triumph of the Socialists, postponing the full political effect of Chirac's victory. The change of government did not, however, contain the shift towards neo-liberalism.

In West Germany, terrorism by the Red Army faction culminated in 1977 in the kidnapping and killing of the head of the employers' organisation BDI, Hans-Martin Schleyer. Terrorism here functioned amidst 'anti-radical' repression on the part of the government (notably the *Berufsverbote*) and served to strengthen state power for dealing with future emergencies. The redefinition of the state role from social compromise towards more authoritarianism was made explicit when Socialist Minister of Justice Vogel, following Schleyer's assassination, affirmed in November 1977 that 'our people have had in these weeks a new and stronger feeling about the relation of a single individual toward the state . . . The people, especially younger people, . . . learned that the state, in order to uphold its functions and protect life, may also demand services and sacrifices.'[18] Against this background, capital accumulation in Germany was gradually re-oriented to monetarism, albeit of a more moderate variety than in the UK or France. The Schmidt government, backed by the powerful trades unions, sought moderate reflation of the Keynesian type. In April 1979, however, the Bundesbank, without consulting the government or the partners in the European Monetary System, shifted towards monetarism by raising the bank rate.[19] Significantly, the Deutsche Bank, opting for a strategy of capital market expansion at high interest rates, saw its profits soar in 1979–80; while its competitors, Commerzbank and Dresdner Bank, having continued to extend investment credits, were themselves caught by the climbing interest rates.[20]

In West German politics, the disintegration of corporate liberalism was an aspect of the shift in economic importance from the north to the south. The two southern states, catholic Bavaria and religiously mixed Baden-Württemberg, were traditionally oriented to specialised, export-oriented production and thus were in a better position to adapt than the coal, steel and other old industries in the north. The main question by 1979 was how the Socialist-Liberal coalition could survive the increasing militancy of the trades unions which, unlike their Italian counterparts, were not intimidated by the anti-terrorist campaign.[21] Under these circumstances, the weight of the south in the Christian Democratic opposition, which in 1980 adopted neo-liberalism in its election programme, increased. Of the two small southern state Prime Ministers, however, the articulate neo-liberal, Lothar Späth of Baden-Württemberg, lacked experience and national stature. This meant that the controversial Franz-Josef Strauss, fiefholder of Bavaria, became the (ultimately unsuccessful) Christian-Democratic candidate in the 1980 elections. Only in 1982, however, would the neo-liberal offensive help to bring down the Schmidt government.

In the USA, the emergence of a New Right which combined vehement anti-communism with various, often mutually contradictory, neo-liberal economic programmes, had been temporarily overshadowed by the trilateral orientation of the Carter Administration. However, the moral emphasis in Carter's posture, coupled to an ongoing arms diplomacy that sought to extend the SALT process, mobilised the Right along a broad front. The activities of the Heritage Foundation, founded by beer magnate Joseph Coors and supported by Mellon heir Richard Scaife, the Chase Manhattan Bank, Mobil and Gulf among others, were complemented by other developments.

These included the formation of the new Committee on the Present Danger (CPD) in 1976 and the shift to a more Cold War line in the influential Council on Foreign Relations (CFR). This occurred after several of the CFR's directors took up posts in the Carter Administration, to be replaced by CPD officers. Professor Richard Pipes, who headed a review team which, early in 1976, produced an alarmist report of Soviet military capabilities commissioned by CIA director George Bush, became a CFR director at this point.[22] These groups contributed to the emergence, on both sides of the Atlantic, of a strong current of opinion which saw the entire trilateral undertaking as too accommodating to the challenges facing the capitalist system. Thus, when, in the course of 1978, the Carter policy ran into trouble, forces of opposition began to stir. UN Ambassador Andrew Young and arms negotiator Paul Warnke were the first casualties to be caught by anti-Third World and Cold War fire. This heralded a shift in the American position on the Third World.[23]

The Cold War trend was complemented by the rise of class forces critical of social compromise and Keynesian spending policies. These forces favoured the money-capital concept. The growing mass of interests dependent on securing the American stake in the international financial markets or seeking to restructure or relocate industrial processes and cut back union power, triumphed in 1979. This triumph was reflected in the appointment of Paul Volcker (a TC member and Rockefeller confidant, but a monetarist first) at the Federal Reserve and by the adoption of the views espoused by the Shadow Open Market Committee. In the labour field, it was to be seen in the Chrysler/United Auto Workers (UAW) contract substituting technology-related 'concession bargaining' for collective wage and benefits bargaining.[24] These agreements in fact led to significant pay cuts for UAW members during the first half of the 1980s.

THE RISE OF NEO-LIBERAL HEGEMONY: NEW FORMS OF ENRICHMENT, NEW MORAL CODES

The process of class formation reflecting the money-capital perspective necessarily involves long-term economic shifts. Thus, while the 1978 turnabout in profit distribution documented in Table 4.1 may be seen as one immediate dimension through which monetarism could come to the fore, it can also be situated in a long-term process of class formation. Table 4.2 illustrates the trend in profit distribution among corporations. With the exception of the UK, the long-term trend is clearly towards increased cash flow of money capital.

Bankers also reinforced their presence in the centres of Atlantic business decision-making. Fennema has documented the increased numbers of bankers and 'finance capitalists' (directors of banks and of industrial companies) in the international network of interlocking directorates between 1970 and 1976. Also, internationalisation as measured in the share of profits from international activities and in the number of foreign subsidiaries of banks (with the exception of the UK) relative to the percentage of industrial investment financed by banks domestically, increased significantly in the course of the 1970s.[25]

The actual rise of the private *rentier* segment in society complementing the rise of corporate finance is brought out in Table 4.3.

The steady rise or, in traditional *rentier* countries like Holland and the UK, the reversal of the post-war decline of *rentier* incomes, adds another dimension to the hegemony of the neo-liberal concept. This is reinforced by the upsurge of popular (speculative) capitalism and the revival of liberal ideology. Whether the contraction of the *rentier* income slice in the USA is part of a tilt back to corporate accumulation, cannot yet be fully assessed. A measure of the widening appeal of the *rentier* or *quasi-rentier* class is the fact that in the UK, privatisation has led to a rise in the number of people owning stock from seven million in 1979 to 19 million in 1987; in France,

Table 4.2 Long-term trend of money capital in profit distribution (percentages)

	1965	1970	1975	1980	1983
USA	7.9	12.2	48.5	54.3	56.6
West Germany	25.4	43.3	30.9	35.6	37.0
United Kingdom	7.3*	9.6	52.8	48.5	40.0
France	0.7	10.9	53.2	58.5	64.4
Netherlands	7.6*	5.0	34.2	41.4	41.7

*1968

Sources: 1975–83, as in Table 4.1; 1965–70: (USA) 'total financial' as a percentage of total corporate profits. Calculated from *Economic Report of the President 1977*, Washington, January 1977, table B–79. (Europe) savings of financial institutions as a percentage of total corporate income. OECD, *National Accounts of OECD Countries 1961–1978*, Paris 1980, vol. II (country tables). To indicate that figures for 1965 and 1970 are based on a different set of data, they are printed in italics.

Table 4.3 Long-term trend of households' property income (rent, dividend and interest)

	1965	1970	1975	1980	1983
USA	9.2	9.1	9.6	11.4	9.8
West Germany	2.2	3.2	3.8	4.5	6.0*
United Kingdom	7.9	6.3	4.3	4.7	9.2†
France	4.2	4.3	5.4	5.4	5.7
Netherlands	17.4	13.9	9.9	12.4	17.2

*Does not include rents
†Interest only
Source: Calculated from OECD, *National Accounts of OECD Countries*, different editions, Paris 1980, 1982, 1985, vol. II (country tables).

the recently denationalised Paribas bank has three million shareowners against 150,000 before its nationalisation in 1981.[26]

To speak of class formation, the social effects produced by the rise in financial and *rentier* income and the trend-setting new forms of enrichment and investment that go with the statistical shifts have to be looked at more closely. The public behaviour of protagonists of these forms of enrichment creates social models, or personification of social success, that mould the aspirations of the most active segments of society. Ultimately, it moulds the behaviour of political elites. Overall, this 'leads' any restratification process.

The rise in bank profits and *rentier* incomes does not simply signify a resurgence of the established bankers' community and the original *rentiers*. At least partly, it represents a new class fraction. In an article on the phenomenon of the 'junk bond' and the Drexel Burnham Lambert investment bank which specialised in its handling, *Business Week* quotes a competing bank officer as saying that Drexel linked up with new tycoons, 'the likes of T. Boone Pickens Jr, Rupert Murdoch, and Ted Turner – . . . brash, entrepreneurial daredevils' as the magazine calls them. And it continues: 'Like the merchant banks of the robber baron era, Drexel doesn't passively finance companies, it creates and molds them. It holds equity positions in more than 100 companies it has financed and seats on as many boards.'[27] The type of high-risk financing pioneered by Drexel Burnham in Wall Street has set the pace for the spread of a basically speculative, 'quick enrichment' economic behaviour. The investment bankers, *Fortune* writes, 'have their own ethic, and it centers on money, as increasingly true for the ethic of the culture at large . . . For the get-rich-quick mergers and acquisitions generation, it sometimes seems that money is the only value.'[28]

At the popular level, it is worth noting a newspaper characterisation of the pop-idol, Madonna. She is 'the very best sort of modern girl' because she 'looks like a whore and thinks like a pimp'. The parallel macho cult exemplified by the *Rambo* and *Rocky* movies lends a new violent quality to egocentric social behaviour.[29] These examples must suffice here to indicate a wider popularisation of neo-liberal culture. It is based on militant micro-economic rationality raised to the level of social philosophy, on an ethic which turns 'an economic theory into a personal moral code, making nonsense of reasonable propositions by exaggeration and distortion'.[30] Such a discourse serves to undermine ideas of social solidarity. The discourse is offset only by occasional media events that present often highly personalised instances of compassion with selected cases, such as Poland or starving Africa, AIDS victims or drug addicts.

The forms of real capital accumulation supporting the neo-liberal trend are characterised partly by the application of new production technologies like robotisation and numerical control, often building on hitherto marginal enclaves of specialised craft production. However, the reactionary implications of automation and small-shop production for traditional labour organisations are amplified by the simultaneous resurgence of a parallel economy characterised by sweatshop labour and low-paid service work. Thus, while the rapid growth of unemployment and new forms of company feudalism have fostered identification with the fate of the company among privileged groups of workers, for others Norbert Wiener's prediction that only slave labour can compete with the automatic machine is becoming a reality.[31]

In the USA, new capital formation and rapid and spectacular enrichment has taken place, notably in media, services and classical light industries like clothing and food. Of the 56 new entries (including returnees) in the 1986 *Forbes 400* list of richest Americans, the financiers and brokers (11) and media people (11) are the two best represented categories; the food and clothing industries together have five, the retail trade also has five entries. The 62 dropouts have diverse backgrounds, but the above sectors are hardly represented. This contrasts with oil (eight dropouts).[32] Sectoral profit distribution in this case is sanctioned, rather than shaped, by tax policies. When the winners and losers by the 1986 US tax reform are compared, the winners seem to be in the typical new tycoon and financial field (securities brokers, insurance brokers, business service, apparel and newspapers), while established industries like automobiles and telecom, next to transport and oil, are among the losers.[33]

In Italy and France, too, the new type of financier has made its appearance, accompanied by the rise of media, electronics and textile tycoons. Benetton, the Italian clothing group, recently recruited the former head of Merrill Lynch's London branch to manage its foray into the financial field. Paradoxically, the new tycoons of southern Europe have often associated themselves with the ascendant Socialist parties. The influx of private Italian capital into France was aided by the coincidence of Socialist rule in the two countries after the French conversion to deflation in 1983. Silvio Berlusconi, the Italian media king close to the Socialist party leader, Craxi, was able to obtain a 25 per cent stake in the new commercial TV channel (*Canal 5*) in France; neo-liberal Socialist Alain Minc was made head of the French holding of Olivetti's De Benedetti. French profits of Raul Gardini's Ferruzzi group (agribusiness, chemicals), which rose to number two private company behind FIAT, were expected to surpass those made at home in 1987.[34]

In France, the most prominent corporate supporters of President Mitterrand were the owners and managers of the American-French Schlumberger group. At the time the Socialists took power, Schlumberger was the fourth biggest corporation in the world after IBM, AT&T and Exxon, while providing its owners with the greatest private fortune in France. Active in the oil drilling business and in electronic control and regulation systems (through subsidiaries like Fairchild), the Schlumberger empire and the mini-empires of the sons of Geneviève Schlumberger and René Seydoux cover textile, transport (Chargeurs Réunis, UTA) and many media ventures, some jointly with Berlusconi.[35]

If less pronounced, in countries like West Germany, the Netherlands and Belgium, the apparently fixed structure of corporate capital has been shaken by newcomers. In Germany, financial tycoons like Karl Miesel of the outsider CSFB-Effectenbank (a subsidiary of Crédit Suisse merged with Warburg), Friedrich Hoyos, and the venture capitalist, Count Albrecht Matuschka, made their appearance in anticipation of liberalising measures of the German capital market dominated by the Deutsche Bank.[36] In Belgium, the new financial scene is dominated by Gérard Eskenazi, a banker made redundant by the nationalisation of Paribas (France) in 1981, and Albert Frère, the former Walloon steel magnate. Their joint holding, Pargesa, has obtained important stakes in the Bruxelles-Lambert Bank, in Drexel Burnham Lambert in the USA, Schneider in France, and the biggest Belgian insurance group, Royal Belge, mostly through take-over battles hitherto unknown in Europe.[37]

Taken together, aggressive entrepreneurship, the adventurousness of the financial raiders, their ostentatious display of wealth, combined with a complementary growth of the money-capital/*rentier* fraction, have fundamentally reshaped the social landscape. These changes have established the hegemony of the bourgeoisie subscribing to the neo-liberal concept of control. This has been reflected, for example, in the handling of strikes and union opposition through mass redundancies, and, on occasion, the use of forms of violence which seemed improbable some 10 to 15 years ago.

INTERNATIONAL MONETARISM AND THE NEW COLD WAR

The spread of the Chilean model to the North Atlantic area culminated in the election of Ronald Reagan to the US presidency. The trilateral experiment in Atlantic relations was characterised by industrial interdependence, social and international compromise, and a high-pitched campaign of human rights observance abroad. These policies were now abandoned completely.

Reagan's revanchism, mobilising domestic frustration over diminishing American international leverage, lent the new American position its aggressive quality. Military spending continued on its upward course, in a marked break with previous Republican practice. In its dealings with western Europe, the Reagan Administration continued the Nixon/Kissinger policy of 1971–73. But whereas the latter had operated in a context of detente and had played the OPEC card by secretly working with the Saudis, Reagan inherited the embargo imposed by Carter after the Soviet intervention in Afghanistan, and confronted the Third World and its NIEO ambitions with a bland rejection.

In its original composition, the Reagan Administration reflected the renewed prominence of the military-industrial complex (MIC) and of speculative finance. This was mediated by the California entourage of the President, which had its backgrounds in both areas. Overall, these interests synthesised their sometimes conflicting positions into a neo-liberal and unilateral concept of foreign policy.[38] The MIC was represented by Secretary of State Haig (former NATO commander and director of United Technologies and the Chase Manhattan Bank) and by Defense Under-, Assistant, and Service Secretaries DeLauer (director of TRW); Perle and Lehman (who both had long-standing ties with Henry Jackson and the anti-Arms Control Lobby, but also ran a multi-million dollar arms procurement agency of their own); and Iklé, a RAND director and consultant of Swiss capital in the USA. Together, 32 CPD members held office in the first Reagan Administration.[39]

Of the financial men who represented the new impact of independent money capital, Donald Regan (Merrill Lynch) and Beryl Sprinkel (Harris Trust) at the Treasury, and John Shad of E. F. Hutton (like Merrill Lynch, catering to the small investor) at the head of the Securities and Exchange Commission, should be mentioned. But CIA head William Casey, too, came from the world of investment advice and quick money-making. These men embodied short-term views that tended to undermine any coordinated Atlantic policy. To their 'functional' predispositions as speculators, an intelligence background (as with Casey or Deputy Defense Secretary, National Security Adviser, and later Secretary of Defense, Frank Carlucci) often added a distinct unilateralist accent.

The men closer to Reagan, such as those who had helped make his career like William French Smith (Attorney General), and those whose career he had made (National Security Advisors, Richard Allen and William Clark, Attorney General Ed Meese), and those Nixon men who later turned to Reagan, like Defense Secretary Caspar Weinberger, were able to synthesise the impulses coming from either side into a concept of militarisation and confrontation. Of the 'New Right' bloc of interests and perspectives behind these men, Mike Davis writes that, apart from having a specific entrepreneurial, anti-union and anti-welfare state perspective, they are expansive towards the Middle East and Central America, while being 'all deeply tied by complex networks of investments, hidden shareholdings and direct activity to Sunbelt land and mineral speculation'. Davis further notes that 'the New Right has been more enamored with supply-side economics, with its reflationary implications, than with a purist monetarism with deflationary consequences'.[40]

A key aspect of the first Reagan Administration was the limited number, and highly circumscribed role, of Republican internationalists with an affinity for the trilateral view like Vice-President George Bush, White House Chief of Staff James Baker, and Secretary of Commerce Malcolm Baldridge.

The programme of the first Reagan Administration consisted of two main elements: international monetarism and a policy of threat and economic warfare against the USSR. Thus two trajectories of neo-liberalism (monetarism and political violence) were relayed into international politics. These policies complemented the ongoing process of neo-liberal class formation in Europe.

As to the first aspect, the application of deflationary policy initially seemed to defy the preferences of 'supply-siders' in the Reagan coalition. With Regan and Sprinkel in command, this policy pushed interest rates upward while bolstering the dollar exchange rate in international currency markets. The resulting recession and, eventually, the global debt crisis, coming on top of the second oil price hike, forced all capitalist countries to apply deflationary policies in order to escape bankruptcy. Simultaneously, Reagan's strategists foresaw that Democrats, with a majority in the House of Representatives, would only consent to welfare cuts if confronted with the need to balance the budget. The 1981–82 recession, however, coming on top of the reduced Federal income due to the initial tax cuts, inflated the deficit beyond the envisaged size. The deficit, higher American interest and exchange rates, and across-the-board military-industrial expansion, turned the USA into the pivot of the world circuit of independent money capital. In 1983, short-term loans to the USA, estimated at 35 billion dollars, were bigger than US government and corporate securities ownership abroad and direct foreign investment in the USA combined.[41]

The second component of the initial Reagan strategy, the new Cold War, combined a projected one trillion dollar defence build-up (over three years) with intentional economic warfare. As Assistant Secretary for Defense Richard Perle put it, the build-up was to be accompanied by 'a well-designed program of economic sanctions [that] can both damage the development of the Soviet economy and slow the growth of their defense industrial base'.[42] However, disrupting the foreign economic supply lines of the USSR also blocked one potential escape route for western European capital. In this field, US policy was to produce the sharpest transatlantic conflict since Suez.

However, the application of this perspective in US policy was not immediate. At the Ottawa Summit of July 1981, Reagan faced strong opposition from Helmut Schmidt over the large Siberian pipeline contract. Schmidt's position was complemented by a bloc of forces in the USA, who were keen to keep the Japanese out of the deal. This bloc included Special Trade Representative William Brock III, Illinois Senator Charles Percy and Secretary of Commerce Baldridge. This bloc prevailed, and Caterpillar Tractor (of which Brock was a stockholder) was allowed to participate in 'the construction of the pipeline'. Brock, a former Chairman of the Republican National committee, was at this point 'basically in control of trade'.[43]

The Polish crisis, however, strengthened the hand of the hard-liners. The USA reacted to the military *coup d'état* of December 1981 by declaring economic sanctions against Poland and the USSR. This move drew a sharp response from Chancellor Schmidt. When Weinberger and UN Ambassador Jeane Kirkpatrick wanted to declare Poland in default, Schmidt's objections were echoed by Secretary of State Haig, who argued that this would cripple the European banking community and gravely prejudice West German economic interests.[44]

The 1981 boycott of the USSR was again an attempt (like earlier boycotts) to delay moves towards greater economic interpenetration of west and east Europe. Given the size of the pipeline deal (six billion dollars worth of gas annually and an equivalent western European export potential, less debt service, for 25 years), a Soviet commentator rightly concluded that 'if the deal succeeds all the US former efforts to restrict the granting of credits to the USSR will be brought to nought'.[45]

At the Versailles Summit of June 1982 based on previous co-operation through the OECD, it was decided that commercial credit to eastern Europe should be extended at a rate of interest of 12.4 per cent. Upon his return to Washington, however, Reagan undid this agreement by extending the embargo decisions of the previous December to American subsidiaries and licenses abroad. Schmidt, hard-pressed domestically, spoke out against this measure in the Bundestag and in July flew to Washington to express his discontent to the new US Secretary of State George Shultz. The Thatcher government and the French Socialist government also opposed US policy, and ordered companies in their jurisdiction to proceed with their contractual obligations. By that time, Atlantic and intra-European relations had been strained by the Falklands war in the spring. In October 1982, Mitterrand and the new German Chancellor Helmut Kohl met to celebrate the Franco-German friendship treaty concluded 19 years before. They declared themselves in favour of its reactivation, including its defence aspect.

NEO-LIBERAL ATLANTIC UNITY: WEST GERMANY AND FRANCE

Meanwhile, by the mid-1980s, a number of political developments in Belgium, Holland and elsewhere cemented the apparent shift towards the hegemony of neo-liberalism. These developments had taken such hold by the mid-1980s that they led the noted commentator, Anthony Sampson, to warn that 'the common-front of the West Europe Leaders – Anti-Communist, Anti-inflation and Anti-union – may well generate common revolts, based on the protest against unemployment'.[46] In this section, I focus on the West German and French cases as illustrations of an inchoate, yet general trend towards neo-liberal hegemony. This existed alongside transatlantic political tensions.

A pivotal shift took place in Germany in 1982, when a change of government occurred. Schmidt's position as Chancellor had been weakened by mounting criticism from within the SPD over military policy, and his inability to sustain his role as an architect of Atlantic unity. However, the decisive issue which led to his demise was deflation of the economy. Unable to develop a policy which satisfied the FDP coalition partners, the Free Democrats crossed the floor and formed a government with the Christian Democrats. Under Helmut Kohl, the new coalition government, with Count Lambsdorff at the helm of economic policy, produced an austerity policy in line with the preferences of money capital. At the same time, a change in military policy occurred, with the CD-FD government supporting both missile deployment and NATO's Follow-On Forces concept (see Chapters 8 and 9).

At this point, however, American unilateralism still undermined Atlantic unity. The Mitterrand–Kohl meeting, referred to above, seemed to indicate that Germany, like France under Mitterrand, was distancing itself from the American line and following a course reflecting national preoccupations. In Sampson's view the perennial danger of West Germany reorienting to the East for economic reasons was particularly acute. Nonetheless, renewed American economic growth and a reinforcement of a trilateral faction within the Reagan Administration would soon promote a realignment back towards greater Atlantic unity.

In France, the Keynesian policy initially embarked upon was abandoned in March 1983. The nationalisation of major corporations (to rationalise the companies involved, to introduce auditing by American firms, and in several cases to save them from bankruptcy) turned out to have been intended to prepare for renewed internationalisation after all; an issue decided before the Socialist election victory.[47] Confronted with grave balance of payments problems and crumbling electoral support, Mitterrand and the groups behind the independent line (Crédit Lyonnais, Schlumberger) first considered fully-fledged protectionism. But pressure by the Socialist Fondation Saint-Simon and its neo-liberal spokesman, Alain Minc (then treasurer of Saint-Gobain) and the Rocardist/CFDT wing of the Socialist Party, succeeded in pushing through deflationary adjustment.[48]

French economic growth henceforth became export-dependent, and Industry Minister Fabius, later Prime Minister, and new managers with a money-capital outlook like Calvet and Besse, subjected the car industry in particular to draconian rationalisation. This policy was inaugurated by mass redundancies at the Talbot-Poissy car plant in 1983–84.[49]

At this juncture, American industrial recovery, at ten per cent in the second quarter of 1983, added an export interest to the *rentier* and Cold War orientation emerging in Europe. This 'locomotive function' of the American economy for European recovery is brought out in Table 4.4.

For other (Latin American, Asian) countries, which also saw their exports increase, this was much less oriented to the American market than the case for the European economies. In Europe, export surpluses for several countries (Germany, France and Belgium) were responsible for 40 to 60 per cent of economic growth in 1984.[50]

The new centrality of the American economy allowed the American internationalists to attempt to somehow pass from wildcat neo-liberalism to a more productive deployment of capital that might sustain a new hegemonic order.

THE STRUGGLE BETWEEN TRILATERALISM AND UNILATERALISM

The initial trilateral strategy, as noted above, was inscribed in a broader corporate liberal framework, which rested on demand-led economic

Table 4.4 Growth of European exports to the USA and to other countries, January/August 1984, percentages

	To USA	To other countries
West Germany	35.9	−1.2
France	39.4	1.0
United Kingdom	15.6	2.3
Italy	46.0	−10.6 (Jan/July)

Source: *NRC-Handelsbad*, 24 October 1984.

growth, nationally orchestrated social compromises, and a universalist political space. In this space, the forces of socialism were incorporated into bourgeois hegemony precisely because this was constructed along apparently peaceful, rational-consensual lines. However, the trilateralism of the Carter period had been unable to overcome the crisis of American imperialism and the Atlantic order. Now that the initial Reagan policy had galvanised the Western position and by various means had exported the crisis to the periphery, trilateralism could be resurrected from a position of strength.

The international deployment of productive capital had assumed new forms. These expressed not only the transformation from corporate liberalism to neo-liberalism, but also the shift from an Atlantic towards a Pacific focus of world capitalism. These forms will undoubtedly give a new and more complete meaning to trilateralism if it comes to prevail. New forms of productive capital have been described by the director of McKinsey in Japan, Kenichi Ohmae, in his book *Triad Power*. The 'triadic' perspective adjusts to the high-technology-oriented, selective industrialisation pattern of neo-liberal vintage, as well as to the creeping protectionism by which metropolitan capitalist states are jockeying for position in the emerging global economy. Industrial corporations, abandoning the product-cycle marketing strategies of the 'multinational' type, have found themselves confronted by the total competition in which their main rivals often are their national counterparts. To secure access to the markets, technological breeding grounds and productive locations that count (that is, the USA, Japan and the EC countries), industrial firms have resorted to a strategy of forming international consortia. Thus in the automobile industry, notwithstanding continuing clamour for protection against excessive imports on the American side, consortia aimed at securing global competitiveness have emerged. General Motors collaborates with Toyota, Isuzu, Suzuki, as well as with non-car producers Hitachi and Fujitsu-Fanuc (robots); Ford co-operates with Mazda, and with NEC and Toshiba; Chrysler's Japanese partner is Mitsubishi, which also collaborates with AMC.[51]

Clearly, the 'triadic' strategy is not only, as Ohmae suggests, a competitive strategy between national rivals, who through the creation of national consortia seek to mutually reinforce their position. It is also a strategy of *national* capitals, and may well be a stage and rationalisation of Japanese expansion, just as the multinational product cycle theory was a rationalisation of American expansion. Critics of the Ohmae thesis claim that the Japanese axis may simply be the specific form of US–Japanese world market competition, just as rival 'multinationalisation' through direct investment was a form of US–European rivalry in the previous period.

The unilateralism central to the first Reagan Administration tended to reinforce rivalry in this sense. The massive American defence build-up worked to undermine European and Soviet economic interdependence. At first sight, this relation would not seem obvious. Direct subsidies to enterprises in the USA, measured as a percentage of GDP, are only between one-third to one-tenth of the comparable figures for Europe and one-half to one-third of Japan's.[52] But the subsidising of 'civilian' industry, anathema to Reaganomics, was compensated for by Pentagon programmes serving roughly the same needs. Under Reagan, military funding of research and development rose from 62 per cent of total government funding in 1980 to 75 per cent in 1983. Pentagon co-ordination served to circumvent anti-trust legislation in industrial co-operation, to cover long-term investment costs, and, through its Manufacturing Technology Program, to encourage the introduction of new production techniques. As a consequence, as Gerd Jünne has shown, current long-term development plans in new technologies are roughly identical for the Pentagon and Japan's MITI.[53]

This strategy of 'Pentagon capitalism', to use Seymour Melman's term, was one in which industrial secrecy and the export embargo policy against the USSR became an instrument of inter-imperialist rivalry as well. This strategy was highly profitable to the major military contractors. In 1984, for example, the average rate of profit for American industry was 12.8 per cent, but profits of General Dynamics, Boeing, Litton, Lockheed, Rockwell and McDonnell Douglas averaged 35 per cent.[54] At the same time, other major American corporations engaged in a triadic strategy (identified by Ohmae as the four automobile concerns; the 12 biggest computer firms; two major airframe producers [Pratt & Whitney and GE]; and a long list of robot makers) were losing ground. The manufacturing trade balance of the USA, which had been positive by $17 billion in 1980, in 1985 was negative by $107.4 billion. More specifically, a Morgan Stanley study noted that whereas in the first half of 1982, the USA still had a high-tech trade surplus of $10.2 billion, the balance was negative by $6.7 billion on an annual basis in the third quarter of 1984.[55]

The sheer scale of the mortgaging of 'fortress America' in trade and capital balance terms prompted the trilateral element in the American bourgeoisie to take the offensive against the military–industrial complex.

In 1981, Paul Thayer, president of LTV (a big military contractor itself) but also chairman of the American Chamber of Commerce, declared that 'defense dollars must be spent wisely. We cannot afford a huge arsenal of weapons at the cost of a sick economy.'[56] In 1982, managers of several major high-tech industries with an internationalist tradition formed Business Executives for National Security (BENS). This organisation, including among its ranks Thomas Watson of IBM, gave voice to the fear that the across-the-board expansion of military power deflected American industry from the course of innovative accumulation necessary for survival in the world market.[57]

THE RESURRECTION OF TRILATERALISM?

The deficits incurred by the USA, coupled to the massive debt crisis that resulted from the industrialisation strategies of Third World countries and their termination by the 1982 interest rate hike, unveiled fundamental global economic imbalances. Therefore, a longer-term political necessity was a reinforcement of global economic management. As such, the trilateral blueprint, adjusted to neo-liberal class relations and triadic corporate strategy, presented itself anew. In June 1982, the appointment as Secretary of State of George Shultz, a board member on some of the most important American investment banks and corporations, reinforced the hitherto marginal trilateral tendency in the Reagan Administration.

Henceforward, the Cold War and international monetarist policies were each, in turn, rolled back. Trimming the influence of the MIC and the national security apparatus on economic and foreign policy was the first line of attack. In 1983, Thayer, whose criticism of across-the-board rearmament was referred to above, replaced Carlucci as Deputy Secretary of Defense. By that time, the critique of the overblown defence budget surfaced in a press uproar over military contract cost overruns and Pentagon mismanagement, which reverberated in a Congressional investigation. Representatives of the foremost American high-tech corporations now moved to centre-stage. In early 1984, Edson Spencer, chairman of Honeywell and a TC member, spoke out for a removal of all non-strategic nuclear weapons from Europe. In 1985, David Packard, a cold warrior and Former Deputy Secretary of Defense under Nixon, chairman of Hewlett-Packard and a member of both the CPD and the TC, was named head of a special Commission of Defense Management to investigate the reform of the armed forces.[58]

The first casualty of the new look at the Pentagon was General Dynamics, the biggest American defence contractor. GD had been responsible for some of the most spectacular cost overruns. Former company president James Beggs (director of NASA) and vice-president George

Sawyer (Assistant Secretary of the Navy) both had to vacate their government posts.[59] On the other hand, in late 1985, Thayer was dealt a four-year prison term following a SEC investigation.[60]

The 'Star Wars' plan, launched in March 1983, also has to be seen in the context of fractional struggles to subordinate defence spending to the needs of advanced American industry. Star Wars fulfilled a campaign promise made by the Republican convention to resume work on an anti-ballistic missile defence. However, an initial version promoted by a group of defence industries, called High Frontier and aimed at the deployment of a space system based on existing technology, had been rejected as unrealistic by both DeLauer and Weinberger. Reagan instead adopted a different version, advocated by Edward Teller, which had a research orientation that could lead to possible technological breakthroughs.[61]

This version of Star Wars served two purposes at once:

1. It served to focus Pentagon research on really promising technology and more clearly demarcated a high-tech sector within the overblown defence budget.
2. By the invitation to other capitalist countries to participate in the project, it sought to adjust Pentagon capitalism to American economic centrality by incorporating more European research capacity. On balance, however, the inclusion of the UK, Japan, Israel, West Germany and Italy into the programme must be viewed as an imposition of American unilateralism rather than as a multilateralisation of Pentagon capitalism, partly because of the extension of export controls to the participating countries. The rival European research programme, EUREKA, launched by French President Mitterrand and involving, nominally, 19 countries and the European Commission, suffered from a lack of funds and therefore remained subordinated to American strategy (see Chapter 9).

Finally, the second Reagan Administration made an ideological shift away from confronting the Soviet 'evil empire' to combating 'international terrorism'. This move was undermined, however, by the Iran Contra scandal, which brought to the surface a covert network involving forces officially designated as the instigators of terrorism. This critically undermined American capacity to enlist European support.

The second target of the trilateralists within the Reagan coalition concerned the role of financial speculators in the monetary policy-making area. American banks were particularly exposed in lending to the Third World at the outset of the Reagan incumbency. Third World debt to private banks was $150 billion in September 1979, offset by $90 billion Third World holdings; the net $60 billion Third World debt to commercial banks, however, was primarily with American banks, since Third World debts and holdings with European banks were almost in balance.[62] Bank liberalisation had accelerated when Reagan took over. In December 1981, 'off-shore' banking was authorised in the USA, allowing banks to set up special-status International Banking Facilities (IBF). In line with the philosophy of the Treasury Secretary, Donald Regan (a champion of total deregulation of the banking business when at Merrill Lynch), the new IBFs were exempt from many Federal Reserve regulations and taxes.[63] Meant to lure Eurocurrency business back to the USA, after four months, American off-shore banking already had assets of more than $100 billion (albeit with a 55 per cent share for non-American banks).[64]

The debt crisis gravely jeopardised the position of American banks, a message brought home in 1984 with the Continental Illinois crisis that came on top of a growing tide of American bank failures. Next to Third World debt, the agricultural crisis as well as pressure on energy prices contributed to this development.[65]

The American budget deficit reached $220 billion in fiscal 1986, net foreign debt was $250 billion and the USA had its worst trade balance ever. Monetarism, all along under fire from the supply-siders, was the first casualty of the original Reagan policy mix. From mid-1982 through 1983, the American money supply expanded by 11·7 per cent on an annual basis. The change of personnel and policy, most importantly the changing places between Treasury Secretary Regan and White House Chief of Staff Baker, interacted with the maturing of a pragmatic rather than ideological trilateral strategy, represented in the Baker Plan.

The Baker Plan aimed at grafting industrial recovery on the Third World circuit of money capital. By its co-ordinated, 'plan' aspect, American policy in this area gravitated somewhat towards the productive capital concept. The plan reflected the influence on economic policy of the bloc of interests associated, materially or ideologically, with the stock exchange, property incomes, and the fraction of capital engaged in handling them. A further sign of a change of orientation was the loss of stature of monetarism.[66] Beryl Sprinkel's demotion from the Treasury to the Council of Economic Advisers fitted into this trend, as did appointments to the Federal Reserve. Of Reagan appointees up to 1987, none was a monetarist, thus further isolating Chairman Volcker. When he resigned in mid-1987, to be replaced by Morgan director Alan Greenspan, monetarism was expected to be replaced by an emphasis on bank deregulation,[67] perhaps signalling a shifting emphasis to industrial expansion.

On the wider, trilateral plane, the re-orientation towards a long-term and multilateral approach was also expressed in various policy planning bodies of the transnational ruling class. At the meeting of the Trilateral Commission in Madrid in May 1986, one report recommended reciprocating the more globalist approach of the new Soviet leadership by a new capitalist globalism that would provide a stable, and favourable setting for systematic co-operation.[68] The new spirit was corroborated in, for example, the Annual Conference of the International Chamber of Commerce held in the same month in Barcelona. At this meeting, the ICC President, Unilever President H. F. van den Hoven, stated that the world market had to be expanded by direct investment in the Third World and by developing East-West trade. An observer saw in the declarations made at the conference a new commitment on the international plane.[69] Significantly, prominent business spokesmen mentioned the drop in oil prices as the basis on which a new relation with the capitalist periphery could be based. Rand Araskog, President of ITT, mentioned this in his opening speech at the ICC Conference, while E. Reviglio, President of ENI, recently pointed to the fall in oil prices as the occasion to renew the western European special relationship with the Mediterranean countries on a new basis.

NOTES

The author wishes to thank Stephen Gill for editorial work, and participants in the panel discussion at the British International Studies Association annual conference in Reading, December 1986, for comments on a draft version of this chapter.
1. R. Bode, 'De Nederlandse bourgeoisie tussen de twee wereldoorlogen', *Cahiers voor de Politieke en sociale Wetenschappen*, II, 2 (1979); K. van der Pijl, *The Making of an Atlantic Ruling Class* (London, Verso, 1984).
2. On the Trilateral Commission, see S. Gill, *American Hegemony and the Trilateral Commission* (Cambridge, Cambridge University Press, 1989).
3. On the connection between the economic crisis and the crisis of bourgeois strategy, see also B. Greiner, *Amerikanische Aussenpolitik von Truman bis heute* (Köln, Pahl-Rugenstein, 1980).
4. P. Chamsol in *Le Monde Diplomatique*, April 1984, p. 1; S. Stuurman, 'A further comment on the energy crisis', *Monthly Review*, XXVI, 5 (1974), p. 56.
5. E. Mandel, *The Second Slump* (London, Verso, 1980), p. 12.
6. A. Lipietz, 'Towards Global Fordism?', *New Left Review*, 132 (1982), p. 37.
7. R. Parboni, *The Dollar and its Rivals* (London, Verso, 1981), p. 13; cf. B. J. Cohen, *In Whose Interest. International Banking and American Foreign Policy* (New York, Yale University Press for the Council on Foreign Relations, 1986), p. 23, table 2.2; *Newsweek*, 26 May 1980.
8. J. K. Javits, 'The MNC as Agent for Peaceful Development', in International Management and Development Institute, *Corporate Citizenship in the Global Community* (Washington 1976), p. 38.
9. E. Altvater, 'Der gar nicht diskrete Charme der neoliberalen Konterrevolution', *Prokla* 44, 1981, pp. 6–7. On the meaning of the Chilean coup, see A. Fernandez Jilberto, *Dictadura Militar y Oposición Politica en Chile 1973–1981* (Dordrecht/Cinnaminson, NJ, Foris, 1985).
10. *Hoy*, November 25, 1981; The interlock between Mont Pélèrin and Heritage is through Ed Feulner, Treasurer and Chairman, respectively, cf. *Who's Who in the World 1982–83* (Chicago, Marquis, 1982).
11. *Newsweek*, 21 July 1986.
12. *Newsweek*, 13 August 1979; *NRC-Handelsblad*, 12 July 1979; H. W. Overbeek,

'The Westland Affair: Collision over the Future of British Capitalism', *Capital and Class*, 29 (1986), p. 22.
13. *El Mercurio*, 30 October/5 November 1980.
14. Giovanni Agnelli, head of FIAT, explained the economic aspect of the emerging 'Historic Compromise' and the 1980 turnabout in dramatic terms in a recent interview. 'We had very strong unions [and] a Communist Party that had more power than they have today', Agnelli told *Newsweek*. 'We could hardly survive in the factories. There was disorder, terrorism – there was even prostitution. I would say that the turning point was the event in Turin in October 1980 . . . From that point discipline came back into the factories.' Interview in *Newsweek*, 16 February 1987.
15. P. Allum in *Le Monde Diplomatique*, March 1984, p. 3; *Newsweek*, 27 July 1987.
16. Quoted in *Gazette de Lausanne*, 23 August 1978; cf. *Financial Times*, 12 March 1979.
17. *NRC Handelsband*, 5 November 1979.
18. *Newsweek*, 21 November 1977.
19. Altvater, 'Der gar nicht diskrete Charme . . .', p. 7; *Le Monde*, 3 April 1979; *Financial Times*, 21 November 1978.
20. *Newsweek*, 22 December 1980.
21. R. Kühnl, 'Carstens, Strauss, und die Offensive der Rechten', *Blätter für deutsche und internationale Politik*, 6 (1979), p. 647.
22. See R. Scheer, *With Enough Shovels. Reagan, Bush & Nuclear War* (New York, Random House, 1982).
23. See G. V. Wright Jr, *A Case Study of US Foreign Policy: The Carter Administration and Angola* (University of Leeds, PhD dissertation, 1987), p. 287 & passim.
24. P. Burch, *Elites in American History* (New York, Holmes & Meier, 1980), vol. III, pp. 340, 356; B. Coriat in *Colloque Automatisation et Mutations Economiques et Sociales* (Paris, Ministère de la Recherche et de la Technologie, 1984), pp. 164, 169–72.
25. M. Fennema, *International Networks of Banks and Industry* (The Hague, Nijhoff, 1982); M. Fennema and K. van der Pijl, *El triunfo del neoliberalismo* (Santo Domingo, Taller, 1987), p. 26, table 4.
26. *Newsweek*, 22 June 1987; Idem, 31 August 1987.
27. *Business Week*, 7 July 1986.
28. *Fortune*, 8 December 1986. One is reminded here of the passage in the *Communist Manifesto* where Marx and Engels write that capitalism has dissolved personal dignity and replaced it by exchange value, *Marx-Engels Werke* (Berlin, Dietz), vol. IV, p. 465.
29. On Madonna, *de Volkskrant*, 21 August 1987, quoting the *Mail on Sunday*.
30. *Fortune*, 8 December 1986.
31. Quoted in A. Roy, 'International Dimensions of "Third World" Struggles in the Present Phase', *The Marxist Review*, XVII, 2 (1984), p. 130. On the craft theory of automation, see M. Piore and C. F. Sabel, *The Second Industrial Divide. Possibilities for Prosperity* (New York, Basic Books, 1984).
32. *Forbes*, 27 October 1986.
33. *Fortune*, 1 September 1986.
34. *Newsweek*, 31 August 1987; *Financial Times*, 10 September 1987.
35. *Newsweek*, 13 October 1986; Schlumberger *Annual Reports*.
36. *Financial Times*, 20 November 1986; *Newsweek*, 31 August 1987.
37. *Newsweek*, 31 August 1987; A. Mommen, 'De lange slagschaduwen van een

Frans holding', *De Nieuwe Maand*, 29, 5 (1986), pp. 38–47.
38. Reagan's own 'selection' from available right-wing candidates has been analysed in T. Ferguson and J. Rogers, 'The Reagan Victory: Corporate Coalitions in the 1980 Campaign' in Ferguson and Rogers (eds), *The Hidden Election* (New York, Pantheon, 1981).
39. All background material on members of the Reagan Administration, unless indicated otherwise, come from R. Brownstein and N. Easton, *Reagan's Ruling Class* (New York, Pantheon, 1983), 2nd edn.
40. M. Davis, *Prisoners of the American Dream* (London, Verso, 1986), pp. 172, 173.
41. *NRC-Handelsblad*, 20 July 1985; *Newsweek*, 7 October 1985.
42. Quoted in Brownstein and Easton, *Reagan's Ruling Class*, p. 459.
43. Brownstein and Easton, *Reagan's Ruling Class*, pp. 46, 87.
44. *NRC-Handelsblad*, 4 August 1982, cf. Brownstein and Easton, *Reagan's Ruling Class*, p. 562.
45. A. Ognev, *Economic Co-operation, an Instrument of Peace* (Moscow, Nauka, 1985), p. 35.
46. *Newsweek*, 6 August 1984.
47. U. Rehfeldt, 'Gemeinsames Programm, Krise und internationale Arbeitsteilung – die Grenzen des Reformismus', *Leviathan*, 6, 1 (1978), pp. 33–5; *Le Monde Diplomatique*, March 1986.
48. *NRC-Handelsblad*, 26 May 1983; A. Lipietz in *Le Monde Diplomatique*, March 1984, p. 16.
49. Thus, the Bank of International Settlements' Annual Report in 1985 could note that net exports had contributed the lion's share (55 per cent) to French economic growth in the 4th quarter 1984/mid-1985 period. *NRC-Handelsblad*, 27 May 1985.
50. Cf. Fennema and van der Pijl, *Triunfo del neoliberalismo*, p. 59, table 11, for comparison with other countries; *NRC-Handelsblad*, 27 May 1985.
51. K. Ohmae, *Macht der Triade. Die neue Form weltweiten Wettbewerbs* (Wiesbaden, Gabler, 1985), pp. 51, 60, 150–3.
52. G. Jünne, 'Der strukturpolitische Wettlauf zwischen den kapitalitistischen Industrieländern', *Politische Vierteljahresschrift*, XXV, 2 (1984), p. 137.
53. G. Jünne, 'Das amerikanische Rüstungsprogramm: Ein Substitut für Industriepolitik', *Leviathan*, XIII, 1 (1985), p. 33.
54. *Le Figaro*, 19 April 1985.
55. *The Times*, 16 April 1985. Overall trade figures from *Newsweek*, 17 November 1986.
56. Quoted in Brownstein and Easton, *Reagan's Ruling Class*, pp. 743–4.
57. *Newsweek*, 24 March 1986.
58. *Newsweek*, 2 April 1984.
59. *Newsweek*, 1 February 1985; *NRC-Handelsblad*, 5 December 1985.
60. *Fortune*, 23 December 1985.
61. C. Julien in *Le Monde Diplomatique*, May 1985, p. 2.
62. See my 'Neoliberalism against a New International Economic Order', *The Marxist Review*, XX, 1 (1987); *NRC-Handelsblad*, 12 November 1985.
63. *Newsweek*, 7 December 1981.
64. *Newsweek*, 10 May 1982.
65. *Newsweek*, 3 September 1984; Idem, 3 March 1986; *NRC-Handelsblad*, 12 November 1985.
66. 'The breadth of the assault is remarkable. Traditional opponents, such as Keynesians in academia, have been joined in monetarist bashing by the U.S.

Chamber of Commerce, Wall Street, Congress and a number of Federal Reserve and Reagan administration economists . . . Few have come so far and then fallen so fast as the monetarists.' *Newsweek,* 23 September 1985.
67. *Newsweek,* 15 June 1987; cf. *Fortune,* 16 September 1985.
68. G. A. Astre in *Le Monde Diplomatique,* August 1986, p. 28.
69. E. Karailiev in *Le Monde Diplomatique,* November 1986, p. 7.

5 · WESTERN EUROPE IN THE ATLANTIC SYSTEM OF THE 1980s
Towards a New Identity?
David Allen and Michael Smith

As several other chapters in this book make plain, images and expectations relating to 'Europe' in Atlantic relations have been critical at many junctures since 1945, and they remain central in the late 1980s. Both the past evolution and the future course of transatlantic issues raise questions about the formation and the development of a specifically European identity, and the main aim of this chapter is to explore such questions. Does the notion of a European identity express the impact of fundamental structural change in the Atlantic system – change which has produced irreversible divergence of American and European positions – or does it rather reflect a series of pragmatic and incremental responses to events? These questions will be explored first through a general assessment of the relationships between the Atlantic system, American policies and a European identity, and then through case studies of two major issues in the diplomatic–strategic sphere – East–West relations and regional conflicts outside the North Atlantic area.[1]

WESTERN EUROPE IN THE ATLANTIC SYSTEM

The history of Atlantic relations in the post-1945 era has been characterised by uncertainty in several dimensions. Whilst the problem is covered elsewhere in this volume, it is appropriate here to point out some of the key features of this uncertainty as it affects the idea of 'western Europe'. Although it may seem paradoxical, the starting point has to be in the nature and evolution of American policies and positions.

From the outset, it has been unclear – often to Americans themselves, and certainly to successive generations of Europeans – what the American role in Atlantic relations has been, is or should be. American policies have expressed a mercurial combination of globalism, isolationism, interventionism and unilateralism. American leaders have preached the virtues – or the inevitability – of Atlantic community, Atlantic partnership and an American empire. Policies, ideologies and events have thus expressed frequent confusion about the position of the Americans *vis-à-vis* western Europe, and as a consequence about the appropriate role for the west Europeans themselves. Are they to form a quasi-united element in a relatively equal partnership? Are they to be the target of divide-and-rule policies and of exploitation? Or are they simply a collection of independent states that happens to cluster around the Americans for protection without having an indissoluble link to them?

The ambiguities are compounded by the nature of developments in western Europe itself. Nowhere is this more so than in the field of 'high politics', where vital national interests come into collision with the need for collaboration. The result has been a series of 'identity crises' for the west Europeans, which have meshed with broader crises of Atlantic relations: the European Defence Community fiasco in the 1950s, the Kennedy–de Gaulle clashes of the 1960s, the 'Year of Europe' in 1973 and its aftermath.[2] Questions of policy and questions of identity are clearly intimately connected and mutually influential, but that is not the whole story: the crises of west European identity have also been affected by broader systemic forces of change and transformation.[3]

At the level of policy, the problems of the Atlantic system are expressed in a number of dilemmas facing its members. Given the complexity, heterogeneity and openness of the transatlantic system, its members have delicate calculations to make about the stakes, risks and consequences attached to specific courses of action. They have similar calculations – or informed guesses – to make about their individual roles, and about their responsiveness to demands made by other members of the system. They have to consider the boundaries of legitimate behaviour not only in the light of established conventions but also in the face of rapidly unfolding events, where the rules of the game may be unclear or themselves contentious. When it comes to the management of the system itself, although there are elaborate institutional frameworks – NATO, the OECD, the EC and others – there are no guarantees as to whether issues will be handled by coercion or consensus, or through unilateral, bilateral or multilateral channels. Such factors explain at least to a limited extent why Atlantic relations since 1945 can plausibly be explained in terms of simultaneous harmony and crisis, of integration and disintegration.[4]

It is arguable that in the 1980s the Atlantic system has been undergoing a crisis more far-reaching than those of previous decades, and that this poses new problems for those wishing to establish positions and roles within it. From a variety of perspectives it is possible to identify a breakdown of hegemonial structures and of the accompanying consensus on objectives and procedures that characterised the 1945–70 period.[5] From the perspective adopted in this chapter, the important feature of the Atlantic system in the 1970s and especially the 1980s is not that the system has been destroyed – for in many respects it has not – but that the establishment of positions and roles within the system by its members has become even more a delicate and fragile process. As others have argued, the breakdown of hegemony in interdependent systems can make collaboration not only more necessary but also more difficult to achieve.[6] Here, that argument can be amended somewhat to state that the breakdown of hegemony can make the establishment of positions, roles and identity by members both more necessary and more difficult to achieve. Nor is this simply a reflection of the shifting internal structure of the Atlantic system: external challenges, especially those posed by developments in the Soviet sphere and by the eruption of regional conflicts, have contributed to the establishment of a new political dynamic among the countries of the North Atlantic area.

One product of this new political dynamic – but also a major contributor to its acceleration – is the phenomenon of Reaganism. As Stephen Gill points out in Chapter 2, it is important to assess the 'Reagan revolution' in the light of the USA's changing position within the international structure, and to analyse it at least in part as a symptom of profound structural dislocations produced by the crises of the 1970s and 1980s.[7] Reaganism can be seen as the manifesto of those who reject the loss of American hegemony and who wish to restore – by coercion if necessary – the Atlantic consensus of the 1950s and 1960s. There is, however, another side to the phenomenon of Reaganism: one of the key features of the 1980s in American foreign policy has been not the ideological consistency which is a striking quality of 'Reaganism in theory', but the untidiness, the confusion and the inconsistencies of 'practical Reaganism'. Here, it is important to note that the challenge of Reaganism – and the American position in terms of which any European identity is partly to be defined – is one which exists in several dimensions. At the level of ideology and broad strategy, it may well be appropriate to see the problem for western Europe as that of a new American drive to domination, but at the level of practical policy the problem can be more accurately defined as that of coping with inconsistencies of 'practical Reaganism'.[8]

Another dimension of the question of Atlanticism is the growth of a distinctive European awareness. In any such process, the presence and the impact of the Americans is crucial both at the European and national levels. Although it has been an article of faith for successive American administrations that the development of collective European structures should be fostered, the reality of American actions has often had the effect of diluting, diverting or disrupting the course of European collaboration. At the west European end, tensions and limitations have often been exacerbated by American actions or postures. This relates to a second tension: the clash between the development of collective procedures (such as those of European Political Co-operation) and the relative reluctance of

European governments to commit themselves to substantive collaboration on issues of vital national interest.

As a result, there is a disparity between the elaboration of procedures and the substance of policy which can make European co-operation appear purely reactive and limited to the lowest common denominator. It is clear that any distinctively European identity in the foreign policy field is likely to be at odds with the values and priorities of the USA, but it is not clear either that a European identity will simply arise from the reaction against American policies. Nor is it apparent that such an identity can be sustained with any consistency when confronted by the harsh reality of the international arena.[9]

For these reasons, there is unlikely to be a simple connection between American policies, European–American disagreements and the growth of a characteristically European foreign policy presence. European collaboration implies a sense of common awareness of national positions and disparities of stakes and risks. A positively European identity may well be encouraged by the system of Atlantic relations in the 1980s; it may well be recognised as a reality within the system; but it will be neither uniform nor cumulative given the tensions that exist with Europe itself and the contradictions of American policy.

This preliminary conclusion, though, requires elaboration and testing. In measuring the extent to which a European identity has been defined and developed during the 1980s, it is possible to adopt a number of indices. First, the notion of a European identity can be seen as the product of a 'learning process', through which the countries of western Europe experience the practicalities of collaboration and produce habits of consultation and communication. Second, the growth of identity can be measured through the expansion of the agenda on which European collaboration takes place, from the procedural to the substantive and the 'low' to the 'high' dimension of policy. Finally, the nature of a European identity can be established in terms of its salience within the structure of Atlantic relations and the extent to which it forms part of the calculations of those engaged in central processes of Atlantic co-operation or conflict. The argument will return to these criteria after exploration of two case studies which raise in an acute form the issues of European identity and policy development: first, the course of East–West relations, and the second, the handling of regional conflicts outside the North Atlantic area.

A FIRST CASE STUDY: EAST–WEST RELATIONS

West European governments confronted Reaganism in 1981 with some broadly shared perceptions, but with wide variations in detailed stances. These variations were accentuated by the development of European–

American diplomacy during the succeeding years. The immediate prospect of the new administration called forth a substantial amount of co-ordinated diplomacy. However, a number of trends in the first Reagan Administration, and in the first half of the second term, made co-ordination difficult to sustain. We discuss these problems with respect to East–West trade and arms control. The latter is most germane to the question of European identity.

East–West trade

East–West economic links have been a focus of European–American relations since the inception of the Marshall Plan. During the 1960s and the 1970s the clash between those who espoused embargoes and 'economic warfare' and those who believed in the beneficial effects of commerce was generally muted, but the politicisation of economic transactions during the 1970s had an inevitable spillover into Atlantic dealings. This came into the open with the crises in Iran and Afghanistan, which created American demands for sanctions even before Reagan took over the White House. Two central questions characterised debate and conditioned responses to American policies in western Europe. First, were economic relations a coercive weapon or a set of incentives to induce co-operation? Second, could economic dealings be insulated from political or strategic judgements?

From the late 1970s on, it was apparent that west European policy makers produced often contradictory answers to these questions. Three essential positions could be discerned on the spectrum of response. At one end were those, especially the West Germans, who were heavily engaged in East–West trade and who held the belief that trade and finance were an essential prop of detente. In the centre were those who held a more pragmatic view, and who saw trade as a two-edged sword – a stance often taken up by the French. At the other end were those with lower material and political stakes who could afford a certain ideological stridency. The British and the Italians found themselves in this position. However, for all west European parties, the tension between ideology and commercial advantage, and between their European and Atlantic priorities, was an established element of policy.[10]

During much of 1981, the sanctions issue remained relatively muted. The British and the West Germans were opposed to the lifting of the grain embargo imposed by the Carter administration, but also to any sanctions directed at the Soviet–west European gas pipeline project – an early target of Reaganite 'hawks'. There was little discussion of these questions at the Ottawa economic summit, where participants were much more concerned with domestic problems. It was in December 1981, with the imposition of martial law in Poland, that the question really came to the fore. Responses in western Europe were predictably diverse. The West Germans gave priority to the economic and social aspects; the French stressed their right to decide as they saw fit; and the British focussed on the need to stave off a possible 'West–West' crisis. Both the French and the West Germans found the issue sensitive within their governing coalitions, whilst the British and the Italians were rather more relaxed (except where specific commercial interests were at stake). These variations were not a matter of intense political concern, given the relatively unassertive initial response from Washington.

Everything changed in June and July 1982, and the crucial element was a shift in the American policy process. The advent of William Clark as National Security Advisor had led, since the spring, to escalating attacks on 'appeasers' – or to put it more kindly, those who favoured multilateral as opposed to unilateral diplomacy. The Versailles economic summit was the last hurrah of the multilateralists: within two weeks Secretary of State Alexander Haig was gone, and the hard unilateralist line was dominant. During July, it appeared that the USA had declared economic war (in the form of sanctions) on its allies as well as on the Soviet bloc. In addition, the East–West issue was superimposed on a number of other festering trade disputes between the USA and the EC, such as those over steel and agriculture. One immediate feature of west European responses was once again their diversity. The West Germans tried their best to ignore the sanctions; the French expressed nationalistic outrage and resistance; the British protested both their Atlantic solidarity and their determination to protect their interests. In these circumstances, positive European solidarity was difficult to discern. Although the EC summit of June 1982 issued a declaration, the British were suspected of neutering it, and the formal protest issued in August was less than dramatic.

During the autumn of 1982 a number of processes combined to defuse – but not fundamentally to resolve – the conflict. First it became apparent that powerful interests in the USA opposed sanctions: their influence over the succeeding two years was to produce a gradual erosion of the measures at the national level. Second, George Shultz, the new Secretary of State, promoted a negotiating process involving the major stakeholders and culminating in an agreement on general principles by the end of the year. Third, the problem was 're-routed': studies in the framework of COCOM, NATO and the OECD diluted the crisis and produced an impression of routine technical adjustment. This did not please everybody, but it was noticeable that on occasions during 1983 and 1984 when the Americans could have raised the stakes afresh, they refrained from doing so. Meanwhile, the Europeans had moved into line in areas such as subsidised export credits, whilst resting firmly on their well-established hostility to American dictat.[11]

Armaments and arms control

The peaks and troughs of European–American conflicts over East–West trade cannot be divorced from armaments and arms control. Two points must be made at once about the arms issue. First, like East–West trade, it has a long and tangled history. Second, more than East–West trade, it demands of the west Europeans an answer to the question, 'what kind of Europe?' The historical context is vital to an understanding of the 1980s, since it reveals a consistent tension between European and American images of the desirable and the practicable in security matters. On the one side, there is the problem of American commitment – a problem summed up for the west Europeans in Michael Mandelbaum's juxtaposition of twin dangers: 'entrapment' and 'abandonment'.[12] On the other hand, for the Americans, there is the problem of the west European contribution. The 'nuclear alliance' has to be legitimised to American domestic audiences, and this is undermined if it appears that the west Europeans are backsliding, hedging or appeasing in the face of the enemy. The problems are compounded by the nature of defence debates and defence policy making in the USA: often it is unclear how far American policy is driven by technological momentum, by the demands of domestic interests or by intellectual debates within the defence community. These uncertainties underline the difficulties for west Europeans, but quite apart from this, Europe has an identity problem. Having arguably grown fat on its status as a 'civilian power', what are the costs and benefits of going beyond that at the European level?

Developments in the late 1970s and early 1980s compounded the problem. The December 1979 NATO commitment on INF, stimulated by west European pressure, heightened the 'abandonment-entrapment' tensions. Reagan came to office committed to the INF decision, but also rejecting SALT II as 'fatally flawed' and dedicated to a policy of 'peace through strength'. His Administration, and Haig in particular, proclaimed their determination to consult the European allies, but consultation in these circumstances ran the risk of exacerbating the structural and political divergences already noted. Thus there was fairly constant European pressure for arms talks; but it was also apparent that each of the major European leaderships perceived priorities differently. For the West Germans talks were vital, not least because of the strength of domestic feeling on nuclear policy. For the French, who shared some parts of the Reaganite response to Soviet threats, the key aim was not to become over-identified with American initiatives. The British, dependent on the Americans for nuclear hardware and conscious of the vestiges of a 'special relationship', were loyal but discreetly critical. All were alarmed by the decision to produce the neutron bomb, taken in mid-1981 by Washington without consultation.[13]

It became clear by late 1981 that Europeans and Americans had divergent views of the linkages on which arms control should be built. The Reagan line was simple: build up strength and offer talks to the Soviets as long as they behaved. West Europeans wanted talks for pressing domestic or regional reasons. Over the winter of 1981–82, however, it appeared that west European pressure had less influence over American policies than domestic budgetary demands and the desire in the White House to choke off the nuclear freeze movement. Although the president's 'zero option' offer to the Soviets in the context of the INF talks was supported by the Europeans, it also became apparent that when talks actually started they might further distance the US–Soviet dialogue from the allies, leaving them as concerned bystanders.

In this context, the events of 1982–83 assumed a peculiar importance both for European–American relations and for the west Europeans themselves. Essentially, a new 'twin-track' process appeared: on the one hand, the Europeans continued to press for shifts in American policy and for consultation, whilst on the other hand, there emerged a series of moves towards a more formal European identity in the security field. The first of these trends built to a climax as the deadline for deployment of cruise and Pershing approached, and as popular pressure in western Europe (with the notable exception of France) became more insistent. There is evidence that the Europeans' pleas were heard in Washington: the assiduous attempts to carry the west Europeans along through such devices as the NATO Special Consultative Group, along with the frequent presence of American emissaries in 'sensitive' countries, testify to the concern in the White House. There still remained, though, the nagging feeling that American commitment to INF deployment outweighed its readiness to negotiate on arms control, and especially to link talks on strategic and theatre weapons. For many west Europeans, the USA appeared more concerned with internal debates and rhetoric than with the impact of policy on the outside world or with the preoccupations of its allies.[14]

European fears of American neglect were accompanied by increasing attention to possibilities for security co-operation on a European basis. One aspect of this trend focussed on the European Community, with the publication in late 1981 of the Genscher–Colombo plan for a 'European Act'. Amongst other things this would have extended the discussion of security issues in an EC context. By the spring of 1982 two lines of further development could be discerned, but both underlined the difficulties attending any such plans. Whilst the British evinced considerable reluctance to subscribe to grand projects for European union, the French and West Germans began actively to pursue avenues of further defence collaboration. Both trends threatened to dilute any EC initiative, and reinforced the continuing conflict between broad plans for a European identity and narrower national orientations.[15]

Whilst it could be claimed that the deployment of INF in the UK, Italy and West Germany from December 1983 was a victory for allied solidarity, it was clear that the process raised questions about the future linkage of strategic and theatre nuclear policies. The threat of 'decoupling' or 'Europeanisation' was underlined by the re-emergence of American doubts about the value of their forces in Europe, especially in Congress, where the Nunn Amendment tied a threat of troop withdrawals to perceived European failings on defence expenditure. At the same time, discussion of 'emergent technologies' in the conventional field provided further food for thought in western Europe, the potential nuclear battlefield. The centrepiece of the developing Reagan strategy in 1984–85, though, was the Strategic Defense Initiative (SDI) which promised – or threatened – to neutralise strategic nuclear weapons through the deployment of techologies which were not only 'emergent' but hardly on the drawing board (see Chapters 8 and 9 for further details).

The emergence of SDI as a central agenda item in European–American relations re-emphasised long-standing problems for west Europeans. Once again the threat of 'decoupling' appeared, an irony in the light of the recent battles over INF. Alongside it was the threat of renewed domination of the continent by superpower strategies. The prospect of greater technological dependence on the USA complicated west European responses. To some European leaders, however, the new challenge further justified the construction of a European defence identity. The keystone of this during 1984 was the resurrection of the moribund Western European Union (WEU). The French were the key proponents of this move. By mid-1984 it was agreed among west European governments that the WEU should be revived, but it was far from clear what the purpose or thrust of the revival should be. Its major members – the UK, France, West Germany and Italy – appeared to agree that WEU was a convenient forum, free of the niggling presence of the Irish and Danes which complicated European Political Co-operation (EPC). But when it came to more positive and material commitments, the members parted company. The French appeared to see WEU as a means of asserting west European separation without espousing integration. West Germany could not decide whether it should be a means of expressing European separatism or a means to counter threats of 'Europeanisation' in NATO. Whereas the fragility of EC and EPC collaboration might well have been exposed by a rejuvenated WEU, it was far from clear where the new identity might lead.[16]

By mid-1985, therefore, the status of the west Europeans – individually and collectively – *vis-à-vis* the security dimensions of European–American relations was marked by continuing ambiguity and uncertainty. Developments in American policies and in US–Soviet relations during 1985–87 were such as to underscore the confusion, and three issues in particular stand out: SDI, arms control and the summits.

The most obviously corrosive factor for a European defence identity during 1985 was SDI, both as a programme and as a focus of debate in domestic or international politics. 'Star Wars' was apparently non-negotiable with the Soviets, but also with the allies, as successive rebuffs dealt to European leaders in Washington appeared to demonstrate. At the same time, the SDI programme itself was inherently divisive with respect to both its strategic and its technological aspects.

Developments in arms control and at the summit level were the most taxing for the west Europeans during 1986 and 1987, reflecting as they did anxieties at both the evolution of Soviet–American relations and a growing uncertainty concerning American policies. A continuing theme was the growing pressures on the established arms control regime: SDI questioned the continued efficacy of the ABM Treaty; the continuing American military build-up threatened to undermine observance of the unratified SALT II agreement. Efforts made by European leaders to communicate concern over these issues were largely bilateral, without an attempt at a pan-European concerting of policies. Where there was an attempt to elevate broader European concerns, this was largely focussed on the field of conventional weapons, with calls for the extension of the CSCE 'umbrella' to cover conventional force reductions – a call met with very little enthusiasm in Washington.[17]

As noted earlier, the development of a closer Soviet–American dialogue has always posed a problem for west Europeans; while they may favour it as a general principle, there is fear that decisions may be taken without their involvement. During 1985–87 the Soviet–American summits not only rekindled these fears but also linked them potently to concrete issues of arms control in ways that threatened a major Atlantic crisis. The roots of the immediate problem lay in a combination of factors: American willingness to negotiate on the basis of their perceived strength and the new mobility of Soviet diplomacy under the leadership of Mikhail Gorbachev. While both leaderships placed a high priority on moves towards a summit in November 1985, they adopted differing postures towards the west Europeans. American policy seemed only reluctantly to have conceded a place to the allies, whereas the Soviets actively worked to stress the west European focus of their diplomacy. The consequences of the Geneva summit were on the whole acceptable to the west Europeans, although the subsequent propaganda battle of competing arms control plans was far less reassuring: once again, it appeared that European concerns might be marginalised or traded away.

Much more concern, amounting to a full-blown Atlantic crisis, was generated by the October 1986 Reykjavik summit. Here, it gradually dawned on leaderships all over western Europe that their security interests had all but been bargained away. Proposals to eliminate nuclear weapons in Europe and to cut strategic arsenals with a view to their abolition threatened to destroy the coupling of European and American strategies, to place renewed pressure on the British and French deterrents and to lay the Europeans open to coercion from superior Soviet conventional forces – and this only three years after the INF deployment struggle. Not surprisingly, national leaderships in western Europe were quick to scramble for reassurance, either in Washington or within the European framework (the French were heard again to urge the beefing up of WEU). The problem was that they found themselves dealing with an embattled and increasingly unsure American Administration, assailed by the fallout of Reykjavik, the adverse results of the mid-term elections and the policy-making chaos unleashed by 'Irangate'. It was not apparent that this Atlantic crisis would be quick to disappear, and although 1987 saw progress towards an INF agreement it was constantly attended by European doubts, reservations and hesitations.[18]

A SECOND CASE STUDY: REGIONAL CONFLICTS OUTSIDE EUROPE

Whilst East–West relations have always provided one of the major testing-grounds of European–American relations (and thus of the notion of a European identity), some of the most obvious challenges to the solidarity of the western alliance have, however, been those arising in the regions less settled and less predictable than those of the 'central balance'.[19] For this reason, regional conflicts provide important evidence relating to the main questions raised in this chapter, enabling an assessment of the extent to which the west Europeans have expanded their capacities and concerns during the 1980s.

The framework for this case study is provided by two sets of factors. First, there has been a continuing tension between the globalism in American policies and the predominantly regional preoccupations of most west European countries.[20] From the west European point of view, it has often seemed that American eagerness to force regional conflicts into a globalist mould does violence to the historical and political nuances of specific areas. On the American side, it has been concluded that Europeans are willing to shirk broader responsibilities and to pursue narrow regional or economic advantages. This set of factors goes alongside a second: within western Europe itself there are important differences of emphasis, often thrown into relief by the development of regional conflicts. The ex-imperial states, or those with special cultural and economic ties to former colonies or dependencies, possess different priorities and reflexes from those with more limited horizons. Just as in the case of East–West relations, the notion of a European identity has to overcome the barriers of history as well as specific challenges from Washington and elsewhere.

Within this broad framework, it is important to note the particular problems posed for the west Europeans by Reaganism. In the first place, the Reagan Administration espoused an extreme variant of the globalist tendency in American foreign policy, defining all regional conflicts in terms of the US–Soviet balance. Secondly, the handling of regional conflicts was envisaged in terms redolent of the 'policy of strength', with military power as the major determining factor. This was accompanied in many cases by the dedication of American forces to support 'freedom fighters' (a stance which came to be formalised in the 'Reagan doctrine'). By adopting these positions, the Americans ensured that they would run up against the interests and the activities of west European governments. But this left open the question of effects: would the American attempt to redefine the limits of the Atlantic system and to link the regional to the global have any measurable effect on the definition of a European identity? In order to pursue this question, the following sections focus on interactions between the USA and the west Europeans in three regions: the Middle East, the Persian Gulf and the Western Hemisphere.

The Middle East

The Middle East – and the Arab–Israeli conflict – forms the longest standing focus of European–American interaction outside Europe itself. Several west European states have major involvements in the region, almost all are heavily dependent on its oil or its markets, and within the European Community it has also formed a significant focus of attempts to produce common policy stances. Not surprisingly, west European initiatives have frequently fallen foul of those made by the USA.[21] During the 1970s, the Americans were irritated by the development of the Euro–Arab Dialogue, which threatened to prevent a co-ordinated Western response to the oil crisis.[22] The movement towards the Camp David Accords under the Carter Administration also caused frictions, and underlying tensions came fully into the open with the Venice Declaration produced by the EC countries in July 1980.

This sought to widen the basis of any future settlement of the Arab–Israeli conflict, in particular by including consideration of the Palestinian case. On the one hand, the Declaration could be seen as a landmark in the development of a common 'European' position. On the other, it generated open criticism from the Israelis and the Americans. Europeans were consciously setting themselves against major tenets of American policy. The key question in relation to any idea of European identity, though, is the extent to which they could go beyond declarations to produce material actions and effects.[23]

In this case, the impact of Reaganism, both on US policies and on the

European position, appears to have been well defined and almost immediate. As soon as the new Administration came into office, it began to work towards the notion of a 'strategic consensus' in the Middle East – a coalition of 'moderate' forces dedicated to the containment of the USSR, which was seen as the major threat in the region. Such a strategy allowed no room for the nuances appreciated by the Europeans, nor for the consideration of the 'Palestinian factor'. It thus flew directly in the face of the Venice Declaration. The Europeans faced even more fundamental obstacles to the implementation of their policies. Whilst they could mount any number of fact-finding missions and assessments of the situation in the Middle East, they were unable to produce any credible initiatives on the ground. Rather then being the beginning of something, it increasingly appeared that Venice was the end, and the narrow national interests of countries such as the UK and France threatened to take over.[24]

During 1982, it appeared that the Europeans were first converted to the American position and overtaken by the new purposefulness of Washington's diplomacy. The 'Reagan Plan' of September 1982 advanced proposals that promised to take account of the Palestinians' interests, and in this and other ways it appeared that there were no longer any significant differences between the USA's and the Europeans' position. Nonetheless, the Europeans continued to desire a more comprehensive settlement of the Arab–Israeli conflict. The fact that both the Reagan Plan and the various attempts to produce a comprehensive peace proved to be stillborn does not dispose of the argument that differences exist between the European and American positions. Nor – unfortunately for the Europeans – does it refute the accusation frequently levelled by Americans, that there is more to policy than declarations and diplomatic sightseeing. The west Europeans have a clear stake in Middle East peace diplomacy, but their ability to translate it into substantive policy during the 1980s has been constrained by a combination of their own inadequacies and the dynamics of the broader situation – among them, American policies.

The diplomatic search for peace is only part of the Middle East situation. Two other, interrelated processes have had a profound impact on the development both of American policies and of European positions. The first is the process by which the USA has become an increasingly active participant in the conflict that beset the region, and the second is the process by which the use and the countering of non-state violence has become the common currency of events therein. They have led to demands that the Europeans take a stand, that they live up to their (often debatable) obligations and that they bear some of the costs of American actions. At the same time, the demands have often exposed precisely the divergent national priorities and calculations which limit the development of any common European stance or any devotion of material resources to the cause.

In this context, the two key words are 'Lebanon' and 'Libya', representing episodes in which the Reagan Administration became embroiled and in which its response was to raise the stakes, creating the probability of increased levels of violence. The Lebanon situation after 1982 admittedly saw the Americans looking for a negotiated solution, but the reality of their entanglement led in an altogether different direction. Although there was no collective European response to American demands for support, a number of individual countries felt obliged to respond by contributing to the multinational force in Beirut. As conditions on the ground deteriorated, and as the Americans found it increasingly difficult to avoid identification with one side in the conflict, the Europeans were anxious to conduct an orderly withdrawal. Whilst this was achieved in dramatic circumstances during early 1984, the dangers created by the American entanglement did not disappear, and many of them made themselves felt directly in west European societies. In particular, the taking of hostages and the perpetration of terrorist attacks was a legacy of European and American policies. In addition to the links between American policies and the escalation of non-state violence, European leaderships had to deal with Washington's definition of terrorism as a form of aggression to which the appropriate response was armed force or coercion. Two particular problems followed. First, there was the need for internal or Europe-centred measures to reduce the risk or the impact of terrorism, and on this the Europeans were able to take some practical measures. Second, and much more sensitive, there was the demand for punishment to be visited upon those held responsible by Washington. It was this that confronted the Europeans with the need to define their position and to do something – even if what they did was to refuse to do anything.[25]

The high point of the tensions thus created came between Christmas 1985 and the early summer of 1986. Increasingly, American leadership came to identify Libya as the sponsor of terrorism and as the legitimate target for revenge. At the same time, the Europeans proved incapable of agreeing on strong collective measures, and this was cited by some as a reason for the Americans' use of force against the Libyan regime in April 1986.[26]

It appeared that the Europeans had failed on two counts: not only had they achieved nothing in the way of common action, they had also forfeited any chance they might have had of exercising a restraining influence on the USA itself. Even as the EC foreign ministers issued an appeal for restraint to both sides, the American strike force had been taking off to bomb Tripoli. Whilst the British went along with the raids and provided the facilities from where they were launched, others refused overflying rights and distanced themselves from the American position (particularly the French). The aftermath was equally instructive, with the British experiencing retaliation and uncovering the 'Syrian connection' and other EC members reluctant to impose diplomatic sanctions. These tensions continued through 1987, and demonstrated that the problem for the west Europeans lay not only in American policies. The issues encountered in the Middle East exposed the limitations of west European collaboration. They question any notion of a developing 'identity'.

The Persian Gulf

It is important to note that tensions between the Americans and the west Europeans in respect of the Gulf are not peculiar to the 1980s, and that the late 1970s in particular had seen significant areas of disagreement, culminating in the Iranian hostages episode of 1979–80. Events in the mid-1980s were to add a new dimension to these long-standing tensions, by heightening the perceived risks in the Gulf at the same time as they undermined the credibility of American policies. Once again, the west Europeans were faced with the dilemmas of collective or individual action and of compliance to, or distance from, the American line.

Up to 1987, the Americans and the Europeans professed some indifference about the Iran–Iraq conflict. As long as neither of the combatants showed any sign of gaining a decisive advantage, and as long as the flow of oil through the Gulf was relatively unimpeded, then policy could be relatively even-handed. The Americans, of course, showed some signs of inclining towards Iraq. The Europeans, meanwhile, issued general declarations of concern. To this extent, the diplomacy of the Gulf conflict was much less active on the surface than that of the Arab–Israeli dispute, and there was markedly less pressure on the Europeans to pursue a coherent line. Matters changed dramatically, however, with the revelations of 'Irangate' in the USA and with the escalation of the 'tanker war' in the Gulf itself during late 1986 and 1987.

The 'Irangate' episode might have been seen as reassuring, if not uplifting, for the Europeans. Having for years endured American accusations of inconsistency, mendacity and ineffectiveness, they could now indulge themselves in self-congratulation. But the collapse of American policy itself raised new problems: quite apart from destroying the credibility of Reaganism, it threatened to destabilise the balance of forces in the Gulf by undermining the Iraqi position. The Europeans once again faced the problems of defining a collective stance in a situation where American policies were a source of disruption and uncertainty, and where events in the Gulf itself were moving unpredictably. The increasing American naval presence in the Gulf and the reflagging of Kuwaiti tankers by the American authorities can in part be explained by the need for the Reagan Administration to regain some of its lost domestic credibility. Whatever the stimulus, it created a potentially explosive situation, one which was replete with possibilities of miscalculation on all sides, as the shooting down of an Iranian airliner by the USA in 1988 was to prove.

For the Europeans, the major immediate impact made itself felt through the Reagan Administration's attempts to legitimise its presence in the Gulf. These took two forms. In the first place, the Americans supported a UN Security Council cease-fire resolution, which was passed on 20 July 1987 and which attracted the enthusiastic support of the British. Although this gave rise to a peacemaking mission by Secretary-General Perez de Cuellar, there was never any hope that a real Western-sponsored diplomatic breakthrough might take place, at least until Ayatollah Khomeini's views concerning absolute victory were changed in mid-1988, when a cease-fire was eventually agreed. More pressing for the west Europeans were American demands for naval support in the Gulf, partly on the grounds that it was the Europeans' oil supplies that were being safeguarded by American efforts. After the first American-escorted convoy suffered mine damage, and a mistaken Iraqi air attack led to a loss of American lives, the demands became very specific and very pressing. By its very nature, the situation was one in which a collective European response was almost out of the question: each west European government might well have felt able to subscribe to general declarations expressing solidarity, but when it came to demands for action only some of their number felt obliged to do anything. Divergent perceptions of interest, of the stakes in the Gulf and the risks attending American policy all made themselves felt.

Within this context, there is little that is surprising about the range of west European responses during and after August 1987. The British and the French already had a presence in or near the Gulf, and after the discovery of mines in the Gulf of Oman they were able to justify the sending of minesweepers. Both, however, were adamant that they would neither be acting in concert with the USA nor constituting part of a collective European effort. This neither prevented Washington from greeting the moves as if they were part of its own policy, nor ended the efforts of the Italians and the Dutch to concoct some kind of joint European force. Eventually, the Italians, the Dutch and the Belgians sent units to the Gulf, but the overall effect created by west European policies was that of prevarication and individual initiative rather than united or coherent action. As in the Middle East conflicts dealt with earlier, the call for substantive commitment and risk-taking was watered down at least as much by European reluctance to assume the joint burden as by suspicions about American policies and their possible implications. When the cease-fire eventually came in the Iran–Iraq war in the summer of 1988, the west European role in its promotion had been virtually negligible, whilst many individual European countries had taken greater risks than they had in the 1970s.

The Western Hemisphere

Although there are similarities between the issues of the Middle East and the Gulf, different questions are raised by European–American interactions in the Western Hemisphere during the 1980s. Whereas the Arab–Israeli conflict and the Gulf War sit uneasily between the spheres of influence of the two superpowers and occupy areas of traditional European interest, the affairs of Central and South America are conducted under the shadow of the USA. Direct European military involvement and influence have for a long time been of secondary importance, although the ties of culture and commerce are extensive. On the basis of the previous cases, it might thus be expected that a policy of declaration would be the only feasible option. Common European positions might therefore be obtained, but they would express only a very limited conception of a European identity. Reaganism emphasised that the whole of the Americas was the USA's 'backyard' and opposed any outside infiltration. As it happens, the 1980s did not conform neatly to this pattern. The two major episodes here are the Falklands War of 1982 and the attempts to reach a settlement in Central American conflicts during the decade.

When Argentina invaded the Falkland Islands in April 1982, the British responded initially through diplomatic attempts to gain support from the United Nations, the EC and the USA. In the first case, they succeeded in obtaining widespread support which then quite rapidly dissipated. When it came to the EC, support was forthcoming not only in the form of declarations but also through sanctions imposed on the Argentinians; to this extent, it represented a step forward in collaborative policy making, although problems later emerged. The speed and extent of the response formed a marked contrast to the disarray in which the Europeans had found themselves when faced with the problems of Afghanistan and Iran, where, of course, the economic and political stakes were higher. It also contrasted favourably with the confusion in Washington, where the contending forces within the Reagan Administration engaged in a protracted internal political struggle. Even though Ireland and Italy felt obliged to opt out of some collective European measures, this did not reduce the impact of European solidarity; whilst the Americans only came down off the fence (with admittedly crucial impact) at a late stage in the build-up to war. The internal divisions of American policy had a material effect on European perceptions. The White House underwent precisely the problems of conflict between different interests and roles which have often disabled the Europeans themselves.[27]

A somewhat different set of problems and interactions is illustrated by the search for a settlement in Central America. Of all regional conflicts, this is the one closest to the heart of the Reagan Administration, embodying the threat of alien infiltration into the 'soft underbelly' of the USA itself. It cannot be said that this was promising terrain for the assertion of a European initiative, but it produced one of the more intriguing confrontations between European diplomacy and American strength during the Reagan era. At the core of this tension was a difference between European analysis of the conflict, based on the belief that indigenous economic and social problems were responsible, and the Reaganite analysis, which stressed the threat of Soviet expansionism and its proxies in Nicaragua or Cuba. The chief expression of the European position was their support (through EPC) for the Contadora peace initiative, which led to formal contacts with the Contadora group and the five Central American republics during 1984.[28] The Europeans put themselves into direct confrontation with American policy – more direct, it could be argued, than in the case of the Venice Declaration on the Middle East conflict. Not surprisingly, American reaction was negative. Henry Kissinger noted that ' . . . in Central America one can only say that several European policies are deliberately designed to, or have the practical consequence of, undercutting what we are attempting to do . . . when a major country acts in an area it considers of vital importance, its allies owe it some respect for its views, as we attempted to show in the Falklands crisis.'[29]

Alongside verbal condemnation of the Europeans' role went some active attempts to obstruct diplomatic contacts between EC and Central American representatives. On one occasion, the British Foreign Secretary, Sir Geoffrey Howe, was heard to reassure the Nicaraguan Foreign Minister that 'the EC does not accept orders from the USA'. Despite this show of assertiveness, contacts between the EC countries and the Central American region remained almost entirely diplomatic in nature. Whilst this marks an advance on purely declaratory policy, and was accompanied by an economic assistance agreement with states in the region, it cannot be claimed that the Europeans exerted a formative influence on events. When the Arias Plan for peace in Central America emerged in the summer of 1987, the Europeans again supported it in the face of American opposition, but throughout their involvement in the affairs of the region during the 1980s they showed neither the inclination nor the ability to modify American policies themselves. At the heart of the Europeans' problem in Central America, as in the Middle East and elsewhere, was the gap between declaratory policy or verbal diplomacy and the ability materially to affect events by collective action. Perhaps the most telling demonstration of this gap came with the American action in Grenada during October 1983, which proceeded without reference to European (and particularly British) views and which ignored the subsequent outrage expressed in many European capitals, and throughout Latin America.

REASSESSMENT AND CONCLUSION

At the beginning of this chapter, it was suggested that while the logic of Atlantic relations during the 1980s might point towards the development of a positive 'European identity', a number of other considerations might stand in its way. In the first place, it could not be assumed that a European identity would emerge from a reaction against Reaganite policies, because it was far from easy to pin down exactly what those policies have been. Secondly, it was argued that the nature of 'Europe' itself constituted a major intervening variable in the process. In particular, the multi-layered character of European collaboration and the inherent tensions between national interests and the need to co-operate stand in the way of any simple linear growth of Europeanism. In a sense, the affairs of western Europe manifest a gap rather like that between 'theoretical' and 'practical' Reaganism. For these reasons, it was necessary to look in more detail at case studies of European–American interaction during the Reagan era.

What do the cases reveal about the evolving place of Europe in Atlantic relations, and in particular about the influence of Reaganism on a developing European identity? There is no doubt that East–West relations during the 1980s have given rise to open competition and important divergences of view between Americans and west Europeans. Nonetheless, the structure within which competition and divergence has taken place remains fundamentally the same as in the 1970s, and Europeans show no material desire to overthrow it. The Americans continue to hold the high cards, and Europeans are neither inclined nor able to take the initiative, not least because of the divergent national orientations in western Europe which can be exploited intentionally or unintentionally by Washington. The record of the 1980s suggests that relatively little has changed, but it will be argued later that this does not prejudge the potential for major transformations in the future.

With respect to regional conflicts, the picture is rather different. Here, the structures and expectations are rather less settled, and the ground rules for European–American interaction less easily accepted. There is thus more room for a 'European voice' to make itself heard, and in western Europe itself the practice of collaboration is less hemmed in by domestic constituencies. Problems are created, though, by the gap between rhetoric or aspiration and substantive policy: the consciousness of a European position is not paralleled by a commitment of resources or the generation of action. Especially in the Middle East and the Gulf, collaboration is undermined by persistent national preferences (the same could be said of European stances in other areas, such as Southern Africa). In this context, American policies under Reagan have compounded the difficulties for the Europeans by raising the stakes and heightening the risks, often in response to domestic needs or in-fighting within the administration.

At the most general level, these assessments of the cases confirm the central part played in the development of a European identity by the USA, by its policies and by its assumptions about the Atlantic and international systems. This centrality and significance, though, is double-edged. On the one hand, there can be no doubt that Reaganite policies have played a vital catalytic role, providing a focus for European perceptions and consciousness and a major element in symbolic diplomacy. On the other hand, American policies have had important constraining effects at the level of substantive policy. Despite the perceptions of risk and costs attached to alignment with Reaganism, the dangers of breaking with Washington have been seen by all west European leaderships as greater than the risks of holding ranks with the USA.

What do these conclusions imply for the definition and the development of a European identity during the 1980s, and for its prospects during the 1990s? As was noted earlier, three indices can be used to chart progress towards a European identity: the 'learning process' inherent in the attempt to collaborate, the expansion of the agenda for collaboration, and the salience of European co-operation within the Atlantic system. From the cases, a number of conclusions can be drawn about the 1980s. First, there has certainly been a consolidation of the 'reflex of co-operation' at the west European level, and this has changed the expectations of those involved in both European collaboration and transatlantic relations. This learning process, though, is severely limited by the role played by American policies. Secondly, there has been an expansion of the agenda for west European collaboration, which partly reflects the need to deal collaboratively with the USA in novel areas of high politics or security. Again, the progress is limited, but it is encouraged by the fact that the Reagan Administration often saw 'Europe' as the target to be persuaded, or divided or coerced. In terms of the Atlantic system, there was an expansion of activities and expectations centring on the notion of European collaboration. But there is a large disparity between expansion of activity and growth of the capacity to manage or to achieve concrete effects. There is still little evidence that American leaders see western Europe as a plausible management partner in the fields of East–West relations or regional conflicts (a contrast with the economic field), although specific west European countries have been seen as useful in this role.

The message of the 1980s is thus one of expansion of consciousness rather than one of material effects and substantive change. As noted earlier, however, this does not mean that change is not on the agenda for the 1990s. Indeed, two major shifts in the context of Atlantic relations have only become apparent in the late 1980s, and may crucially affect the prospects for a future European identity. The first of these is the changing nature of the USA and the USSR, and the changing strategic environment. For a variety of reasons, it is now possible and even necessary to think of 'Europe without America', and some west European leaders have shown themselves willing to consider such an eventuality. Secondly, there has been a major shift in Europeans' perceptions of the costs and benefits attached to alignment with the USA in specific situations, and automatic convergence of European and American preferences is no longer to be assumed.[30]

In both these shifts, Reaganism has played a decisive role, and in so doing has opened up at least some of the alternative futures which can and must be contemplated by the west Europeans. What might those futures be? One which can be ruled out is the reassertion of pervasive American dominance. Inasmuch as this was part of the Reaganite programme, it has been tried and failed, and in so doing it has ensured that European leaderships will think twice about the dangers. More plausible, in the short to medium term, is an attempt on both sides of the Atlantic to reconstruct a form of pluralistic partnership, in which the nature of demands and obligations is redefined and the Europeans are given a more formally-recognised role in line with their growing experience and awareness of the benefits of collaboration at the European level. Such moves, though, might have unintended consequences in the long term, precisely because of the shifts in perceptions and calculations of costs and benefits which have been identified here. It is this factor which creates at least the possibility that 'Europe without America' expresses the long-term logic of Atlantic relations. By the mid-1990s, the costs of defection may well look very different to both sides, and one central element in such a change would undoubtedly be the further consolidation of a substantive European identity.

NOTES

1. Although it could be argued that a diplomatic-strategic focus excludes the area in which a 'European identity' is most fully developed – the economic sphere – the assumption here is that treatment of these 'high policy' issues is most likely to provide a searching test of significant trends in the growth of such an identity.
2. For a treatment of these issues, see M. Smith, *Western Europe and the United States: the uncertain alliance* (London, Allen and Unwin, 1984), especially Chapters 2 and 5.
3. See M. Smith, 'Atlanticism and North Atlantic Interdependence: the widening gap?' in R. J. Barry Jones and P. Willetts (eds) *Interdependence on Trial: studies in the theory and reality of contemporary interdependence* (London, Frances Pinter, 1984), pp. 167–99; and J. Pinder, 'Interdependence: problem or solution', in L. Freedman (ed.) *The Troubled Alliance: Atlantic Relations in the 1980s* (London, Heinemann, 1983), pp. 67–87.
4. See Smith, *Western Europe and the United States, op. cit.*, Chapter 5; Smith, 'Atlanticism and North Atlantic Interdependence', *op. cit.*
5. See the chapters by Stephen Gill and Kees van der Pijl in this volume and also, for example: R. Keohane, *After Hegemony: co-operation and discord in the world political economy* (Princeton, Princeton UP, 1984); D. Calleo and B. Rowland, *America and the World Political Economy* (Bloomington,

Indiana UP, 1973); M. Kaldor, *The Disintegrating West* (Harmondsworth, Penguin, 1979); I. Wallerstein, 'Friends as Foes', *Foreign Policy*, no. 40, autumn 1980, pp. 119–31.
6. See Keohane, *After Hegemony, op. cit.*, especially Part I.
7. For a different interpretation at the structural level, see K. Oye, 'International systems structure and American foreign policy', in K. Oye *et al.* (eds) *Eagle Defiant: United States Foreign Policy in the 1980s* (Boston, Little, Brown, 1983), pp. 3–32.
8. See M. Smith, 'Ronald Reagan's disintegrating world', *The World Today*, vol. 43(2), February 1987, pp. 24–7; S. Serfaty, 'Lost Illusions', *Foreign Policy*, no. 66, spring 1987, pp. 3–19; I. M. Destler *et al.*, *Our Own Worst Enemy: the unmaking of American Foreign Policy* (New York, Simon and Schuster, 1984).
9. See C. Hill (ed.) *National Foreign Policies and European Political Co-operation* (London, Allen and Unwin, 1983); D. Allen *et al.* (eds) *European Political Co-operation: towards a foreign policy for Western Europe* (London, Butterworth, 1982).
10. On the issue of East–West trade in Atlantic relations, see especially S. Woolcock, *Western Policies on East–West Trade* (London, Routledge and Kegan Paul for the Royal Institute of International Affairs, 1982); E. Frost and A. Stent, 'NATO's Troubles with East–West Trade', *International Security*, vol. 8(1), summer 1983, pp. 179–200; A. Stent, 'East–West Trade and Technology Transfer: the West's search for consensus', *The World Today*, vol. 40(11), November 1984, pp. 452–62.
11. See Woolcock, *Western Policies on East–West Trade, op. cit.*; S. Woolcock, 'East–West Trade after Williamsburg: an issue shelved but not solved', *The World Today*, vol. 39(7), July–August 1983, pp. 291–6; J. Joffe, 'Europe and America: the politics of resentment (cont'd)' *Foreign Affairs*, vol. 61(3), 1983, *America and the World 1982*, pp. 569–90.
12. M. Mandelbaum, *The Nuclear Revolution: international politics since Hiroshima* (Cambridge, CUP, 1981), Ch. 6.
13. For a helpful discussion of the early west European impact of Reaganism, see M. Kahler, 'The United States and Western Europe: the diplomatic consequences of President Reagan', in Oye *et al.* (eds) *Eagle Defiant, op. cit.*, pp. 273–309; also F. Lewis, 'Alarm Bells in the West', *Foreign Affairs*, vol. 60(3), 1982, *America and the World 1981*, pp. 551–72.
14. See D. Watt, 'As a European saw it', *Foreign Affairs*, vol. 62(3), 1984, *America and the World 1983*, pp. 521–32.
15. R. McGeehan, 'European Defence Co-operation: a political perspective', *The World Today*, vol. 41(6), June 1985, pp. 116–19. As McGeehan noted, European collaboration 'may be back on the agenda, but it is not on the cards' (p. 119).
16. See McGeehan, 'European Defence Co-operation', *op cit.*; also S. May, 'West European Security Collaboration: driving forces and prospects', *International Journal*, vol. 40(1), winter 1984–85, pp. 104–27. On the particular challenge posed by SDI see (among many others) A. Kanter, 'Thinking about the Strategic Defence Initiative: an Alliance perspective', *International Affairs*, vol. 61(3), Summer 1985, pp. 449–64.
17. On the impact of SDI, see Kanter, 'Thinking about the Strategic Defence Initiative', *op cit.*; also three articles on 'European Allies and SDI' in *International Affairs*, vol. 62(2), Spring 1986 (by Trevor Taylor, John Fenske and Christoph Bluth). The issue of SALT II is covered in L. Sartori, 'Will SALT II Survive?', *International Security*, vol. 10(3), winter 1985–86,

pp. 147–74, and M. Dando and P. Rogers, 'Why SALT II Failed', *ADIU Report*, vol. 8(4), August 1986, pp. 4–6. On conventional weapons, see R. Darilek, 'The Future of Conventional Arms Control in Europe', *Survival*, vol. 29(1), January–February 1987, pp. 5–20.
18. For European reactions to Reykjavik and other developments, see for example J. Sharp, 'After Reykjavik: arms control and the allies', *International Affairs*, vol. 63(2), spring 1987, pp. 239–58; and S. Croft and P. Williams, 'SDI and the Path from Reykjavik', *ADIU Report*, vol. 8(6), November 1986, pp. 1–3.
19. For a general review of these episodes, see D. Allen, 'The Alliance and Extra-European Challenges', *Harvard International Review*, vol. IX(1), November/December 1986, pp. 6–9.
20. The most explicit criticisms have been made by Americans. See for example H. Kissinger, 'The Year of Europe', address to the Associated Press, New York, 23 April 1973, reprinted in H. Kissinger, *American Foreign Policy*, 3rd edn (New York, Norton, 1977), pp. 101–13; and L. Eagleburger, 'The Transatlantic Relationship: a long term perspective', address before the National Newspaper Association, Washington DC, 7 March 1984. United States Information Service *Official Text*, 9 March 1984.
21. D. Allen and M. Smith, 'Europe, the United States and the Middle East: a case study in comparative foreign policy making', *Journal of Common Market Studies*, vol. XXII(2), December 1983, pp. 125–46.
22. For an assessment of the Euro–Arab Dialogue, see D. Allen, 'The Euro–Arab Dialogue', *Journal of Common Market Studies*, vol. XVI(4), June 1978.
23. Many of the issues raised here are dealt with in detail in D. Allen and A. Pijpers (eds) *European Foreign Policy Making and the Arab–Israeli Conflict* (The Hague, Nijhoff, 1984).
24. On the changing nature of US involvement, see M. Smith, 'Taking up Arms . . . ? The Implementation of United States Policy in the Middle East', in P. Shearman and P. Williams (eds) *The Superpowers, Central America and the Middle East* (London, Brasseys, 1988). On the development of the European position, see Allen and Smith, 'Europe, the United States and the Middle East', *op. cit.*
25. On the issues in general, see L. Freedman *et al.*, *Terrorism and International Order* (London, Routledge and Kegan Paul for the Royal Institute of International Affairs, 1986), and particularly the chapter by P. Wilkinson, 'Trends in International Terrorism and the American Response'.
26. See E. Schumacher, 'The United States and Libya', *Foreign Affairs*, vol. 65(2), 1986, pp. 329–48.
27. See G. Edwards, 'Europe and the Falkland Islands Crisis, 1982', *Journal of Common Market Studies*, vol. XXII(4), June 1984, pp. 295–313.
28. See *Bulletin of the European Communities*, 6/1983, 9/1984 and 12/1984 for details of the contacts.
29. H. Kissinger, 'Challenges to the West in the 1980s', in *Observations: Selected Speeches and Essays, 1982–1984* (London, Michael Joseph and Weidenfeld and Nicolson, 1985), p. 86.
30. On the general issues raised here, see J. Palmer, *Europe without America? The Crisis in Atlantic Relations* (Oxford, OUP, 1987).

6 · ECONOMIC CONFLICTS AND THE TRANSFORMATION OF THE ATLANTIC ORDER
The US, Europe and the Liberalisation of Agriculture and Services

Alan W. Cafruny

Since its inception in 1947, the General Agreement on Tariffs and Trade (GATT) has regulated trading conflicts among advanced capitalist nations. While seven previous rounds of trade negotiations have focused primarily on the reduction of barriers to trade in manufactured goods, the present 'Uruguay Round' is directed mainly to the proposed liberalisation of services and agriculture, sectors of the world economy that have traditionally been subject to extensive national regulation and protection, and have enjoyed exemptions from most GATT rules. The Uruguay Round has major significance for the international economy, and for relations between the USA and western Europe.

This chapter describes the main economic and political changes that are taking place in agriculture and services, and considers the implications of these changes for Euro–American relations. The first part discusses a number of theoretical difficulties that have arisen in attempts to explain the crisis of Atlanticism. Although it is commonly assumed that the changing balance of power between the USA and Europe is a key factor in the growth of conflict, attempts to develop a satisfactory theory of power relations have not been wholly successful. Antonio Gramsci's perspective on hegemony, when applied to international relations, helps to resolve important theoretical problems. As the second part of this essay indicates, it provides a conceptual framework for characterising the evolution of US–European relations since the war. The third part reviews the main developments in agriculture, while the final part describes changes in the service sector, focusing on the pivotal telecommunications industry. Although agriculture and services occupy opposite ends of the industrial cycle, they share a common political logic: in each, a relatively stable and highly regulated post-war regime was constructed after World War II that was consistent with the USA's domestic practices and policies. At the present time, dramatic changes are taking place in each sector, largely in response to developments in the USA. Although the tendency towards liberalisation is partly a result of technological developments, especially in telecommunications, it is also symptomatic of fundamental changes that are taking place in the world political economy, and in the USA's relations with western Europe.

INTERPRETING THE RISE AND DECLINE OF ATLANTICISM

The persistence of transatlantic economic conflict in the post-World War II era hardly gives cause for surprise: the pace of economic and technological development among the advanced capitalist nations has been rapid, yet highly uneven, and the institutions that have been established to regulate uneven development have had to contend with very different national expectations and objectives. Moreover, the limited mandate of key international economic institutions has encouraged the USA to assume many of the responsibilities – and privileges – of global economic leadership, thereby complicating the management of the system by making it dependent on the idiosyncracies of American politics and, increasingly, on the realisation of particular American objectives and interests: even as the American economy has weakened, the fundamental asymmetry in power between the USA and Europe has become more striking. Finally, economic and strategic policies have tended to overlap, further contributing to instability. As relations in one sphere have changed, specific arrangements in the other sphere have lost their *raison d'être*.

The Atlantic relationship

Although the concept of Atlanticism has preoccupied American statesmen since World War I, it has not offered a systematic or clearly-defined theory of world politics. During some periods Atlanticism has supplied a highly-idealised vision of Atlantic economic and political community or even confederation, while in other periods it has simply expressed the determination of businessmen and statesmen on each side of the Atlantic to nurture close economic, cultural and political links. Examples of the former include the idea of an 'Atlantic Union' that gained currency in the early 1950s. Examples of the latter include the 'Atlantic Partnership' of the Kennedy era, and the efforts of the Trilateral Commission to arrest centrifugal tendencies and rekindle a sense of transatlantic (and Pacific) elite unity.

Atlanticism emerged as the USA tentatively grasped the mantle of international economic leadership surrendered by the UK during the period 1918–1931. It gathered support on both sides of the Atlantic as American interests in Europe expanded, and as Europe began to rely more heavily on American capital and technology. During the inter-war period, however, Atlanticism in the USA co-existed uneasily with isolationism and rabid Anglophobia, and its *laissez faire* approach to the global economy was incompatible with the global leadership role that the USA would adopt after World War II.[1] Atlanticists remained, for the most part, on the political sidelines until Cordell Hull's sponsorship of tripartite trade and monetary co-ordination during the 1930s indicated that the USA had adopted a vision of Atlanticism that was consistent with New Deal policies.

After World War II Atlanticists became ascendant in the USA. Through aid, trade, investment and political intervention, the USA sought to reconstruct European society in accordance with a pragmatic conception of Atlanticism that stressed not economic and political union, but rather the virtues of political and economic interdependence, the receptivity of Europe to American capital, and a Cold War alliance against communism. In the USA, Atlanticism was instrumental in quelling isolationist sentiments and mobilising public opinion behind the USA's global role. In Europe, the success of the Marshall Plan propelled pro-American politicians to the forefront and helped to defeat the Left. Atlanticism meant, in practical terms, the 'extrapolation of the New Deal'.[2] Whereas pre-war Atlanticism reflected the dominance of money capital, the post-war vision expressed the interests of productive capital and emphasised demand management and Fordism, a system based on mass production and consumption, and corporatist labour relations.[3] However, as the USA's industrial base erodes, support for Atlanticism has weakened.

As the level of transatlantic conflict has increased, there has been no shortage of analyses of the economic and political dimensions of the schism. Observers have attributed growing conflict to the emergence of a more plural distribution of power, marked by the rise of the European Community as a rival to the USA;[4] the re-orientation of the USA towards the Pacific;[5] the American challenge in the form of capital and superior technology;[6] and the exploitation of the USA's structural power, especially in monetary affairs.[7] To be sure, some observers continue to emphasise the high level of co-operation between Europe and the USA, a thesis which finds its leftist reflection in the Kautskian hypothesis of 'ultra-imperialism'.[8] Nevertheless, there can be little doubt that the level and stakes of transatlantic economic conflict have increased and that the international structural basis of Atlanticism as it emerged out of World War II is now becoming obsolete. Fundamental conflicts over trade, monetary policy and macro-economic policy co-ordination have divided the Alliance since the early 1970s. Western European statesmen are seriously contemplating the establishment of an independent defence force, and the cultural and social bases of Atlanticism in the USA appear to be eroding.[9] Although it would be premature to predict the death of the Atlanticist concept, it seems clear that the US–European relationship is in a phase of crisis, and is being recast by a combination of economic and political changes.

The changing face of American power

The influence of the changing distribution of international power has been central to discussions of the crisis of US–European economic affairs. Yet attempts to theorise about international power have encountered a host of empirical and conceptual difficulties. Since the early 1970s, a number of American scholars have sought to explain the growth of conflict with reference to the USA's loss of power and resulting inability to continue to provide collective goods and prevent Europe and Japan from taking undue advantages of the system. Pointing to the rise of the European Community, they have assumed the emergence of more or less plural structure of international power, and cast the problem of international co-operation in terms of the ability of roughly equal actors to co-operate in the absence of a hegemonic leader.[10]

In recent years, however, the assumption of the USA's hegemonic decline has generated a great deal of criticism.[11] American scholars and officials have lamented the alleged loss of power, yet Europe's poor economic record over the last decade must be attributed, in part, to the effect of American monetary and fiscal policies, which have elicited widespread opposition in Europe.[12] Although few dispute the fact of the USA's loss of relative power, there is great disagreement over the extent of the loss, and the significance for international co-operation. American power has declined, but it remains very great. The USA's GNP is three times the size of Japan, and five times as large as that of West Germany. While it is true that it no longer controls the international agenda as previously, the substantial residue of power available to the USA can hardly be overlooked.

Is it possible to reconcile these seemingly contradictory views about the decline of American hegemony and its consequences? Because it draws an important distinction between 'power-as-preponderance' and 'hegemonic power', the Gramscian approach provides a means of conceptualising the increasing application of American power even as its overall hegemony declines.[13] For Gramsci, power had many forms and variants, ranging from the purely coercive and visible to the consensual and invisible. Hegemonic power was a progressive relation of domination among competing social classes. In a hegemonic system, the ruling group governs primarily by eliciting consensus from subordinate groups, even though the long-range objective interests of these groups may not be served. The possibility of reaching a consensus depends, however, on the ability of a ruling group to transcend its economic corporate or particular interests and thereby to induce subordinate groups to participate in its own economic programme.

When hegemony is firmly implanted, the ruling group can afford to define its interests not in narrow, exclusionary terms, but rather as embodying and leading a larger, societal interest. The ruling group does not simply exploit state power for parochial ends, but rather incorporates at least some of the aspirations of subordinate groups within its economic project. Gramsci's theory of hegemony includes elements of domination and leadership within its frame of reference, thus helping to conceptualise the combination of benevolence and exploitation that realists have observed but had difficulty placing within their theoretical framework.[14]

The Gramscian perspective on power also has a second advantage. Realist conceptions of international power have generally maintained a sharp distinction between domestic and international levels of analysis. Gramsci's approach, however, makes it possible to develop a more systematic account of the linkage between domestic and international power relations.[15] Hegemonic periods reflect and reinforce the ascendancy of a hegemonic class that is capable of transforming domestic structures of its own and allied states, making them compatible with the requirements of an expanding international system. Scholars of the 'regulation' school have documented the transition of European political economies following World War II from accumulation structures based on intensive regulation and high levels of market competition, to one of extensive regulation, grounded in monopolistic structures and characterised by mass production and mass consumption.[16] The extensive mode of regulation emerged in Europe in the context of American hegemony, but it appears doubtful that it can outlive the decline of that hegemony.

THE DECLINE OF AMERICAN HEGEMONY

Gramsci's model of hegemonic power assumed that after the 'founding', a phase of integral or organic co-operation, hegemony gradually decays as economic and political contradictions unfold.[17] Although the hegemon-in-decline may actually be capable of projecting a great deal of power, such power is no longer utilised in ways that promote systemic stability. The following sketch of Euro–American economic relations since World War II demonstrates the utility of this model.

The construction of transatlantic hegemony, 1944–60

The formation of the Bretton Woods system itself resulted from an 'organic crisis', or a crisis of authority embracing global ideological, economic and political structures. The construction of the post-war hegemonic system involved the reintegration of these structures in ways that accommodated the disparate interests and needs of the USA, Europe and

Japan, and provided for stability and growth. It vividly exemplified the combination of leadership and domination that characterised strong hegemonic rule.

At the end of World War II, the USA possessed 70 per cent of global financial assets. Its high rate of industrial productivity ensured that concern for the balance of payments would not constrain efforts to rebuild the system. Industrial supremacy and relative insulation from the world economy maximised the freedom of action of American policymakers, allowing them to devote substantial resources to military spending and foreign aid in order to reconstruct and re-integrate Europe into a unified, Atlantic order.

The USA bore many of the costs of the system, but its large banks, multinational corporations and, for a time, a substantial segment of organised labour derived significant and visible benefits. For western European ruling classes, economic aid and investment were viewed as essential to modernisation and to undercutting support for the Left. The USA's primary economic objective was to establish a world economy open to American exports of goods and capital. In order to re-integrate Europe and Japan into a capitalist world order it was necessary for the USA to accept restraints on the use of power. In both the trade and monetary spheres, the USA granted important concessions. In trade, it tolerated widespread discrimination and, eventually, the formation of a European tariff bloc, although this bloc also had the effect of sheltering American multinational corporations. It also encouraged the implementation of statist/corporatist and neo-mercantilist policies throughout western Europe predicated, to varying degrees, on export-led growth. In monetary affairs, it accepted the fact that currencies would need to remain inconvertible until reconstruction was completed and despite, or perhaps because of, the conservatism of the IMF, supplied the world with liquidity through foreign investment, defence spending and high levels of aid.

The decline of hegemony, 1960–71

During the 1950s, the high degree of Atlantic unity derived, above all, from the universal interest in maintaining a flow of dollars from the USA to Europe to resolve the anticipated 'liquidity problem'. In 1960, however, a speculative attack on the dollar precipitated a run on gold, resulting in multilateral agreement to form the London Gold Pool, whereby governments agreed to regulate the gold supply to maintain price stability.[18] Although minor by the standards of the 1970s and 1980s, nonetheless the gold crisis signified the beginning of the decline of American hegemony, and marked an important shift in the way in which American power was exercised. It heralded, along with the return to convertibility, the fact of European and Japanese recovery, resulting in the first rumblings of discontent with the dollar. Henceforth, the value of the dollar would be determined through negotiations. The formal and informal arrangements to deal with the problem indicated both change and continuity in the USA's hegemonic role.

The contradictions of the Atlantic order as they unfolded during the 1960s were best captured by the 'Triffin Paradox': the USA's balance of payments deficits provided the world with liquidity; yet as the supply of dollars outraced existing gold stocks, the growing 'dollar overhang' undermined confidence in the dollar. As Triffin argued, a 'long-range shortage of liquidity', with serious deflationary consequences, would inevitably result from either the USA's attempt to equilibrate its balance of payments or Europe and Japan's refusal 'to pile up further IOUs from them'.[19] However, the continuation of balance of payments deficits would lead to severe deflation if surplus countries were 'called upon to finance indefinitely US deficits through unpredictable accumulations of dollar claims'. Inflation and deflation thus represented international political as well as economic relationships, expressing changes in the balance of Atlantic economic power and the particular ways in which international and national conflicts were played out.[20]

The USA's willingness and ability to bear a disproportionate share of the costs of the system diminished during the 1960s, although there was no corresponding effort to distribute the benefits more broadly. The USA continued to fulful the responsibilities of financial stewardship and the open market, albeit with growing difficulty, still largely tolerating the neo-mercantilist policies of its trading partners. However, lacking a mechanism to control uneven development and, in particular, to alleviate the burdens placed on deficit nations, the system generated growing costs, and these needed to be distributed among states as well as classes. As the USA's balance of payments position eroded, limits were placed on the concessions which it could make. Whereas during the 1950s and early 1960s Europe welcomed American capital export, by the late 1960s foreign investment caused a great deal of resentment as dollars were no longer in short supply and various constraints on the convertibility of dollars to gold were introduced. In 1968 American firms controlled 75 per cent of the European computer market, one-half of France's telecommunications equipment, 40 per cent of the West German car industry and 33 per cent of its tyre industry.[21] Hence the 1960s witnessed intense conflict over the status of the dollar: beginning with the establishment of the London Gold Pool (1961); bilateral diplomacy over convertibility, continuing in President de Gaulle's refusal to hold dollars in 1965; the devaluation of sterling in 1967, negotiations over creation of IMF Special Drawing Rights (SDRs) and the full-blown gold crisis of 1968. At this time the USA tried to devalue its currency, but Europeans threatened to do likewise, resulting in a negotiated 'two-tier' market for gold.[22] President Nixon's decision to remove the dollar from its gold standard would mark the beginning of a new phase, characterised by a more unilateral and nationalist strategy on the part of the USA.

Minimal hegemony: 1971 to the present

Washington's 'benign neglect' of the dollar expressed the contradictory nature of American power. On one hand, it indicated that the USA was no longer powerful enough to enforce or manage a return to unchallenged dollar supremacy. On the other hand, it lay bare the extraordinary power of the USA, given its structural position in the world economy, to act unilaterally and, within very wide bounds, with impunity. Here the comparison with the UK's inter-war experience is instructive: in 1931 the British government, after having subjected the working class to five years of austerity through currency revaluation, finally abandoned the gold standard and the world splintered into currency blocs. In 1971, in contrast, the USA removed the dollar from gold, but the dollar would remain unchallenged and the rest of the world would bear much of the cost of adjustment.

Clearly, the relative decline of American industry, the cause of speculative attacks on the dollar, was the immediate target of Nixon's decision to abandon the dollar–gold standard. The decision signified, however, not so much the development of a more plural system of international relations, as is often assumed, but rather the tendency of the USA to use power in ways that reflected national objectives and interests, often at the expense of the allies. The decoupling of the dollar from gold thus represented a strategic decision to respond to the reality of hegemonic decline, but one in which the USA's freedom of action and influence over the system would be maximised.[23]

Between 1971 and 1978, American monetary policy was directed primarily towards competitive depreciation. On a trade-weighted basis, the dollar declined by more than one-third against the yen and mark.[24] In conjunction with oil price increases, which proved far more damaging to Europe than to the USA, American exports actually increased as a percentage of world trade and the balance of trade became favourable, especially in relation to the European Community.[25] However, the inflationary results of depreciation reduced confidence in the dollar, raising the spectre of a rival Eurocurrency. Partly in response to this challenge, in 1979 the USA adopted a strategy of monetarism, precipitated by Federal Reserve Board Chairman Paul Volcker's decision to restrict the money supply. Monetarism shored up the dollar, but it had a massively deflationary impact on global economic activity via high real interest rates, the attraction of large amounts of capital to the USA and the resulting trade deficit. Although the resort to 'domesticism',[26] in Henry Nau's terminology reasserted American power and precipitated a boom in the American economy, it did not resolve deeper contradictions in either the American or the global economy. Domestic economic expansion was not accompanied by an improvement in industrial productivity. The dependence on foreign capital and eventual transition of the USA to debtor status have exacerbated the global debt crisis. Since 1985 the USA has once again allowed the dollar to depreciate substantially. However, it is unlikely that dollar depreciation will, in itself, be sufficient to restore the USA's industrial competitiveness. Efforts to improve the trade balance (and deflect protectionist sentiments) through dollar depreciation undermine the role of the dollar as the major world currency, but attempts to fortify the dollar through tight money precipitate national and international recession.

American trade policy since 1971 has followed a logic that is closely connected to developments in the monetary sphere. Monetary and trade instability are inversely related. On the one hand, as the dollar depreciates, the protectionist impulse in the USA diminishes. The Tokyo Round, for example, was concluded in the context of a relatively weak dollar. On the other hand, as the dollar appreciates, demands for protectionism have increased. Monetarism has also slowed down world trade, especially in Latin America, by contributing to the debt burden. Hence protectionism is avoided at least partly at the cost of global monetary instability.

Is a return to integral hegemony possible, or is minimal hegemony likely to degenerate further? The efforts of the Trilateral Commission to reorganise the international economy on the basis of tripartite leadership reflect an awareness of the need to institutionalise important shifts in the distribution of power, and to restore the position within the USA of Atlanticists, who have seen their power undermined by the loss of industrial competitiveness. However, the failure of the Trilateral Commission to influence policies illustrates both the strength and weakness of the USA in the present period: its willingness and ability to provide leadership have been reduced, but West Germany and Japan remain unable or unwilling to take the risks entailed by tripartite leadership. The failure of trilateralism, which appeared to depend on the viability of Keynesian and social democratic policies, including a commitment to industrial planning in the USA, has led to the adoption of neo-liberalism, and its subsequent acceptance elsewhere either through economic necessity or co-option of elites. The USA's decision to combat inflation through monetarism has made it impossible for European governments to sustain Keynesian/social democratic forms of legitimation.

Nevertheless, although the distribution of power has changed, with important consequences for the world economy, the system has not broken down; it is not non-hegemonic. The USA has not completely renounced or abrogated leadership, which remains evident in qualified support for existing international economic institutions, a determination to limit the scope of currency wars, maintenance of the primacy of the dollar and the extension of the GATT to more areas of the global economy. The USA's efforts to deregulate national and international financial markets, coupled with high interest rates, has promoted a great deal of cross-investment, much of it into the USA. Hence, even as the USA's macro-economic policies damage and antagonise Europe and the Third World, they help to consolidate its central position within a world economy that is growing more, and not less, interdependent.

Here again the contrast between the British and American experience is instructive. Unlike the UK, the USA is greatly aided by the fact that its principal economic rivals appear incapable of developing an alternative to American tutelage, despite the fact that the distribution of costs and benefits has become much less favourable to them. As the cases of services and agriculture illustrate, change is taking place largely on the USA's terms. Europe's attempt to adopt an independent role or even define its common interest is fraught with obstacles and contradictions: Europe requires regional unity to act as a counterweight to the USA, yet remains constrained by national divisions. Ironically, the policies which appear essential to the modernisation of its industrial base and infrastructure, including the weakening of the common agricultural policy (CAP) and joint venture strategies with non-European firms in telecommunications, would seem to call into question the very existence of the community.

EUROPE, THE USA AND THE LIBERALISATION OF AGRICULTURE

Transatlantic conflict over agricultural issues is not new. The common agricultural policy has served as the 'marriage contract' of the European Community, in the words of the Commission,[27] and divorce has been avoided by pursuing measures that affect the USA, which is the largest exporter of agricultural commodities: a high tariff wall, in the form of variable levies, to exclude imports of crops produced by European farmers and, increasingly, policies designed to sell community crops to the rest of the world. Nevertheless, the community remains the leading market for global and American agricultural exports, especially corn, cereals, soyabeans and cotton. Of course, the USA also protects a number of crops, including sugar, dairy products and meat.

The USA's post-war agricultural policy: a global New Deal

Despite persistent skirmishing over various agricultural commodities, for the first 25 years after World War II the USA contributed to global agricultural stability and minimised the scope of conflict by renouncing certain inherent advantages while permitting the nations of western Europe to exploit opportunities afforded by American policies that were elaborated during the New Deal. Confronted with falling commodity prices during the 1930s, American policymakers diagnosed the problem of American agriculture as one of overproduction, and not international barriers to trade. The government established agricultural programmes designed to limit exports and provide price supports for farmers, including reduction of the area of cultivation; loans to farmers through the Commodities Credit Corporation; marketing quotas; guaranteed prices; foreign aid to distribute surplus production; and outright protectionism. These policies were framed by the Agricultural Adjustment Act of 1933, the New Deal for American farmers.[28]

As a result, American farmers turned inward, and the central element of American policy from the 1930s to the 1970s was the reduction of exports, the maintenance of income levels and support for the 'family farm'. By increasing prices paid to farmers and linking these to production limits, net income was raised. Acreage was reduced in six major commodities: wheat, corn, cotton, rice, peanuts and tobacco. 'Autarchy' served, however, to promote global stability because it encouraged American farmers to renounce an export strategy in which they could exploit their comparative advantage.

European agricultural policies also developed in response to the Great Depression. In the major countries, agricultural output had expanded dramatically in the aftermath of World War I, only to plummet during the 1930s as commodity prices collapsed. At first, most governments introduced import quotas; in France and Germany the domestic market was gradually insulated from the world market. However, import quotas were insufficient to raise output, and governments were compelled to organise markets. State policy focused not on the problem of overproduction, as in the USA, but rather on increasing output through subsidies and price supports. While the USA has traditionally sought to curtail production, western European governments have sought to expand output, a response in part to the post-war famines.[29]

The CAP harmonised individual European policies. France, with its large number of small farmers, was the principal beneficiary, but farmers throughout the community also received high levels of subsidies and protection. Although West Germany initially acquiesced to high price supports as a means of gaining access for its industry to French markets, ironically south German grain producers are now the most ardent defenders of high price supports for grain.

The CAP was intended to slow down, but not to eliminate, the exodus of Europe's rural population to the cities, and it succeeded in this objective: between 1964 and 1984 productivity in agriculture increased by 2.5 per cent per year, while the number of agricultural workers declined by 31 per cent between 1972 to 1983. During that time Europe's self-sufficiency in agricultural products increased from 79 per cent to 87 per cent, while Europe's trade deficit in agricultural products declined from 8.4 million ECU to 7.8 million ECU.[30] Article 39 of the Treaty of Rome called for 'a fair standard of living' for farmers and 'reasonable prices'. However, stabilisation and security have been achieved partly through productivity gains, but also through subsidies and protection.

The breakdown of the New Deal settlement

The post-war international regime was relatively stable because different policies were being followed on each side of the Atlantic. However, the system contained two important and mutually-reinforcing contradictions, the first having to do with the long-range impact of European agricultural policies, and the second concerning the continuing ability and willingness of the USA to pursue practices and policies which renounced the temptation to conquer international markets. On the one hand, the CAP was designed to ensure that agricultural output would rise. The existence of the CAP, and the power of entrenched interest groups dependent on subsidies, set in motion powerful forces that would eventually not only increase self-sufficiency, but gradually push western European agricultural production into world markets. Pressure on the EC budget mounted as output expanded. As the European market for American exports diminished and European exports flowed in increasing quantities into markets which America opened up in the 1970s, transatlantic conflict intensified.[31] Price supports were substantially above the world price for most commodities, and they also exceeded the average internal price. This gave European farmers an incentive to increase production and made expansion of exports a logical extension of the CAP. Export subsidies, pioneered during the 1950s by individual countries, were gradually introduced and increased over time. By 1986 the EC had captured 15 per cent of the world wheat market; it is the world's leading dairy exporter, and in 1984 exported 800,000 tons of beef.[32] Many embarrassing 'mountains' (butter) and 'lakes' (wine) are disposed of by dumping on the world market.

The CAP was, nonetheless, not incompatible with the USA's New Deal settlement, which minimised the need for export markets and focused on crop reduction. The USA held export prices above the world average by maintaining large buffer stocks. When these stocks became too large, production was curtailed. This stabilised food prices, but encouraged other countries to achieve a growing share of world markets. During the 1960s, 90 per cent of all surplus stocks of wheat and coarse grain were either American or Canadian. By refraining from placing restrictions on purchases of grain, the USA maintained confidence in world grain markets and thus indirectly discouraged protectionism.[33] Finally, the USA was also by far the largest food donor. To sum up: 'The United States permitted the EC to subsidize its own much less efficient grain producers, to protect those producers from US exports, and even to dump some of the resulting surplus production onto the world market for US grain'.[34]

Since the early 1970s, however, international food markets have become increasingly unstable. Instability has taken the form of large price fluctuations, subsidy wars, and a decrease in food aid. Although many factors contribute to a comprehensive explanation for these phenomena, the USA's changing role in the world economy has been important. Beset by growing balance of payments problems, the USA has begun to mobilise its underlying 'green power'.[35]

The USA's changing policies can be traced to the mid-1960s, although the major innovations did not occur until the early 1970s. At that time, it began to increase commercial grain exports by raising export subsidies. However, 1972 is generally regarded as a turning point for international grain markets because the USA liquidated one-half of its grain stocks in order to sell wheat to the USSR. Following this, exports of soyabeans were temporarily halted (1973); the world grain market became increasingly politicised, and many countries began to adopt self-sufficiency policies.[36]

The depreciation of the dollar during the 1970s helped American grain exports, which grew from $7.7 billion in 1971 to $21 billion in 1975, and to $44 billion in 1980. American policy became predicated on the assumption of a continually expanding world market; by 1980 over a third of the USA's cropland was producing for export. The boom in international trade increased land values and despite rising interest rates many invested in farm land both for its productive value and also as speculation. However, the global recession, the debt crisis, dramatic appreciation of the dollar and the post-Afghanistan grain embargo sparked a major crisis for agriculture, turning the virtuous cycle of increasing exports, rising profits and increase in the value of farmland into its opposite, and setting the USA on a collision course with the EC.

By the early 1980s the change in the world agricultural situation, coupled with the rising dollar, was causing severe distress for American farmers. By the 1980s stocks had reached record levels, and farm incomes collapsed just as interest rates were rising. Land values have continued to plummet; and farmers have been driven into bankruptcy in record numbers.[37]

The USA, Europe and the GATT

Initially, the Reagan Administration responded to the farm crisis by strengthening traditional programmes. In 1983 an ambitious 'payment in kind' programme was introduced, which sought to reduce output by granting farmers compensation in kind from public stocks, provided they kept a certain proportion of acreage out of cultivation. However, the new strategy of the Reagan Administration, encapsulated in the 1985 Farm Bill, is one of national and international liberalisation. Reductions in domestic spending programmes will bring farm prices down. As domestic output increases as a result of phasing out crop reduction schemes, the liberalisation of global agriculture will open up markets abroad. The Farm Bill rejects supply management (crop reduction) as wasteful, statist and expensive for the consumer.

The 1985 Farm Bill has brought about a fundamental change in American agricultural politics, and promises to have major international significance. It has reduced subsidies for grain, cotton and soyabeans by lowering the loan rate, and provided export subsidies in order to win back markets lost to the European Community. The Uruguay Round of the GATT negotiations is intended to be the international counterpart to the 1985 Farm Bill.

Prior to the Dillon Round of the GATT (1960–61), agriculture was excluded from GATT negotiations. Although the GATT officially applies to agricultural trade (but not trade in services), the GATT articles themselves have been worded vaguely, and both the USA and western Europe have circumvented them. Article XI prohibits quantitative restrictions on imports and exports. Article XVI enjoins members of the GATT to 'seek to avoid' export subsidies for primary products. However, in 1955, the USA was granted a waiver from Article XI, permitting it to apply quantitative restrictions on a range of agricultural imports in keeping with domestic laws. The provisions of Article XVI allow export subsidies, provided they do not give countries 'more than an equitable share of world export trade' in the commodity concerned. In practice, 'equitable share' is impossible to define.[38]

During the 1960s, the GATT began to look more closely at agricultural trade. However, in neither the Dillon nor the Kennedy Rounds was much progress made on the key issues of American access to European markets. The European Community decreed in 1973 that 'Elements Basic to Community Unity'[39] may not be subject to negotiation, and defined the CAP as such a basic element, whose 'principles and mechanisms shall not be called into question and are, therefore, in no way a matter for negotiation'.[40] The EC has traditionally favoured cartelisation and international supply management, based on price fixing, market sharing and supply management. The USA has consistently opposed this.

The Tokyo Round, concluded in 1979, did not contain major initiatives in agriculture. Since that time, however, the USA has pushed hard to have agricultural issues considered in the GATT. American proposals for the liberalisation of global agriculture include abolition of export subsidies and the abolition of tariff and non-tariff barriers, including various kinds of price support. Such a task presents numerous conceptual problems, not the least of which is the definition of a subsidy.[41] The USA has called for the abolition of all subsidies over a ten-year period. In the meantime, however, the 1985 Farm Bill has authorised substantial export subsidies designed to compete with Europe and bring Europe to the bargaining table. The result has been a subsidy war that has drained treasuries on each side of the Atlantic, and proved damaging to many Third World countries, as domestic production became uncompetitive with subsidised imports.[42]

The European Community maintains that export subsidies are a core element of the CAP, that they have not, in any case, brought the EC more than an 'equitable share' of the market in the commodity concerned, and that in any case the USA also violates the subsidies code.[43] Nevertheless, at Uruguay the Commission accepted the legitimacy of negotiations on these issues, prodded by the USA and other wheat-exporting nations. The USA regarded this as a major achievement and hoped to place agricultural negotiations on a 'fast track', with agreements concluded by the end of 1988. The outcome would be determined by Europe's willingness to accelerate the pace of structural reform embarked on in 1982, and to accept a fundamental revision of the CAP. It would also depend on American willingness to continue to tolerate the high levels of rural distress that result from the reduction in farm support programmes, and to continue to subsidise exports, a strategy which, at least in the short term, was even more expensive than previous programmes.

THE USA, EUROPE AND THE LIBERALISATION OF SERVICES

The service sector encompasses a group of disparate industries, including shipping, insurance, telecommunications and banking, that are characterised by their perishability at the point of consumption. A commonly-accepted definition of a service is:

> a change in the condition of a person, or of a good belonging to some economic unit, which is brought about as a result of the activity of some other economic unit, with the prior agreement of the former person or economic unit. Services are consumed as they are produced in the sense that the change in the condition of the consumer unit must occur simultaneously with the production of that change by the producer.[44]

Services represent the largest and fastest growing sector of economic activity in the advanced capitalist countries. Although all schools of economic theory have, until recently, neglected services as unproductive and a drag on economic growth, their importance as engines of economic development is now widely recognised.[45]

International trade in services may be defined as 'international transactions in services between the residents of one country and the residents of another country, irrespective of where the transaction takes place'.[46] Historically, the localised character of services, the difficulty of separating the issue of trade in services from that of foreign direct investment and the fact that so many services are owned or supervised by governments, has meant that services, like agriculture, were largely excluded from post-war trade negotiations and ignored by the GATT. The growth of international trade in services has lagged behind the growth of the sector in national economies.[47]

During the 1970s, American service industries, especially in telecommunications and insurance, took the lead in seeking to establish an international legal regime for free trade. In 1974, Congress was persuaded to include services within its definition of international trade in the Trade Act of 1974. Under the amended Trade Agreements Act of 1979, service firms began to file grievances with the government, and the Department of Commerce and the Office of the US Trade Representative added services to their concerns.[48] Services were not discussed during the Tokyo Round. However, the 1982 GATT Ministerial Meeting established a work programme for services, despite Third World opposition. The Ministerial also authorised national studies of service industries, which have now been completed, in order to provide an empirical and conceptual basis for negotiations. The US Trade and Tariff Act of 1984 clearly states the objectives of American policy. Unlike the GATT charter, it defines international trade as comprising trade in goods as well as services, and it calls for equal treatment of service corporations abroad, a policy that would effectively make foreign direct investment a trade issue covered by existing GATT rules. It calls on the US Trade Representative to seek to open global markets.[49]

American domestic and international policy: telecommunications

It is possible to argue that a domestic regime for services, comparable to that for agriculture, developed during the New Deal era. At that time most services became subject to national regulation. For example, important legislation in shipping, insurance, telecommunications and banking services originated in New Deal reforms. Banking functions were separated in an effort to promote stability and prevent monopolies, and numerous constraints were placed on the ability of banks to offer various services. Close regulation of banking, which largely restricted banking services to the national domain, corresponded to the Keynesian international monetary paradigm, which regulated capital flows and maximised government control over monetary affairs. The movement to deregulation began during the 1960s, but gained considerable momentum under the Reagan Administration. The telecommunications industry exemplifies both the tendency towards deregulation in the USA and its implications for western Europe.

The telecommunications industry represents a large and increasing proportion of world trade. There is a growing recognition that innovation and development of telecommunications are major determinants of economic growth, not only in the advanced countries, but also in the Third World. As the US Council for International Business has stated:

> It is increasingly evident that efficient and effective telecommunications systems are essential to the growth and development of the economy as a whole. Telecommunications and information products and services, as high-technology, high-growth industries, not only make contributions to healthy innovation and expansion in the economy in their own right, but they also promote increased productivity, greater competitiveness, and higher employment and growth rates throughout the economy.[50]

In most advanced capitalist countries the role of telecommunications and the related informatics sector is large, accounting for no less than 9 per cent of the GDP in France, Japan and the USA.[51]

Telecommunications industries have traditionally been subject to a high degree of governmental regulation and control. In the USA, the Communications Act of 1934 vested regulatory authority in the Federal Communications Commission (FCC), an independent governmental agency, American Telegraph and Telephones (ATT), although privately owned, enjoyed monopoly status but was subject to FCC regulation. In western Europe, government-owned Post, Telegraph and Telephone Corporations or Ministries (PTTs) controlled communications networks. Prior to the 1960s, there was very little conflict in this sector. Technological innovation was slow, in part a function of monopolistic practices, and telecommunications was not seen as a growth industry.[52]

In the last two decades, however, change and conflict have been precipitated by dramatic technological breakthroughs, most of which have originated in the USA. In the 1960s, the development of data processing had a dynamic impact on telecommunications, which is the carrier of information technology. The development of digital computers sent shock waves throughout the industry; it rendered existing national and international regulatory regimes obsolete by making possible not only simple communications, but also the storage and transmission of massive volumes of data. In 1984, the break-up of ATT marked the culmination of ten years of gradual deregulatory activity. American firms are now expanding abroad, even as Japanese and European firms are seeking to gain a foothold in newly deregulated markets in the USA.[53] American firms seek an international regime which enables them to gain access to local markets in both Europe and the Third World.

These pressures pose a substantial challenge to western European telecommunications industries, which lack national economies of scale.

Although in telecommunications itself the EC runs a trade surplus, in the broader informatics market, Europe is very weak. In 1982, for example, Europe had a trade deficit of $4.6 billion with the USA; 70 per cent of Europe's computers were produced by American subsidiaries, and eight of the top ten companies were American. The EC produced less than 5 per cent of the world's integrated circuits, compared to 70 per cent for the USA and 25 per cent for Japan.[54]

Individual European countries have pursued different strategies. In the UK, a substantial degree of deregulation has already occurred, along the lines of the American pattern. The denationalisation of British Telecom in 1984 staked out one European strategy of deregulation, and marked a bid for the UK to become the hub of Europe's telecommunications network. West Germany occupies the opposite end of the spectrum. The Bundespost continues to enjoy national monopoly status, although it is expanding its network of suppliers. Western European governments contend that the size of the American market supports competition, whereas the limited capacity of individual European markets means that, without governmental protection, Europe's telecommunications industries will succumb to American firms. The average regional 'baby bell' (Bell Telephone Company) in the USA is as large as the major European national PTTs.[55] Moreover, conflicts exist between Europe and the USA, but also among individual firms, anxious to establish joint ventures with Americans, and governments which seek to retain control.

The importance of economies of scale suggests that European competitiveness will be determined by the ability to establish a community-wide telecommunications policy. At the present time, for example, PTTs use their monopolistic power for national industrial policy, increasing the fragmentation of the market and duplicating research and development efforts. The EC has excluded telecommunications from its liberalisation of public contracts and secured an exemption from the GATT Code on government procurement.

Throughout the 1970s, efforts to integrate European telecommunications failed, largely as a result of PTT monopolies and nationalism. More recently, however, the European Commission has aggressively sought to develop a common approach and to stimulate research and development. In 1984, the European Community launched the $2 billion European Strategic Programme for Research and Development in Information Technologies (ESPRIT), whose objective is 'to assist European industry to develop the indigenous technological capability needed to design, manufacture and use profitable and highly competitive information products, systems and services able within ten years to compete successfully and profitably with the USA and Japan.' In telecommunications, the EC established the Research and Development in Advanced Communications Technologies for Europe programme (RACE) to create an integrated

European communications grid. The European Research Co-ordinating Agency (EUREKA) was created in 1985 when 17 western European countries, led by France, established a research programme along the lines of the Strategic Defense Initiative.[56] Although all of these bodies are directed primarily to telecommunications and information, they will have a broader impact on the modernisation of Europe's industrial base.

The USA perceives the GATT negotiations as an opportunity to establish a more liberal regime providing access for American service multinationals. It seeks to extend existing GATT rules to services: national treatment of foreign suppliers; non-discrimination (or most favoured nation treatment), giving foreign suppliers favourable treatment; and 'least restrictive regulations'. A liberal regime would establish principles pertaining to market access: the right to set up operations in a foreign country; intellectual property rights; and greater freedom for transborder data flows.[57] Many obstacles to an international agreement remain. Conceptually, the difference between trade in services and foreign direct investment is fuzzy, and the Third World is acutely conscious of the need to maintain regulation in order to establish infant industries in this sector. Hence, although the Uruguay Declaration was adopted as 'a single political undertaking launching the Uruguay Round', services are to be dealt with technically outside the GATT negotiations.[58] The interpretations of, say, India, are markedly different to the public pronouncements of the OECD countries, and especially the USA. However, if the USA cannot secure agreements through the GATT, then it will continue to promote liberalisation by actively seeking bilateral agreements, as it has done with Israel and Canada.

CONCLUSION

The commencement of the Uruguay Round marked the end of the first stage of a protracted American campaign, spearheaded by large agribusiness and service corporations, to reduce barriers to trade in these sectors. The liberalisation of agriculture and services is explicable in terms of two related processes: first, the determination and ability of the USA to respond to the decline of hegemony by constructing international regimes in which it can exploit its remaining comparative advantages; second, changes in the political–economic basis of advanced capitalism in the USA, including the gradual eclipse of the corporate liberal sector and the Fordist regulatory model that emerged from the New Deal by the forces of transnationally-oriented capital, and the extension of the deregulatory, liberal model to Europe, Japan and the Third World.

The tendency towards liberalisation gives evidence, contrary to much conventional wisdom, that protectionism does not represent the dominant tendency of the international political economy. It is also true, however, that liberalisation is taking place in the context of the rapid concentration and centralisation of capital, and that it reflects the strategies of oligopolistic actors seeking to extend their share of the world market.[59]

The USA's agricultural sector has become increasingly dependent on foreign markets. Whereas prior to World War II American farm policy was largely oriented to domestic forces and markets, by 1981 30 per cent of gross farm income was derived from exports. The importance of agriculture for the American economy can only be fully appreciated if related industries, including food processing, fertiliser and farm machinery are included. The EC continues to account for a large share of world agricultural imports (approximately one-quarter of global imports), and it is determined to maintain or expand its growing share of exports (now approximately 10 per cent).

The liberalisation of agriculture faces many more political constraints than services, where the desire to open world markets enjoys the support of most parties in the USA and western Europe. The 1985 Farm Bill has dealt a crushing blow to small and medium-sized farmers in the USA, creating widespread bankruptcy and rural poverty, and accelerating the trend towards concentration of land and income. Moreover, the budgetary costs of export subsidies are themselves substantial. There is some doubt that the USA will be able to stay the course. The Harkin–Gephardt 'Save the Family Farm Act', which calls for national and international supply management, has attracted widespread support from small and medium-sized farmers, and it was possible that if a Democratic Administration had been elected in 1988, it would probably have adopted some of the provisions of this bill.[60]

In 1980, services constituted over 60 per cent of the gross world product, but only 8 per cent of these services were traded internationally.[61] Exports of services, like agricultural commodities, loom especially large for the USA, which is running a large trade deficit in manufactured goods. The strong support for the GATT initiatives in the USA, and the fragmented nature of the opposition in Europe and the USA suggest that the political impediments to liberalisation are weak.

Europe's willingness to include these sectors in GATT negotiations reflects both the continuing power of the USA, and the existence of uncertainty and division in Europe. Europe's resistance to agricultural liberalisation is legendary. Even victims of the CAP, such as the UK, have not sought to alter basic principles of the Community by demanding wholesale revision of its provisions. Traditionally, France has generated the bedrock of support for the CAP, but the institutional momentum of more than two decades remains a serious obstacle to change.

Thus the Commission's acceptance of the Uruguay Round, however tentative and qualified, gives evidence of fundamental changes in the

European Community. First, the community itself is beset by a severe budgetary crisis as it faces the need to devote resources to the development of new technologies. Since 1982 structural reform, including limitations on subsidies, have been implemented. Perhaps more important, however, are changes within the composition of agriculture, especially in France. Once the bastion of protection, French agriculture has become much more concentrated and much more productive. As a result, France has become less concerned about domestic protection, and more concerned about access to foreign markets, both externally and within the community. The most ardent supporters of existing supports are small farmers, especially in West Germany. Steps towards the phasing out of the CAP would be likely to lead to the 'renationalisation' of agricultural policy, a challenge to the fundamental tenets of the EC.

Initially opposed to service liberalisation, in recent years both the EC Commission and member governments, including France, have changed their views. In part, this can be attributed to the completion of national studies, mandated by the GATT in 1982, which revealed the scope and extent of Europe's participation in international trade in services. Moreover, there is a strong 'spillover' dynamic: once liberalisation has begun in some domestic markets, especially in the USA, it becomes necessary for governments elsewhere to liberalise in order to remain competitive. However, although Europe has supported the GATT process, it is to be expected that actual negotiations will highlight significant areas of conflict.

The importance of services and agriculture for the contemporary global economy, finally, illustrates the great power of the USA, despite its relative decline, and suggests that this power is based not simply on residual monetary supremacy. As with all previous GATT rounds, the USA has taken the initiative in calling for negotiations and setting the agenda; its agribusiness and service multinationals have been the agents of change and will be its prime beneficiaries.[61] Liberalisation thus gives evidence of the waning of the New Deal system, and the crumbling of the national and international regimes to which it gave rise in favour of a system in which conflicts are resolved in the interests of holders of market power, and one in which the USA is less inclined to underwrite stability.

EPILOGUE

The first draft of this chapter was completed in June, 1987. During the last 18 months, the Uruguay Round has proceeded against a background of continuing serious transatlantic conflict. In agriculture, the USA has undertaken a bold negotiating initiative, and international agricultural markets have experienced a great deal of turbulence, partly as a result of American policies. In services, on the other hand, negotiations have been bogged down in complexities. Finally, the decision of the European Community to eliminate internal trade barriers by 1992 under the terms of the Single European Act has opened up a new avenue of potential transatlantic conflict, provoking charges from the USA and Japan of a 'fortress Europe'.

In July, 1987 the USA issued a sweeping proposal in Geneva for the abolition of farm subsidies, tariffs, and other border measures by the year 2000. The USA hoped to reap an 'early harvest' at the mid-term Uruguay Round review in Montreal, in December 1988, by achieving consensus on its proposals among GATT participants. However, the EC, emboldened by the summer drought of 1988, has categorically rejected what it considers to be an idealistic solution to the problem of agricultural overproduction. Europe has instead proposed a 'framework approach' endorsing gradual reductions in subsidies on a step-by-step basis, an approach which would not fundamentally alter the status quo and which would preserve the essential features of the CAP. The EC budget compromise of February 1988, although widely touted as constituting a reform of the CAP, is not likely to reduce European export subsidies or enhance budget discipline. At the Toronto summit, President Reagan was unable to secure European agreement on a deadline for liberalisation.

Thus Europe's intransigence appears to sound the death knell of a dramatic, negotiated repeal of modern 'corn laws', and it is doubtful that the USA will achieve a breakthrough in Montreal. Although it is likely that the new American president, George Bush, will adopt a more pragmatic approach to the reduction of subsidies and trade barriers, the impetus for liberalisation can be expected to persist throughout the 1990s, driven by the particular interests of the large grain corporations, the budgetary consequences of commodity programmes, and the growing role assigned to agriculture in America's international economic strategy.

The GATT stalemate indicates the limitations of American power in international institutions. However, as a result of its resource endowment, productivity, and presence in foreign markets, the USA does wield enormous market power and American policy remains the central factor in the world price for grain. By establishing export subsidy programmes and reducing the world price of many commodities, the USA has destabilised global agricultural markets in an attempt to compel the EC to reduce its own subsidies and to lower trade barriers. Between 1985 and 1987, export subsidies for wheat, feedgrains, rice and cotton totalled more than $17 billion, although these subsidies have in general been targeted to larger farmers and have not compensated even these farmers fully for low prices. Against this figure, the total value of these export crops was just $9.2 billion. During this time, although the volume of exports rose, export earnings actually decreased. Yet the EC has responded by also raising subsidies in order to protect markets for its own producers. Euro-

American farm trade wars have devastated Third World countries as poor farmers' incomes have been slashed as a result of cheap food imports.

It is likely that President Bush will enjoy substantial bi-partisan support for continuing efforts to liberalise agriculture, and that a breakdown of GATT negotiations will induce the USA to step up export subsidies as a means of pressuring the EC. Coupled with new USA–EC conflicts over specific commodities (e.g. the EC ban on US exports of meat containing growth hormones), and the inability to make progress in services, such an outcome might jeopardise the Uruguay Round itself and have serious consequences for transatlantic economic and political co-operation in the 1990s.

The most important provisions of the Single European Act are those which eliminate all barriers to trade in goods and services within the community. The Act has raised the spectre in both the USA and Japan of a protectionist trade bloc employing import quotas, anti-dumping rules, and reciprocity requirements. In recent months, actions by the European Commission have given some evidence of a 'fortress Europe', and the media have widely publicised a number of actual and potential instances of protection. Under rules recently drafted by the Commission, foreign banks and financial service corporations would be prevented from establishing themselves in Europe unless their host government granted 'reciprocity' to European banks. This rule would create major problems for American banks because of the separation of commercial and investment banking under the Glass-Steagall Act. In addition, American telecommunications firms have charged that Commission rules will allow national governments to continue to discriminate against them in government procurement contracts.

The Single European Act represents a new phase of European integration. As such, it expresses, in heightened form, existing contradictions both at the level of US–European relations, and within Europe. On one hand, manifestations of 'fortress Europe' reveal the persistence of inter-state and transatlantic rivalry. Originally supported by the USA during its integral hegemonic phase as a means of blunting the power of the Soviet Union, an integrated Europe is viewed as an increasingly serious rival by a declining hegemon. Yet, the walls of 'fortress Europe' are porous, and protectionism has brought forth equally strong countervailing, that is, liberalising, tendencies. The Single European Act does not appear to represent a fundamental threat to the internationalisation of capital. Just as American multinationals entered Europe in the 1960s as a means of leapfrogging trade barriers, so today American service corporations are establishing European subsidiaries and joint ventures in anticipation of the implementation of the Single European Act in 1992.

Within the community, the effects of the Single European Act will also exacerbate existing conflicts. Integration is favoured by the most productive states, regions and sectors. Here, integration is viewed as a means of enhancing Europe's international stature. Yet despite provisions of the Single Act designed to promote growth in less-developed regions of the community, greater liberalisation is likely to accelerate uneven development. The pace and scope of internal liberalisation will be limited by the less productive states, sectors and regions.

NOTES

1. Kees van der Pijl, *The Making of an Atlantic Ruling Class* (London, Verso, 1984), especially Chapter 3.
2. *Ibid.*, p. 138.
3. *Ibid.* See also Thomas Ferguson, 'From Normalcy to New Deal: Industrial Structure, Party Competition, and American Public Policy in the Great Depression', *International Organization*, vol. 38, winter 1984.
4. Bob Rowthorn, 'Imperialism in the 1970s – Unity or Rivalry?' in Hugo Radice (ed.) *International Firms and Modern Imperialism* (Harmondsworth, Penguin, 1975); Ernest Mandel, *Late Capitalism* (London, New Left Books, 1975); Charles P. Kindleberger, *The World in Depression, 1929–39* (Berkeley, University of California Press, 1973). Mary Kaldor, *The Disintegrating West* (New York, Hill and Wang, 1978). Ernest Mandel, *Europe vs America?* (London, New Left Books, 1970).
5. John N. Yochelson, 'Outlook for US Economic Diplomacy: Europe and the Pacific Basin', in Yochelson (ed.) *The United States and the World Economy: Policy Alternatives for New Realities* (Boulder, Colo., Westview Press, 1985).
6. For the classic statement see Jean Jacques Servan-Schreiber, *The American Challenge* (Harmondsworth, Penguin, 1967).
7. See especially David P. Calleo, *The Imperious Economy* (Cambridge, Harvard University Press, 1982); and Riccardo Parboni, *The Dollar and its Rivals: Recession, Inflation, and International Finance* (London, Verso, 1981).
8. See, for example, Giovanni Arrighi, 'A Crisis of Hegemony', in Samir Amin, Giovanni Arrighi, Andre Gunder Frank and Immanuel Wallerstein (eds) *Dynamics of Global Crisis* (New York, Monthly Review Press, 1982).
9. See, for example, Theodore C. Sorensen, 'A Changing America', in Andrew J. Pierre (ed.) *A Widening Atlantic? Domestic Change and Foreign Policy* (New York, Council on Foreign Relations, 1986); and David P. Calleo, 'The Atlantic Alliance: A View from America', in Frans A. M. Alting von Geusau (ed.) *Allies in a Turbulent World: Challenges to US and Western European Cooperation* (Lexington, Mass., Heath, 1982).
10. Robert Gilpin, *U.S. Power and the Multinational Corporations* (New York, Basic Books, 1975); Charles P. Kindleberger, 'Dominance and Leadership in the International Economy: Exploitation, Public Goods, and Free Rides', *International Studies Quarterly*, vol. 25, June 1981; Robert O. Keohane, *After Hegemony: Cooperation and Discord in the World Political Economy* (Princeton, Princeton University Press, 1984).
11. Susan Strange, 'Still an Extraordinary Power: America's Role in the International Monetary System', in Ray E. Lombra and William E. Witte (eds) *The Political Economy of International and Domestic Monetary Relations* (Ames, Iowa, Iowa State University Press, 1982); Calleo, *The Imperious Economy;*

Bruce Russett, 'The Mysterious Case of Vanishing Hegemony: Or, Is Mark Twain Really Dead?' *International Organization*, vol. 39, spring 1985; Stephen Gill, 'American Hegemony: Its Limits and Prospects in the Reagan Era', *Millenium*, vol. 15, autumn 1986.

12. Olivier Blanchard and Rudiger Dornbusch, 'US Deficits, the Dollar, and Europe', in Olivier Blanchard, Rudiger Dornbusch and Richard Layard (eds) *Restoring Europe's Prosperity* (Cambridge, MIT Press, 1986); J. P. Fitoussi and E. S. Phelps, 'Causes of the 1980s Slump in Europe', in William C. Brainard and George L. Perry (eds) *Brookings Papers on Economic Activity 2* (Washington DC, The Brookings Institutions, 1986); see also Calleo, *The Imperious Economy;* and Parboni, *The Dollar and its Rivals*.

13. Gramsci's discussion of hegemony appears in Quintin Hoare and Geoffrey Nowell Smith, *Selections from the Prison Notebooks* (London, Lawrence and Wishart, 1971).

14. For an application of Gramsci's theory of power to the international system see Robert W. Cox, 'Social Forces, States, and World Orders: Beyond International Relations Theory', in Robert O. Keohane (ed.) *Neorealism and its Critics* (New York, Columbia University Press, 1986). Stephen Gill applies this theory to the activities of the Trilateral Commission.

15. Van der Pijl's work is especially useful in showing the connections between domestic and international political and economic events.

16. For a review of this literature, very little of which is published in English, see Alain Noel, 'Accumulation, Regulation, and Social Change: An Essay on French Political Economy', *International Organization*, vol. 41, spring 1987. See also Mike Davis, *Prisoners of the American Dream* (London, Verso, 1986).

17. Joseph Femia, *Gramsci's Political Thought: Hegemony, Consciousness, and the Revolutionary Process* (Oxford, Clarendon Press, 1981), pp. 45–7.

18. E. A. Brett, *International Money and Capitalist Crisis: The Anatomy of Global Disintegration* (London, Heinemann, 1983), pp. 193–4.

19. Robert Triffin, *The World Money Maze* (New Haven, Yale University Press, 1966), p. 288.

20. David P. Calleo, 'Inflation and American Power', *Foreign Affairs*, no. 59, spring, 1981; Richard J. Barnet, *The Alliance: America, Europe, Japan: Makers of the Postwar World* (New York, Simon and Schuster, 1983), p. 251.

21. Barnet, p. 255.

22. Brett, p. 176.

23. Susan Strange, 'The Monetary Tangle', in F. A. M. Alting von Geusau, pp. 117–19.

24. Federal Reserve Bank of Cleveland, *Economic Trends*, January, 1987, Table 22.

25. Calleo, *The Imperious Economy*, pp. 115–16.

26. Henry Nau, 'Where Reaganomics Works', *Foreign Policy*, no. 57, winter 1984–5.

27. European Community Commission, *Perspectives for the Common Agricultural Policy – the Green Paper of the Commission*, Brussels, July/85, p. II.

28. For an introduction to American agricultural policies see Raymond Hopkins, *Global Food Interdependence: Challenge to American Foreign Policy* (New York, Columbia University Press, 1980). On the New Deal, see especially Don Paarlberg, *Farm and Food Policy: Issues of the 1980s* (Lincoln, University of Nebraska Press, 1980), especially Chapters 2–4.

29. On Western European farm policies see M. Tracy, *Agriculture in Western Europe: Challenge and Response 1880–1980* (London, Granada, 1982).

30. European Community, *Green Europe Newsletter*, 'The Outlook for Europe's Agricultural Policy', Brussels, 1984.
31. Tracy, p. 368. As the COGECA (Comité Général de la Coopération Agricole) has noted, 'With the prospect of a reasonable and moderate expansion of European agricultural output – which corresponds to the basic needs of the people and farmers in Community countries – regular export of a substantial part of this production is a need which cannot be disputed.' See also John Cathie, 'US and EEC Agricultural Trade Policies: A long-run View of the Present Conflict', *Food Policy*, February 1985.
32. David Curry, 'Farm Policy is Fundamental to European Community', *Europe*, July/August, 1985, p. 36.
33. Robert Paarlberg, 'Three Political Explanations for Crisis in the World Grain Market', in William P. Avery and David P. Rapkin (eds) *America in a Changing World Political Economy* (New York, Longman, 1982).
34. *Ibid.*, p. 123.
35. Emma Rothschild, 'Food Politics', *Foreign Affairs*, no. 54, January 1976. A number of observers, including GATT officials, believe that American food power has been exaggerated, and that the USA's comparative advantage in grain production is eroding. See, for example, Barbara Insel, 'A World Awash in Grain', *Foreign Affairs*, spring 1985. For a rebuttal to this argument see W. Patrick Nichols, 'US Agriculture: Another Slumbering Giant', *Food Policy*, May 1986. See also Alain Revel and Christophe Riboud, *American Green Power* (Baltimore, Johns Hopkins University Press, 1986), who strongly emphasise the centrality of American agriculture in the domestic and international economies.
36. Green Europe, *Agriculture in the US and EC: A Comparison*, Brussels, April 1984, p. 14.
37. For details on the magnitude of the domestic crisis see Mark Ritchie and Kevin Ristau, 'US Farm Policy', *World Policy Journal*, no. 4, winter 1986–7.
38. Article XVI enjoins GATT members to 'seek to avoid' export subsidies. Domestic production subsidies are not prohibited.
39. US Congress, Congressional Research Service, *Agriculture in the GATT: Toward the Next Round of Multilateral Trade Negotiations*, 99th Congress, 2nd Session (Washington, US Government Printing Office, 1986), p. 16.
40. *Ibid.*
41. Recently, the OECD has devised a system for comparing national farm programmes. The 'producer subsidy equivalent' (PSE) includes all government support, including import restrictions, subsidies, and price supports. A PSE of 10 per cent means that subsidies are equal to 10 per cent of a farmer's income. The US Department of Agriculture estimates the following PSEs for the period 1982–4: Japan, 72 per cent; EC, 33 per cent; USA, 22 per cent; Australia, 9 per cent.
42. The 1985 Farm Bill, for example, makes special provision for rice in the form of 'marketing loans'. The US government provides a subsidy of $17 for each hundredweight of rice, which sells for $3.50 on the open market. Rice accounts for 15 per cent of Thailand's foreign exchange, and is the principal source of income for 4 million farmers. The drop in world prices has meant a $60 million fall in Thailand's export earnings. See Ritchie and Ristau, pp. 124–5.
43. European Community, 'EC Issues Updated List of US Trade Barriers' (Washington DC, Office of Press and Public Affairs, 2 April 1987).
44. T. P. Hill, 'On Goods and Services', *Review of Income and Wealth*, vol. 1, December 1977. Both marxists and neo-classicists (e.g. Adam Smith) have

drawn a distinction between productive and unproductive (i.e. tertiary sector or services) labour.
45. See, for example, UNCTAD, *Services and the Development Process* (New York, United Nations, 1985); and subsequent work by the UNCTAD Secretariat.
46. Deepak Nayyar, *International Trade in Services: Implications for Developing Countries* (Bombay, Eximbank of India, 1986). Work on international trade in services has proliferated, especially in the USA. Useful introductions to the issues include Jonathan David Aronson and Peter F. Cowhey, *Trade in Services: A Case for Open Markets* (Washington, American Enterprise Institute, 1986); Mario A. Kakabadse, *International Trade in Services: Prospects for Liberalisation in the 1990s* (London, Atlantic Institute for International Affairs, 1986); and Karl Sauvant, *International Transactions in Services: The Politics of Transborder Data Flows* (Boulder, Colo., Westview Press, 1986).
47. Aronson and Cowhey, p. 6.
48. Sauvant documents the lobbying role of American service firms during the 1970s and early 1980s, *op cit.*, especially pp. 183–215.
49. *Ibid.*, pp. 185–9.
50. Quoted in *ibid.*, p. 183.
51. 'Telecommunications: The Global Battle', *Business Week Special Report*, 24 October 1983, p. 126.
52. For a discussion of post-war developments see especially Stephen Woolcock, Jeffrey Hart and Hans Van Der Ven, *Interdependence in the Post-Multilateral Era: Trends in US–European Trade Relations* (Lanham, Md., Center for International Affairs, Harvard University and University Press of America, 1985), pp. 97–9 and 106–9. See also Pascal Petit, *Slow Growth and the Service Economy* (New York, St Martins Press, 1986).
53. Recent joint ventures include ITT and France's state-owned Cie. Générale d'Eléctricité; ATT and Philips (Netherlands); GET (USA)–Siemens (FRG); Plessey (UK)–Stromberg–Carlson (USA); Ericsson (Sweden) and General Electric (UK).
54. Woolcock *et al.*, p. 102.
55. *Ibid.*, 112. See also Godefroy Dang Nguyen, 'Telecommunications: A Challenge to the Old Order', in Margaret Sharp (ed.) *Europe and the New Technologies: Six Case Studies in Innovation and Adjustment* (London, Frances Pinter, 1983).
56. On developments in the EC see Sauvant, pp. 168–9.
57. Aronson and Cowhey, pp. 24–30; Kakabadse, p. 73–9.
58. India and Brazil will continue to oppose the inclusion of services within the GATT, laying emphasis on the technical separation of service sector negotiations and GATT negotiations. See, for example, GATT Secretariat, Group of Negotiations on Services, *Communication* from India, 11 March 1987 (mimeo).
59. Of the top 200 global corporations, 82 can be classified as service corporations, whose total sales account for two-fifths of the sales of the top 200 corporations. 94 per cent of the sales of these corporations were from corporations originating in the USA, Japan, France, the UK and FRG. 75 per cent of the sales were from corporations originating in the USA and Japan. F. Clairmonte and J. Cavanagh, 'Transnational Corporation and Services: The final Frontier', *Trade and Development*, vol. 5, 1984. David Holland and Joe Carvalho document the increasing concentration of income, the growth of average farm size and the increasing importance of forward linkages (e.g. sales by contract to large corporations) in 'The Changing Mode of Production in American

Agriculture: Emerging Conflicts in Agriculture's Role in the Reproduction of Advanced Capitalism', *Review of Radical Political Economics*, no. 17, winter 1985.
60. The Harkin–Gephardt Bill authorises the President to seek multilateral supply management. If agreements with other countries cannot be reached, then the USA is to adopt export-enhancement programmes to secure its market share, based on the American share of the 1985 crop. Although Democrats have been quick to blame rural distress on the Republicans, the 1985 Farm Bill was a product of the Democratic-controlled House Agriculture Committee as well as the Administration and the Senate Agriculture Committee.
61. UNCTAD, *Services and the Development Process*, p. viii.

7 · TRANSATLANTIC ECONOMIC CO-OPERATION
The Baker Initiatives and Beyond

David Law

INTRODUCTION

The Baker Initiatives on the debt crisis and exchange rate management in the autumn of 1985 marked a change in American policy. Macro-economic co-operation and some joint management of the world economy by the leading capitalist states was deemed desirable and feasible. By the time of the stock market crash of October 1987, the Initiatives appeared to be falling apart. World economic growth seemed set to slow down, trade barriers about to rise. Some saw that, in the long-term, the world economy might fracture into regional blocs.[1]

In some senses, the Initiatives were seen as the reassertion of a fading American internationalism, with a renewed commitment to the provision of international public goods such as monetary stability, liquidity and an orderly trading system. At the same time, there was no guarantee that the other leading countries would reciprocate, particularly since their commitment to internationalism had been shaken by the way in which global interdependence had imposed significant costs on entrenched interests.[2] Further, the USA might yet relapse into a self-centred unilateralism: the Initiatives might be tactical, temporary and self-serving, seen from a realist viewpoint.

In this essay I argue that a pessimistic verdict on the Initiatives would be hasty and perhaps over-simplified. However, it would also be premature to conclude that they were a turning point on the road to the establishment of an institutionalised steering mechanism for the capitalist world economy. An examination of the Initiatives, their sources, successes, failures and prospects, serves to highlight a number of questions concerning the possibilities for capitalist international economic co-operation at the end of the twentieth century. Such considerations are made more relevant, of course, by the 1988 Presidential election victory of George Bush. James Baker III was Bush's most trusted advisor, his campaign manager and the President-elect's first appointee, as Secretary of State.

STRUCTURAL CHANGE AND THE BACKGROUND TO THE INITIATIVES

Major structural changes in the capitalist world economy have made attempts at economic co-operation both difficult and inevitable. These changes have resulted in an increasingly integrated global political economy in which huge capital flows and the activities of transnational firms are major features. Capital flows across the foreign exchanges have been thought to dwarf trade flows by as much as 20– or 30–fold. These capital flows (especially short term flows) are the major driving force behind exchange rate movements. One consequence for floating rates has been that fluctuations have been very great, far more so than their advocates had expected. While this has partly reflected bandwagon effects and the relatively quick-adjusting character of financial and foreign exchange markets, it has also been due to major international imbalances in monetary and fiscal policy and also in saving rates. Traders, investors and tourists have been exposed to increased risks as a result of volatile exchange rates and/or to increased costs as they seek to cover themselves against these risks. As such, they have an interest in a reduction of imbalances and in more policy co-operation.

However, one option – the reimposition of wide-ranging capital controls – is unlikely because of the growth of economic interdependence. Trade has outgrown output since World War II and despite protectionist measures could well continue to do so because of changes in technology and communications. Trade can be a vehicle for capital flows: notably through the under – and over – invoicing of imports and exports. In addition transnational firms can use transfer pricing techniques in intra-company trade to shift capital between countries. Hence capital controls become less effective (see Table 7.1).

A second option – a return to fixed exchange rates – is also unlikely mainly because of increased capital mobility since the 1950s and 1960s. They are far less feasible technically since central banks need much larger foreign exchange reserves relative to national output in order to cope with enormous short-term capital flows. They are less feasible politically since to defend fixed rates, countries would have to give up most of their autonomy in economic policy-making, even more so than under the Bretton Woods system. In the USA's case, since it had more autonomy than other countries under that system, the loss of autonomy for monetary and fiscal policy would be especially great.

The rise of international capital mobility has made use of Keynesian policies to expand demand both more and less feasible. On the one hand a budget deficit can be more readily financed from abroad, as leading Latin American debtor countries found in the 1970s (when there was a glut of capital and the American budget deficit was much smaller than in the

Table 7.1 Proportions of merchandise trade to national product for major developed countries (percentages)

Ranked by economic size	Pre-World War 1	1950s	1984
USA	11.0	7.9	15.2
Japan	29.5	18.8	24.2
Germany	38.3	35.1	52.8
France	35.2	n/a	40.2
UK	43.5	30.4	47.0
Italy	28.1	25.0	44.6
Canada	32.2	31.2	47.3

Source: Simon Kuznets and *World Development Report 1986;* cited in *Financial Times,* 16 November 1987.

1980s). Such borrowed funds can limit the rise in interest rates and avoid the crowding out of investment. On the other hand expansionary policies, if not matched by other countries, can lead to a weaker trade balance and a large capital outflow, as France found in 1981–2. Further, even if capital is attracted, under floating exchange rates it will drive up the exchange rate, so reducing the price competitiveness of domestic producers and worsening the trade balance. This happened in the American case in the 1980s. The USA's current account was in surplus in the recession years of 1980 and 1981 ($6.6 billion and $10.7 billion) but went into deficit in 1982 ($3.8 billion). By 1984 and 1985 the deficit was as high as $93.4 billion and $117.5 billion, respectively.[3] By contrast, West Germany had a current account surplus of $17.7 billion and Japan of $40.9 billion in 1985.[4]

The USA's ability to draw in funds was unique. This was due to its huge financial markets and the international currency role of the dollar. More than any other country it could make Keynesian policies work (though some would stress the supply-side effects of income tax cuts and deregulation). The success of American expansion in the 1980s was bought at the price of high interest rates (real as well as nominal) and a worsening trade deficit. The normal Keynesian recipe would have been for the USA to substantially reduce its budget deficit in 1985–6 as the boom led to lower levels of unemployment. Then, American borrowing from abroad could have been sharply reduced, so bringing down both interest rate levels and the value of the dollar. This did not happen due to the devotion of the Reagan Administration to both low taxes and high military spending combined with a reluctance by Congress to continue slashing social welfare expenditures. Thus the USA, far more than its leading capitalist allies, pursued an active fiscal policy.

On the other hand, American monetary policy from 1979 was much more disciplined. In this respect the USA was more in line with Europe and Japan. American officials had learned in the 1970s how a lax monetary policy could lead to a falling dollar and inflation. Indeed if the USA was much more inflation-prone than Japan and Germany, then the special status of the dollar might be seriously weakened. Hence while the USA was increasingly 'interdependent' with other countries in the global political economy, it continued to occupy a unique and privileged position in monetary (as well as military) relations. The USA had simultaneously unique capacities to give long-term leadership and to cause major macro-economic imbalances with far-reaching consequences. It is common to stress the USA's relative economic decline as undermining its will and ability to provide hegemonic leadership. However, another line of argument may deserve more consideration: namely that this decline has not gone far enough for the effects of growing economic interdependence to reshape American policies and its policy frameworks of thought. In many ways the Reagan years (up to 1985) were an attempt to reassert American primacy and a belief in its exceptionalism, and old habits lived on, not least in the form of neglect of the balance of payments.

Apart from trade and short term capital flows another aspect of structural change was transnationalisation. Although foreign investments were important in the world economy before 1914 they were usually in the form of portfolio rather than direct investment. Most of the latter was in primary products. Since 1945 direct investment and, later, portfolio investment have revived. The greater part of the investment by transnational firms was in manufacturing and related services, such as banking. Much of this was in the developed countries. Firms based in different countries 'invaded' each other's home territory. A new kind of cross-cutting interdependence was emerging. Even some of the more industrialised countries from what used to be called the Third World have firms with subsidiaries in Western countries. These trends have led some writers to conclude that in an age of research-intensive industry and mass consumption products, firms in many industries need to operate in, and sell to, the three major market areas of North America, western Europe and Japan. The political counterpart to this is the emergence of a set of forces concerned to sustain and extend the transnationalisation process, forming, in effect, a transnational historic bloc (see Chapters 1 and 2).

THE BAKER INITIATIVES

In the summer of 1985, Reagan's White House Chief-of-Staff, James Baker, swapped jobs with Donald Regan, the Treasury Secretary. In a remarkably short space of time he came to question the complacent confidence in 'market place magic' and American economic performance which had been a feature of the outlook of the first Reagan Administration's economic policy. Then the official view had been that the high dollar exchange rate reflected the basic strength of the American economy.

According to the prevailing view in the Administration, the renewed growth of 1982–5 was attributed to tax cuts. As a consequence, it was up to each country to put its own house in order. National virtue rather than international co-operation was the key requirement for sustained world economic growth. This whole approach was rationalised by Henry Nau under the label of 'domesticism'.[5] Amongst the domestic virtues were low taxes, monetary discipline and low (or zero) budget deficits – at least with the economy at or near full employment. Ironically it was Reagan's 1984 challenger for the Presidency, Walter Mondale, who pointed to the growing size of the budget deficit and the need for tax increases and/or spending cuts. It won him few votes.

Against this background, two problems were soon identified by Baker, problems which had been the subject of much attention from economists in the 1980s, both in the USA and Europe. One concerned the volatility of floating exchange rates and what was seen as a marked tendency towards short-sighted bandwagon effects. The strong dollar of the mid-1980s was seen by some as an extreme example of this tendency. Others argued that the American budget deficit was a sufficient cause without invoking bandwagon effects.[6] The strength of the dollar was not sustainable in the long term since it involved both a huge deficit on current account and massive borrowing from abroad to finance the government budget deficit. The USA's external debt and interest payments to foreigners were rising faster than its gross national product.

For the Reagan Administration, the high dollar became a political problem in several ways. It meant cheaper imports which threatened certain sections of American industry. If American economic growth was to be sustained a lower dollar and a more favourable trade balance was desirable. Last but not least was concern over the dramatic increase in demands for protection as evidenced in hundreds of bills introduced into Congress.[7] Given the commitment of the Administration to an open trading system, a managed decline in the dollar became an immediate necessity.

This last concern was related to the other problem, that of the debt crisis. From August 1982 a series of *ad hoc* expedients (such as the USA's oil purchases from Mexico, rescheduling of debts and short-term, case-by-case conditional loans organised by the IMF) had prevented major defaults. Debtor countries continued to make large interest payments to Western and Japanese banks so averting a threat to the latter's solvency (notably some of the largest American ones). By 1985 this crisis management approach was seen as inadequate. It assumed that the crisis was merely one of liquidity not solvency. Yet the debt-to-exports ratio remained very high for many countries. Despite the boost to world economic growth given by American expansion in 1982–5, the prices of commodities exported by the Third World continued to remain depressed in real terms.

Japan, western Europe and some Far Eastern newly industrialising countries benefited most from America's import appetite (although Brazilian manufacturing exports did well too). Increased American protectionism would further hit Third World exports of manufacturers. In these circumstances many developing countries, including much of Latin America, suffered a substantial fall in the living standards of the majority of their population.[8] Continuing stagnation and decline was a recipe for political unrest and instability. It was thought that left-wing movements might gain increased influence in these nations.

With regard to exchange rates, Baker attempted to gain an agreement between the Group of Five countries (the USA, Japan, Germany, the UK and France) to facilitate a gradual, but substantial, depreciation of the dollar. The means to this end were to be co-ordinated monetary policy, especially on interest rates, co-ordinated intervention in foreign exchange markets, and an attempt to 'talk down' the market. The aim was to achieve a 'soft landing' for the dollar rather than a precipitous drop leading to overshooting on the downside. Early success was achieved in the Plaza agreement negotiated in September 1985.

Prior to this agreement the western European governments had been critical of American policies which led to high real interest rates from 1980 onwards, an outcome which forced them to raise their own interest rates because of fears of a sharp depreciation of their currencies against the dollar. Such depreciation might undermine their efforts to reduce inflation. West Germany was especially concerned to squeeze inflation out of the system. With inflation coming down fast in 1982–3, but unemployment at persistently high levels, western Europe had reason to be thankful for the American expansion of the 1983–5 period. A high dollar made exporting to the USA very profitable. So extreme was the overvaluation of the dollar that the European countries and Japan could readily agree to some dollar depreciation. Indeed by helping to limit the pace and extent of the decline of the dollar's value they could ensure that their export interests were not severely damaged.

In general, the European countries had been more sympathetic to frequent and co-ordinated intervention in foreign exchange markets than the USA in the early 1980s. The European preference for managed floating was embodied in the European Monetary System (EMS), which began in 1979.

American neglect of the foreign exchange markets until the Plaza agreement can be traced to more than a belief in 'market place magic'. American advocates of floating exchange rates had been influential since the 1960s. Imports and exports made up a much smaller proportion of American GNP than was the case for the west European countries (see Table 7.1). Hence sharp movements in exchange rates had a less dramatic effect on American output, employment and inflation than on the

European countries. However, the rise in trade-intensity in the 1960s and 1970s affected the USA, not least as it became less self-reliant in a range of minerals, notably oil. Thus by the mid-1980s, faced with the possibility of a plunging dollar, the USA had more to gain than before from co-operation with other leading capitalist states.

The massive size and centrality of the American economy helps to explain not only the contrast between American and European attitudes to exchange rate policy, but also why the Europeans and Japanese waited for the USA to take the initiative. Without the active co-operation of the two leading capitalist states, European attempts to influence the dollar rate (downwards) were unlikely to be effective, unless they adopted highly deflationary policies. Given that monetary and fiscal policies were already 'tight' and unemployment very high, this was not an attractive option. In addition, the need for American leadership also reflected the continuing primacy of the dollar as an international currency (see Table 7.2) and European dependence on the USA for security.

The Initiatives of autumn 1985 were meant to be mutually supportive of world economic growth and global tendencies towards economic liberalisation. While continued growth in the leading capitalist countries was vital for the exports of less developed countries, a revival of growth in the Third World would benefit the exports of the developed countries. In particular, the USA had a large interest in the Latin American market which had been depressed since 1982 with the outbreak of the debt crisis. Brazil and Mexico, each with debts close to $100 billion, were not only the biggest Third World debtors, but were of major geopolitical importance for the USA.

The 'Baker Plan' on Third World debts built on the substantial cooperation between leading capitalist governments and banks in 1982–85. It was more a strategy than a blueprint since all the details were to be worked out later, partly in negotiation with particular debtor countries. Multilateral development financial institutions (MDFIs) were to play a key part in these negotiations since increased long-term loans, especially from the World Bank, were seen by Baker as underpinning renewed growth. These loans were to be conditional on a commitment to market-orientated reforms such as competitive interest rates, an easing of exchange controls, devaluation, trade liberalisation and privatisation. Thus conditionality was to become a major feature of World Bank loans as it already was for the International Monetary Fund. The role of the latter was to continue, not least as the leader of the commercial banks whose loans were tied to IMF loans. Baker proposed that commercial banks and MDFIs should extend an additional US $29 billion in credit to less developed countries in 1986–88. The involvement of the MDFIs was supposed to alleviate the short-term and somewhat deflationary character of IMF loans and conditions. The Baker Plan thus signified a shift from short-term crisis management towards a sense of long-term strategy.

Table 7.2 International role of the United States dollar
(percentage of official reserves)

	End 1974	End 1984
US dollar	75.0	57.0
Japanese yen	0	4.8
West German deutschmark	5.8	11.0
British sterling	5.4	2.6
Swiss franc	1.4	1.9
French franc	1.0	1.0
ECU	0	11.0
Other	11.4	10.6

Source: *Financial Times*, 8 April 1987.
Based on IMF Annual Reports.

THE FATE OF THE INITIATIVE ON EXCHANGE RATES

The Plaza agreement was successful in bringing down the value of the dollar in a gradual manner. In the case of the yen, the rate against the dollar strengthened from over $1:200 yen in 1985 to about $1:140 to $1:150 yen in 1987. The Deutschmark strengthened from over $1:2.4 marks in 1985 to $1:1.8 marks for the first three-quarters of 1987.[9] However, the American budget deficit remained high so that given rough equality between American saving (personal and corporate) and investment, a current account deficit continued along with capital inflows (see Table 7.3).

Success in devaluing the dollar was made easier by a consensus on the case for a fall. By contrast, managing a stabilisation of the dollar at a lower level posed more difficulties. Economists differed in their estimates of what rate for the dollar would eliminate the American current account deficit (and hence the capital inflow). Much depended on how large American foreign debts became and the rate of interest on these debts, since debt servicing is part of the current account. These magnitudes, in turn, vary with the size of the budget deficit. In addition, much rested on the responsiveness of American imports and exports to a lower dollar. Yet another factor was the growth of demand in other major countries, notably West Germany and Japan. Apart from these sources of uncertainty there was the mercantilist preference of surplus countries for a dollar devaluation which was insufficient to eliminate the American deficit. They had an interest in underestimating the required fall in the dollar for a situation of balance to be achieved. In so far as mercantilist considerations influenced the American government, then an overestimate of the 'necessary fall' would be logical.

In practice the path from the Plaza to the Louvre agreement and on to the global stock market crash of October 1987 was marked by Japanese attempts to limit the decline of the dollar (lest their export sector be

Table 7.3 Relationship between American foreign investment and national saving and investment, selected years

Year	Per cent of GNP			
	Net foreign investment	Gross private saving	Government budget surplus	Gross domestic investment
1966	0.5	17.0	−0.2	16.7
1973	0.6	18.0	0.6	17.6
1979	0.1	17.8	0.5	18.1
1984	−2.4	18.4	−2.9	17.9
1985	−2.9	17.4	−3.5	16.8

(Net foreign investment = Gross private saving + Government budget surplus − Gross domestic investment)

Source: Adapted from R. N. Cooper; 'Dealing with the Trade Deficit in a Floating Rate System', *Brookings Economic Papers* 1986, Vol. 1, p. 298.

severely squeezed) and by American attempts to get Japan and West Germany to adopt expansionary policies. At the end of 1986 there was a yen–dollar pact which, however, was soon followed in 1987 by further dollar depreciation. The Americans let it be known that they thought the Germans and Japanese were not doing enough to expand. The Louvre Accord of February 1987 renewed co-operation in exchange markets but did little to change 'fundamentals', that is the imbalances of saving and investment plus taxation and government spending between the major industrialised countries. Its apparent success until October was only made possible by large scale purchases of dollars by European and Japanese central banks. Private capital inflows into the USA showed signs of faltering. In effect West Germany and Japan were buying time for their exporters to adjust to a lower dollar as well as limiting the immediate squeeze on their profit rates.

Western Europe and Japan resisted American suggestions made from spring 1986 that more detailed rules for managed floating were needed. West Germany was wary of the notion of 'automaticity', whereby countries would have to lower their interest rates and increase their budget deficits if world growth slowed and they were still in current account surplus. (By contrast France had long favoured the idea of reference rates.) West Germany feared that tighter links to the dollar would make the EMS more vulnerable to erratic American policy (and potentially to American inflationary tendencies). In effect, American commitment to monetary and fiscal discipline and to a reduction in its economic sovereignty was doubted. After all, it was but a short time since the USA had proclaimed a self-centred indifference to exchange rate movements. However, the large-scale purchase of dollars by the European G5 countries and Japan in 1987 boosted their monetary growth, so that their economies grew faster – as Baker wished. It went far to finance the USA's budget deficit.

In October and November 1987, following the stock market crash, the dollar depreciated further, especially against the yen and the Deutschmark

Once again the European and Japanese central banks attempted to check the fall, but without American support. Indeed, some of Secretary Baker's remarks seemed designed to hasten the decline of the dollar. If the exchange rates of the Louvre agreement went with too high a dollar then this gave speculators a one-way option. Thus the dollar might need to be reduced to a more credible level. Such a level would also give a further boost to American exports and restrain the volume of imports. Given the 'melt-down' on the American stock market, consumer spending was likely to fall due to an adverse 'wealth effect'. Hence higher exports and an improved trade balance were one way for the USA to avoid a recession in 1988 – a Presidential and Congressional election year. Domestic politics thus ruled out a major (though not a modest) reduction of the American budget deficit. In the face of nervous stock and foreign exchange markets, President Reagan and Congress embarked on talks which resulted in a plan to cut the budget deficit by $30 billion in 1988.

American pressure on Europe to help keep the world economy growing bore some fruit. In December 1987, the leading European countries lowered their interest rates, allowing the USA to avoid increasing its interest rates in a defence of the dollar. Some commentators saw these moves as long overdue because of the prevailing high real rates in the OECD countries and evidence of a marked slowing down of American monetary growth.[10]

Thus by December 1987, while attempts at co-operation continued, American domestic politics, German caution and Japanese mercantilism complicated the efforts. At the same time European divisions were highlighted by calls from France and the UK for West Germany to expand, and by British refusal to become an active member of the EMS, that is to join the exchange rate mechanism.

The scale of the Baker proposals was inadequate, given slower growth in the major economies. In addition, the commercial banks were increasingly reluctant to commit new funds to heavily indebted borrowers. Even so, the banks contributed the amounts of new money called for under the Baker Plan.[11] As a result the debt/export ratios of the 14 main countries which were the object of the Baker plan rose from 300 per cent to 370 per cent in 1986, primarily because of lower export revenues which were down to about three-quarters of their 1980–81 peak.[12]

The World Bank expanded its loans to debtor countries, notably in Latin America: by September 1987 Baker said the Bank had increased disbursements to major Third World debtors by over 40 per cent (about $8 billion). Baker dropped American opposition to an early increase in the Bank's capital. However, the decline in the dollar brought the Bank up against its lending limits. Thus Baker made complimentary remarks about World Bank efforts so as to lower Congressional resistance to his moves: in previous years Congress had substantially cut American outlays to the Bank.

The inadequacy of the Baker strategy was related to its failure either to effect a conversion of Third World debt into forms which were long term or to face up to the need to write off (or write down) large portions of the debt. As it was, commercial banks increased their own capital while boosting bad debt provisions. A 'menu of choice' emerged, whereby banks could dispose of (or securitise) their debts. Debt-equity swaps began to play a modest but growing role.

In December 1987 there was a further initiative which opened up opportunities for the writing down of Latin American debts and the reduction of the debt servicing burden. The USA and Mexico announced plans to retire up to $20 billion of Mexico's $105 billion foreign debt. The scheme involved Mexico purchasing United States Treasury bonds as a basis for its repurchasing of debts to commercial banks at a discount which might be as high as 40 per cent. In return the banks were to receive a new 20-year security, the principal of which was secured by the United States Treasury bonds. The Brazilian government was quick to express an interest in this kind of arrangement. However, the willingness of banks to get involved in the Mexican scheme proved very limited.

American internationalism in this case went beyond a concern for world economic growth and the position of American banks. In an election year a worsening of the Latin American debt crisis could have embarrassed the Republican party, not least with the growing number of Hispanic voters. American 'internationalism' could therefore be seen as gaining new domestic roots.

By contrast the African debt crisis has been of more concern to western Europe than the United States – in line with African links to the European Community. The USA decided, in December 1987, to support in principle, but not back financially, a new IMF fund for the world's poorest countries, many of them in sub-Saharan Africa. The USA cited its balance of payments problems as a reason for not putting up funds. However, it backed a capital increase of $80 billion for the World Bank. Of the $8.4 billion for the IMF fund, Japan was expected to contribute about $2 billion. Hence this fund (involving Canada, too) does not necessarily imply the development of a regional economic sphere of interest. What is significant, and likely in the long term, is an increase in the role of Japan in the IMF and the World Bank, relative to that of the USA and other nations.

PROSPECTS FOR TRANSATLANTIC ECONOMIC INTERNATIONALISM

By internationalism is meant the awareness of, and policy sensitivity to, the economic interdependence of countries by their governments. How far do governments allow for the external effects of their economic policies? How far do they anticipate and incorporate the reactions of other states? How far do they take a long-term view of the repercussions of their actions? To suggest that governments could act in a more internationalist way does not mean that they have completely to transcend rivalries and differences in national priorities. Rather it implies that they recognise the potentially positive and variable-sum game character of international economic relations, practise effective communication and take a more long-term view, especially with regard to the maintenance and establishment of international institutions.

In the case of transatlantic relations, the limits to internationalism in 1987 were much in evidence. While the USA was anxious to maintain economic growth, West Germany seemed more concerned about inflation (even though it was only about one per cent per annum) and its relatively high ratio of national debt to GNP. Other west European countries pressed the Federal Republic to expand but with little response. Given that it had a high ratio of exports to gross domestic product (about 27 per cent), West Germany had strong reasons to be interested in world economic growth. However, with generous welfare state provision and a high national output per head, in 1987 West Germany seemed content with an annual growth rate below two per cent, despite high and rising unemployment.

This contrast highlights the different priorities which existed within Europe, as well as across the Atlantic (and the Pacific). Compared to West Germany, the governments of France, the UK and Italy were anxious to achieve economic growth. West Germany has been happy to pump more money into domestic subsidies (often into declining sectors), which the Kiel Institute has estimated as 6.75 per cent of GNP.[13] Thus the German case does not neatly fit into the category of traditional mercantilism. Rather it is better seen as a case of 'social' mercantilism, where a concern for social cohesion is stressed. Given the memories of the collapse of the Weimar Republic and its aftermath, West Germany is still rather strongly attached to the mix of social democracy and qualified liberalism so common in OECD countries in the 30 years after World War II. The industrial structure, vested interests and policies of that period are very much intact.

It is often suggested that co-operation between the USA and Europe in the 1950s and 1960s was easier not just because of American hegemonic dominance but because socio-economic structures were congruent. In the 1970s and 1980s the compromise of what John Ruggie calls 'embedded liberalism' has unravelled in varying ways and at varying rates in different countries.[14] More monetarist policies were adopted in many countries. This facilitated some European co-operation, for example in the EMS. For West Germany this was not such a major shift, in that its monetary policies had long been geared to checking inflation. This meant other countries fell into line with West German policy, rather than *vice versa*. The EMS case has lessons for transatlantic macro-economic co-operation. For the latter to be more effective, a sharing of priorities and a readiness by some states to forgo some of their monetary autonomy is essential. On this basis the prospect for a new system of managed floating is clearly distant.

However, what now seems remote may eventually transpire if certain changes occur which result in a new and more liberal economic consensus on both sides of the Atlantic. This is where the structural changes discussed earlier may be crucial, especially that of transnationalisation. Cross-cutting foreign investments are tending to result in industries in North America, western Europe and Japan being dominated by the same transnational firms. Purely national firms (with no foreign subsidiaries) are increasingly playing a more marginal role. Such changes have been associated with, and reinforced by, the integration and liberalisation of financial markets.

A key question is how far such material changes can and will be matched by changes in political outlook and practice. The growing structural power of internationally-mobile, large-scale capital puts added pressure on governments to supply an attractive business climate. On the other hand the power of traditional labour unions is reduced. Such tendencies are already apparent in the decline of Keynesian politics and greater stress on the supply side, notably in the UK under Margaret Thatcher. However, in West Germany the compromise of embedded liberalism remains deeply entrenched. Both labour and national capital, for example coal, steel and farming, remain highly influential, with the latter gaining large subsidies and support from the Common Agricultural Policy (CAP). Indeed, by 1987 Germany had emerged as the principal opponent of liberal reforms of the CAP, despite its position as the largest net contributor to European Community funds. Similarly, the state monopoly in telecommunications appeared more entrenched in West Germany than in the UK or France. In both these instances, the German position added to transatlantic economic tensions, given American opposition to the dumping of Community food surpluses and preference for a more open telecommunications market (see Chapter 6).

In the USA, despite tax cuts and deregulation, high spending policies have survived with the powerful backing of the military-industrial complex. As a result the economic liberalism of the Reagan Administration was beset by contradictions, as manifested in the high budget deficits after a period of rapid growth. The high dollar stoked up demands for protection and exacerbated the debt crisis. In the USA's case the path to a neo-liberal internationalism would seem to require some reining back of the military-industrial complex. This would only be possible if there were a series of major arms reduction agreements going well beyond the INF Treaty negotiated in 1987. In addition, the internationalist elements within the USA would need to make substantial headway. Macro-economic and exchange rate co-operation between Europe and the USA are central to this strategy. So is a successful conclusion to the Uruguay Round of trade negotiations begun in 1987.

Thus the emergence of a new international monetary order with institutionalised macro-economic co-operation faces major hurdles. One of these is American economic exceptionalism, embodied in a hegemonic habit that Robert Gilpin calls 'malign neglect'.[15] Further American economic decline might modify this exceptionalism. A circulating European currency (the ECU as a medium of exchange) could also contribute to such a change by weakening the special position of the dollar. This, however, would require the United Kingdom to join the EMS exchange rate mechanism and West Germany to surrender some of its monetary autonomy to an EC central bank. In addition, as Susan Strange has argued, such a European monetary challenge is inhibited by continuing European dependence on the USA for security.[16] Thus increased west European co-operation on defence is of significance for monetary as well as security relations (see Chapter 5). While the USA is likely to be suspicious of such developments, its budgetary difficulties drive it to seek an increased military effort from both western Europe and Japan. Indeed, questions about transatlantic economic relations usually have a Japanese dimension in the background, given the massive and growing importance of Japan in world banking, finance and production.

CONCLUSIONS

The Baker Initiatives have been one of several attempts at transatlantic economic co-operation since the breakdown of the Bretton Woods system. American efforts to get West Germany to act as an economic 'locomotive' in the late 1970s soon broke down. By contrast collaboration over exchange rates in the later 1980s has not collapsed even though it has been fitful and half-hearted. There has been a reluctance to get 'fundamentals' (monetary and fiscal policy) into line. Further imperfect attempts at managed floating are to be expected in the 1990s as countries have become more aware of the hazards of free floating and unco-ordinated policies. This is not to deny that these attempts will be beset by major difficulties, partly due to the sheer scale of the USA's twin deficits.

In the very long term, of 20 to 30 years, the conditions for a more effective and institutionalised co-operation may well develop. This is because of structural changes producing a more integrated global political economy. Very gradually, political and economic ideas and institutions can be expected to change. German memories of Weimar and hyperinflation could fade, while the social democratic compromise of the 1960s to the 1980s erodes. The UK (after Thatcher) will probably join the EMS, facilitating more effective European monetary co-operation, while the EC budgetary crisis will eventually be resolved. A European rival currency may well be in circulation. These tendencies towards a more cohesive western Europe could simplify transatlantic co-operation. They could also provide lessons for future transatlantic and trilateral macro-economic co-operation.

Already such co-operation has been successful in keeping the debt crisis at bay. With the latest Baker initiative the crisis may be on the way to resolution. The roles of the IMF and the World Bank have been expanded. This might be taken further if countries come to place less value on their monetary autonomy in the future. Experience of floating rates in an age of capital mobility has shown the limits to such autonomy. With further economic integration through financial links, direct investments and trade these limits are likely to tighten, even for the USA – especially if there is some relative decline of the dollar as a reserve currency. However, American habits of hegemony, the influence of its military-industrial complex and the comparative self-sufficiency of the American economy need to be modified if a new international monetary order involving a large measure of what Benjamin Cohen calls 'automaticity' is to be realised.[17] In the 1990s the scope for American initiatives will be constrained by the burden of servicing a debt of nearly a trillion dollars.[18] In consequence, the USA will have greater need of international private and governmental support, while its deficits are being corrected. The successors to the Baker Initiatives may come from a more self-confident and internationalist Japan. They are less likely to come for the European Community, so long as it is caught up in the struggle for more economic and political integration.

POSTSCRIPT

We have seen how the USA not only took the Baker Initiatives, but also how James Baker acted in 1987 to undermine the Louvre Agreement so as to get a further devaluation of the dollar. Given the size of the American trade deficit, this American 'power play' came to be seen as necessary for long-term balance of payments adjustment by the other G5 countries. Ironically, in the summer of 1988, the West German Bundesbank, aided by other European central banks, was active in selling dollars, so as to check a strong *upward* movement in the dollar. The strength of the dollar owed something to suspicions that James Baker would not act to halt this rise. Foreign exchange market operators thought that Baker favoured a strong dollar in the run-up to the American Presidential election in November 1988, so that inflation and growth figures would help his old friend, Vice-President George Bush, to win the election against Michael Dukakis, as indeed they did, since Bush ran on a platform stressing the Republicans' economic successes and as the party of peace. This episode illustrated the short-term character of 'rational expectations' and how highly political is the question of the level of exchange rates. As it turned out, the speculators underestimated how strong the European reaction would be. The Japanese government did not rush to sell dollars. It was thought that they (like Baker) were anxious to assist a Bush victory. The reason for this was that they feared that a Dukakis triumph would result in more protection against their exports, a fear which began to materialise in Dukakis' speeches in the last weeks of the campaign.[19] Hence, while Baker may have done much in 1985–7 to promote a longer-term, co-ordinated approach, his party and personal allegiances may have worked to favour 'short-termism' in 1988. Politics is a complicated and contradictory business, not least since elections are not synchronised between the leading capitalist countries. Even if the long-term desirability of international policy co-ordination were generally accepted, short-term political factors might hinder agreement.

Another cautionary note from this saga derives from the widespread disagreements between economists (including American ones) as to how low a dollar was needed for long-term adjustment. Estimates varied between 100 and 185 yen to the dollar.[20] Such differences are symptomatic of both the lack of theoretical consensus within macro-economics, and of the complex and changing nature of the global political economy. As a result, as Richard Cooper has argued, international macro-economic co-operation will continue to be unsettled and imperfect even if awareness of policy interdependence increases.[21] In practice, domestic political pressures have sometimes impeded the growth of such an awareness. For example, the American Presidential candidates in 1988 were wary of opening up debate on the twin deficits, recalling the heavy defeat of Walter Mondale by Reagan in 1984. The Baker Initiatives derived from a shift at the top, rather than from a major change in public attitudes, understanding and priorities.

NOTES

I would like to thank Stephen Gill for his suggestions, comments and editorial work on drafts of this chapter.

1. This scenario has been stressed by Robert Gilpin in *The Political Economy of International Relations* (Princeton NJ, Princeton University Press, 1987).
2. See Robert O. Keohane, 'The World Political Economy and the Crisis of Embedded Liberalism', in John Goldthorpe (ed.) *Order and Conflict in Contemporary Capitalism* (Oxford, Oxford University Press, 1984), p. 35.
3. See IMF, *World Economic Outlook* (Washington DC, IMF, 1985), Table 30, p. 239.

4. *Ibid.*
5. See Henry Nau, 'Where Reaganomics Works', *Foreign Policy,* winter 1984–5, no. 57, pp. 14–37.
6. See R. Dornbusch, 'Flexible Exchange Rates and Excess Capital Mobility', *Brookings Economic Papers* (Washington DC, Brookings Institution, 1986), pp. 209–35.
7. Cited by Richard N. Cooper, 'Dealing with the Trade Deficit in a Floating Rate System', *Brookings Economic Papers* (Washington DC, Brookings Institution, 1986), p. 196.
8. See P. Korner *et al., The IMF and the Debt Crisis* (London, Zed Books, 1986).
9. Philip Stevens, 'Private Smiles, Public Unease', *Financial Times,* 22 September 1987.
10. Cited by P. Craig Roberts, 'Europe's Dangerous Obsession', *Financial Times,* 11 November 1987.
11. See *The Amex Bank Review* (1988), vol. 15, no. 5, pp. 1–2.
12. Stevens, *op. cit.*
13. Cited in 'Unmiraculous West Germany', *Financial Times,* 20 July 1987.
14. John Gerard Ruggie, 'International Regimes, Transactions and Change: Embedded Liberalism in the Post-War Economic Order', *International Organisation* (1982), vol. 36, pp. 379–415.
15. Gilpin, *op. cit.*
16. Susan Strange, 'Politics, Trade and Money', in L. Tsoukalis (ed.) *Europe, America and the World Economy* (Oxford, Blackwell, 1986).
17. Benjamin Cohen, *Organising the World's Money: The Political Economy of International Monetary Relations* (London, Macmillan, 1978). In principle the nineteenth century Gold Standard was an automatic system of balance of payments adjustment. For a discussion of this, in the context of other types of international monetary order, see Stephen Gill and David Law, *The Global Political Economy: Perspectives, Problems and Policies* (Hemel Hempstead and Baltimore, Harvester Wheatsheaf/Johns Hopkins University Press, 1988), pp. 165–74.
18. *South,* July 1988, p. 15.
19. See Irwin Stelzer, 'Traders try to make sense of the rise in the dollar', *Sunday Times,* 10 July 1988.
20. *Ibid.*
21. Richard N. Cooper, 'International Economic Co-operation: Is it Desirable? Is it Likely?' *Bulletin of the American Academy of Arts and Sciences* (1985), vol. 39, pp. 11–35.

8 · STRATEGIC ASPECTS OF ATLANTIC RELATIONS IN THE REAGAN ERA

Steve Smith

As the Reagan era drew to its close there is an evident paradox about the state of the Atlantic Alliance: for most of the Reagan years NATO has been involved in one short-term crisis after another, from Cruise/Pershing II deployment via the impact of President Reagan's Strategic Defense Initiative (SDI) to the prospects of a Europe without intermediate-range nuclear missiles (INF). In addition there were the questions of widely differing US–European perceptions of the Soviet 'threat', the move towards raising the nuclear threshold in NATO's strategy, the attempt to redefine Flexible Response via notions of Air–Land Battle and Deep Strike, and the prospect in Europe of the electoral victory of parties with very different defence policies than those that have been commonplace since the birth of the Alliance. Yet, despite these problems and challenges, the Alliance had survived, and in many ways looked a lot stronger than it did in the early 1980s or the late 1970s. The paradox, then, is that the challenges seem to have been successfully met, resulting in a more stable NATO. However, this chapter is concerned with the future of US–European relations within NATO and the main theme I want to advance is that there are in fact very serious problems that the Alliance will face in the remainder of this century: many of these are structural, and reflect the simple geographical fact that the USA is only part of Europe by reason of alliance; others, though, may be traced to the policies of the Reagan Administration. There is a clear inter-relationship between the structural and the historically specific factors, and together they result in a rather serious threat to the long-term stability of the Alliance.

In a crucial sense, NATO has always reflected the essentially bipolar nature of the international strategic system: whatever the public statements, and whatever the dreams or aspirations of European leaders, the Alliance has always been based on American hegemony amongst the Western powers. It was that hegemony that enabled, or required, past differences and tensions between the European members of the Alliance to be resolved or relaxed; and it was that hegemony that provided the strategic mechanism whereby consensus between European governments could be achieved for almost 40 years following the founding of the Alliance. At the end of the day, NATO hangs together because the USSR perceives a linkage between the defence of Europe and American strategic systems; note that I write that NATO hangs together because of a *Soviet* perception – the reason is central to the theme of this chapter: it is because European governments require much more explicit indicators of this linkage than seems to be required by the Soviets. Of course, this in turn takes us into the notoriously difficult area of imputing intentions to Soviet behaviour in Europe. The point, though, is simply that the geographical facts of the US–European relationship have posed an ongoing problem for NATO, that is how to keep all Alliance members happy that the guarantees offered by the US to come to the defence of Europe will be met. It is the intersection between this structural problem and the policies of the Reagan Administration which is the focus of this chapter.

The problem can be stated simply: on the one hand the geography of an alliance split by an ocean creates a worry amongst the European governments that the linkage between the two parts of the Alliance is not sufficiently strong to prevent an attempt by the Soviets to exploit it. The scenario is a well-known one, and involves a Soviet invasion of western Europe using conventional forces: in the face of this an American president decides not to use nuclear systems to stop the attack for fear of retaliation on American territory. No-one – or certainly only a very few – imagines such an incident as likely, but it is important to note that the real worry is of the *political* consequences of such a doubt, both within the Alliance and between NATO and the Warsaw Treaty Organisation (WTO). The problem, then, is not the actual threat of attack, but the impact on NATO's resolve, as well as the resolve of its member countries, in the face of crises in all parts of the world. Accordingly, the fact that very few think that the Soviets are even contemplating such an attack is really not the issue at all: linkage is crucial to the Alliance because it is through linkage that the range of Soviet leverage (from influence via pressure through to blackmail and actual invasion) is held in check. The actual linkage that exists after a Soviet action is irrelevant if the action is what you wish to prevent: this, of course, is the commonplace world of deterrence.

To achieve this linkage a number of measures are utilised, ranging from legal obligations (such as Article V of the North Atlantic Treaty) through political statements to the deployment of American military personnel and weapons systems in Europe. Of these, the latter is by far and away the most important, and we will return to the future of the American military commitment to Europe later on. In fact, many observers and political activists misunderstand the role of these military symbols of linkage, examining them within primarily a military framework. Discussion therefore turns on the range of certain American INF systems or the kind of targets they can hit. However, the critical role of these symbols is political, in that they indicate the commitment of the USA to the defence of Europe, and carry the clear implication that if war did occur then American forces would soon become engaged, thereby involving the threat of escalation up to the strategic nuclear level. Military systems and personnel are therefore crucial because they serve as an unmistakeable link between what happens in Europe and the American strategic nuclear arsenal. Their targets and roles are less important than their political significance.

But if one problem for NATO involves trying to strengthen the link between the American strategic nuclear arsenal and the defence of Europe, the other main one results from a form of reverse linkage. One result of the Reagan Administration has been to remind Europeans that linkages go both ways, and whilst in an era of detente this may not be particularly worrying, a period of renewed Cold War links the Europeans to the hegemonic power within the Alliance in a way that worries large sections of European public opinion. The Reagan era has seen a very wide gap emerging between American and European views of the Soviet threat, and this has led some in Europe to drift towards a 'moral equivalence' view of the superpowers and many to be concerned that the Reagan Administration might utilise NATO to further its political campaigning against the 'evil empire'. Now, there have indeed always been differences between American and many European definitions of the Soviet threat (as well as a whole variety of European views at any given time), but these differences have been more marked during the Reagan era than at any other time in NATO's history. Not only does such a difference result in diverging views of how to deal with the USSR (and in this sense it is a 'neighbour' to the European members of NATO, in a way that it is not to North American members) but more saliently it leads to the European fear of being dragged into an American political (even military) crusade against the USSR. Such a crusade involves risks, and in this light the very systems (Cruise/Pershing II) that were installed to calm the fears of some European leaders, as the linkage between the USA and Europe loosened, became symbols of a desired or intended American campaign to achieve military superiority. Incautious statements by senior members of the Reagan Administration as to the possibility of fighting a limited nuclear war in Europe served only to worry both those Europeans who were concerned that NATO might be used to put pressure on the Soviets and those who wanted Cruise and Pershing II in the first place precisely in order to prevent any notions that nuclear war could be limited to Europe. It is for this reason, the concurrent surfacing of both these aspects of NATO's security dilemma, that the Reagan years are distinct. And it is in this light that, as the Reagan years draw to a close, the Alliance looks on the verge of the most potentially destabilising period in its history.

Before turning to examine what can be termed the 'Reagan shocks', it is helpful to say a little about the pre-Reagan years. Why was consensus within and between NATO member countries so relatively easy to achieve then? There seem to be four main reasons: first, the strategic situation was, from NATO's inception until the late 1970s, very much in NATO's favour. It was only towards the very end of the 1950s that the USSR could attack the American homeland with nuclear forces, and until the mid-1960s Soviet strategic forces were very small in number. Even when rough numerical strategic parity was achieved in the mid-1970s, the USA continued (and still continues) to lead in virtually all measures of strategic capability. Such a lopsided strategic bipolarity was very conducive to the requirements for extended deterrence. The USA was in a position of hegemony within NATO, and was on any count the superior nuclear power. Note that this made NATO's strategy relatively easy to maintain despite Soviet conventional superiority: the reason, of course, is that NATO's strategy was always based upon the dual threat of the *first use* of nuclear weapons and the escalation of conventional conflict to strategic nuclear war.[1] Even when American numerical nuclear superiority began to be eroded, it remained the case that NATO's threat to escalate conventional conflict to strategic nuclear war had considerable credibility. American nuclear capabilities provided the backdrop for extended deterrence, and NATO, based as it was on exactly such a linkage between conventional and nuclear systems, seemed to have no worries in maintaining internal consensus on the adequacy and credibility of its strategic posture.

Yet, the strategic situation has to be seen in the light of a second factor, the wider political climate. Crucially, the years of the Cold War (which we can classify as occurring roughly from 1947 to the mid-1960s) were the years of overwhelming American superiority, if not monopoly. So, when US–Soviet relations were bad, it happened to be the case that the USA had a very clear margin of superiority. It is irrelevant that this superiority has no real meaning in a military sense, since once assured destruction is achieved there is little strategic importance in increasing levels of destructive capability. It is rather that perceptions of American superiority made the process of achieving consensus within NATO all the easier. It matters not a jot that strategic superiority may be meaningless if war occurs; it is, however, crucial to the attainment of Alliance consensus that American nuclear superiority makes the task of offering extended deterrence guarantees rather easier than in a period of essential equivalence. What deters the Soviets is not the issue (they may well not need deterring at all); what is critical is how credible American guarantees look to those whose security is being guaranteed. In this light, American superiority made the guarantees seem credible. When this numerical superiority was eroded, the reason why there was not a massive crisis in the Alliance was simply because the political climate (as a result?) had improved. Whatever detente meant to the Soviets or to the USA it did signal a sea-change in East–West relations to many European governments: indeed, several of these (in the UK, France and West Germany) had played an important role in developing better relations with the Soviets. Viewed on a superpower level, detente may have concentrated on arms agreements, such as SALT I and SALT II; viewed from Europe, it resulted in a considerable number of agreements that seemed to lessen East–West tension in Europe (the Four Power Agreement on Berlin, Ostpolitik and the CSCE are clear examples). For many Europeans, detente was a process, one that lowered the possibility of war between NATO and the WTO. In such a political climate, the decline of American numerical strategic superiority was not a major cause for concern.

A third reason for consensus within NATO resulted from the combination of the first two, and this was the nature of NATO's strategic doctrine during these years. Following the failure of NATO countries to meet the Lisbon Force Goals (set down in 1952), which were an attempt to match Soviet conventional forces, NATO's strategy soon evolved into one of sheltering behind the American declaratory policy of massive retaliation (and this became enshrined in NATO's guidance on strategy, MC 14/2, in 1957). In an era of effective American nuclear monopoly this was relatively straightforward: there was no need to match Soviet conventional force levels if deterrence could be maintained by the threat of massive retaliation to any Soviet conventional advance. The loss of American nuclear monopoly provoked a widespread rethink in the Alliance at the same time as the lack of American support for the British and French action in Suez led to concerns as to the reliability of American support for European interests. Together these factors led to American attempts to reassure Europeans of their commitment and, although there were problems associated with these attempts (especially the American proposals for a multilateral force (MLF) and for the placing of Thor and Jupiter missiles in Europe), they eventually led to NATO's acceptance of a new guidance on strategy, MC14/3, adopted in 1967.[2] MC14/3 is based upon the American strategic posture of Flexible Response, and central to it is the linkage between conventional and nuclear forces. In military terms, this was to be achieved by the presence of over 7,000 American nuclear warheads in Europe. But the most important point about MC14/3 is that it was deliberately ambiguous over the crucial issue: under what circumstances would NATO go nuclear?

The answer to this question depends upon whom you ask: for an American leader the answer, removed of all the necessary qualifications about flexibility, must surely be that the resort to nuclear systems, certainly strategic nuclear systems, should come as late as possible. For European leaders, the opposite would be argued. Certainly for those in West Germany, the concern was to avoid *any* conflict, not just nuclear ones, and so Flexible Response became caught up with notions of Forward Defence, with conventional forces essentially serving the function of being a tripwire. Now, again it is worth remembering that the issue is not what would happen if conflict occurred, nor what the Soviets believe, but rather what the members of the Alliance believe: critically, are their beliefs compatible? The great advantage of Flexible Response is that it allows very different ideas of how to respond to a Soviet attack to coexist. It is essentially ambiguous, and therefore was ideal for dealing with the structural dilemma of the Alliance. The USA could maintain that what flexible meant was that the USA could exhaust the other rungs of the ladder of escalation before turning to nuclear systems, thereby implying that the resulting cease-fire might lead to a different division of territory between East and West, as the ultimate threat of nuclear usage would seem to be consistent with halting an advance. For the Europeans, especially the West Germans, what Flexible Response meant was that a variety of systems would be used to make Forward Defence credible. Precisely because of its ambiguity, MC14/3 could allow everyone to define the strategy in a way that suited them. In short, consensus could be maintained within the Alliance because declaratory strategy was vague; Flexible Response was a good way to manage the Alliance.

A final reason why consensus was possible shifts the level of analysis a little. The first three reasons have to do with intergovernmental consensus, and it is an interesting reflection of the silences of international relations theory and strategic studies that the people of the countries concerned only enter into the discussion at this stage. The point, however, is simply that for all intents and purposes, defence, and certainly NATO, was not a major political issue within the countries of NATO throughout this period. On those occasions when defence intruded into political debate, it was either met with a cross-party divide or had an essentially bipartisan nature. Of course there are exceptions, but it is generally the case that defence was not a contentious political issue within the members of the Alliance. This meant that fundamentally problematic issues, such as those concerned with defining NATO's strategy, never had to be exposed to public scrutiny: they were rarely major issues *within* governments. Thus, it was not difficult to remove defence and NATO issues from the hurly-burly of political debate, and governments were therefore given virtually a free hand in their determination of policy towards the Alliance.

The combination of these four factors meant that it was not difficult to obtain consensus within and between the members of the Alliance. The events since the late 1970s have told a different story. There are many aspects of the problems facing the Alliance in the last few years, but it is evident that each of the four factors that made for consensus changed, and together these constitute the backdrop for the currrent dilemmas facing the Alliance. The strategic situation changed during the 1970s, so that although essential equivalence may well have been the reality, there were significant groups in the USA and Europe (and probably in the USSR as well) who saw American power waning. Not that this was concerned solely with the nuclear balance, where the USA in fact maintained a technical superiority; rather it was the numerical growth of Soviet nuclear forces combined with a loss of political resolve in the USA that led to claims about Soviet superiority. This caused major problems for those Europeans who were concerned with the possible political consequences of doubts over the credibility of American extended deterrence guarantees.This was especially so given the desire of successive American administrations in the 1970s for arms control agreements with the Soviets: these were widely seen in Europe as threatening to freeze superpower strategic arsenals, yet doing nothing to counter a Soviet strategic European advantage: again, extended deterrence looked less credible.

Combined with this change in the strategic situation was the nature of political relationships between the superpowers. As the 1970s drew to a close it was clear that detente was in very serious trouble, and the Soviet invasion of Afghanistan was simply the last nail in its coffin. International tension seemed to be increasing and this resulted in a heightened concern within European countries both of the dangers of linkage to the USA and of the instabilities introduced into East–West relations by the series of crises that marked the decline of detente. As a result of the changing political and strategic situation, NATO began to re-examine its strategic doctrine: partly, this was a response to a perceived need to modernise NATO's INF; partly, it reflected Soviet modernisation of its own INF (in the shape of the SS20); crucially, though, the whole INF issue reflected the political concern of several key European politicians, a concern to strengthen linkage. There were other efforts to modernise and strengthen NATO forces (notably the issue of deploying the neutron bomb, and the 3 per cent growth in defence expenditure commitment), but none had the effect of the INF issue; because it forced the Alliance to discuss the military role of the systems, it did what NATO had avoided doing for many years – it required a re-examination and a clarification of what Flexible Response actually meant. Finally, the attempt to modernise NATO's INF occurred at a juncture when the political situation between the superpowers was deteriorating and, by choosing to justify Cruise/Pershing II deployment by reference to the Soviet's deployment of the SS20, the issue became politicised in a way that had never previously been the case. The INF issue saw the final breakdown of the consensus on defence that had existed within most European countries.

By the late 1970s, then, all four factors that had until then encouraged consensus within the Alliance were undergoing change. It would be pointlessly mechanistic to argue for a specific set of causal relationships, since what is important for the argument of this chapter is that these four factors, the strategic situation, the political climate, NATO's strategy, and the domestic setting, were inter-related in such a way that the ramifying changes amongst them exacerbated the structural tensions inherent in the Alliance. In all of this, the underlying problem remained that of how to keep in balance the dual pressures of ensuring linkage so as to satisfy European leaders, without worrying the European public about the possibility of a nuclear war starting in Europe. Such are the inherent problems of deterrence theory, and it was exactly the weapons that were seen by European leaders as crucial symbols of linkage that were seen by large sections of European public opinion as raising the spectre of nuclear war. Such a structural problem was not the fault of any American or European administration, nor of a specific set of policies; rather it was endemic in the nature of extended deterrence. Even the Carter Administration, despite its essentially close ties with Europe (through, for example, the Trilateral Commission), had a very serious problem in reassuring European leaders that the American commitment was firm. That successive attempts to achieve this during 1977–79 led to European leaders seeing Carter as a weak leader, and American resolve as declining, indicates the potential for serious problems for the Alliance arising out of geopolitics. In this period, after all, what was feared was a *loss* of American military hegemony, a lack of American leadership in the Alliance. The ultimate remedy to the issue of linkage was, of course, the INF deployment decision anounced by NATO on 12 December 1979, and it was the manner in which this was justified (by reference to the SS20) and the technical characteristics of the systems to be deployed (which were deliberately chosen since their basing mode – on land – was considered to be a more visible sign of American commitment than deploying the systems at sea) that finally led to a break in the public consensus on NATO issues. The lesson of the late 1970s is surely that structural factors make it problematic to achieve intergovernmental consensus at the same time as achieving consensus within member countries if the *status quo* is disturbed. In fact, it may well be the case that the nature of any disturbance to the *status quo* is less important than the rate of change involved, since too great a pace of change makes it progressively more difficult to maintain intergovernmental and intrasocietal consensus. Indeed, the very factors that make the one easier to achieve seem to make the other more difficult to achieve.

Such a conclusion about the nature of pre-Reagan consensus should come as no surprise to those who see the foreign and defence policies of states as adaptive mechanisms, with these policies having the critical characteristic of being formulated in one environment yet implemented in another. But, if the combination of the geopolitical structure of the Alliance and the nature of the intergovernmental and intrasocietal consensus lay at the heart of the problems of the Alliance in the late 1970s, it is now appropriate to consider the Reagan era, to see the effect of the policies of that administration on the underlying structural tensions within the Alliance. If the problems inherent in achieving consensus within an alliance which is both geographically split and is hierarchically organised (in contrast to the nature of alliances in previous international systems) are difficult to resolve anyway, what has been the impact of the Reagan Administration on an already problematic US–European relationship?

My argument is that the Reagan years have witnessed a set of awkward issues being discussed by NATO, issues that have not led to obvious crises within the Alliance, but issues that, nevertheless, threaten long-term consensus both within member countries and between them. This is not so much because the policies pursued by the Reagan Administration are wildly at variance with the concerns of European leaders (although some certainly are), but more because they have either or both of two characteristics: either they threaten the key linkage between American strategic forces and Europe or they envisage quite rapid change in the European strategic environment. Before discussing them, it is important to note that in many cases these problems are not simply caused by the policies of the Reagan Administration but are rather the result of American *and* European actions. It would be a typical act of European myopia to claim that everything is the fault of the current American administration – a popular ploy for many European politicians and activists – when in reality the European governments are capable of introducing enough shocks of their own (think, for example, of the potential impact on the Alliance had the British Labour Party won the 1987 election). And in all candour we should note that all European leaders have a history of complaining in turn about a lack of American leadership and then about American dominance in NATO. So when I write of the 'Reagan shocks', I mean the issues that have arisen during the years of the Reagan Administration. Essentially, there are six issues that NATO had to grapple with during the Reagan era: none proved in itself to be impossible for the Alliance to deal with, but together these factors created, and will continue to create, a fundamentally problematic agenda for the Alliance in the remainder of this century. These 'Reagan shocks' will be addressed starting with the most general and moving to the more specific.

THE RISE OF A SECOND COLD WAR

It would be grossly misleading to claim that the Reagan Administration was responsible for the decline of detente and the rise of a second Cold War (although one must note that many public opinion polls revealed that in western Europe a large section of the general public saw the Reagan Administration as either the main or the joint cause of the downturn in US–Soviet relations). Not only did the decline of detente have something to do with Soviet foreign policy behaviour, especially in the Third World, but it is also clear that detente was in very serious trouble by the mid-1970s; some see it as in decline as early as the 1973 Yom Kippur war. But whilst the Soviets did try to exploit both their own attainment of strategic parity and the loss of political will in the USA, and although it was President Carter who began the counter attack in terms of increasing defence expenditure and in his response to Soviet activities in the Ogaden and in Afghanistan, the Reagan years saw a qualitative change in US–Soviet relations.

There were two main aspects of this: first, the Reagan Administration had a rather different view of the Soviet threat than had either its immediate predecessor or most European governments. Put simply, the Reagan Administration, certainly during its first term of office, assessed and portrayed the Soviet threat in a far more extreme light than was the view on the European side of the Atlantic. The USSR was an empire with an aggressive (and co-ordinated) foreign policy, essentially and irretrievably expansionist, with an ideologically informed world view that saw an inevitable triumph of the Soviet system. Furthermore, this was reflected in a commitment to defence that was almost double (in percentage of GNP) that of the USA, a nuclear strategy that emphasised victory, and a superiority in nuclear forces such that American ICBMs were vulnerable to a disarming first strike.[3] It is not important that these were massively exaggerated claims; what is critical is that such an assessment of the Soviet threat was bound to cause tension with the European members of the Alliance, whose governments tended to have a rather different view. European governments may well have accepted elements of the Reagan Administration's assessment, but this was always tempered by a realisation that Western Europe had no alternative but to try and work with the Soviets to reach some kind of accommodation in Europe.

The second aspect of the first Reagan Administration's approach to US–Soviet relations was a very marked change in the tone of American statements. A war of words was unleashed, and although some of the more intemperate statements by members of the Reagan Administration could be seen as being more to do with domestic than international politics, it is nonetheless clear that the war of words did lead to a considerable chilling in US–Soviet relations.[4] This is because the constant themes were that the USSR was not a legitimate superpower, that it would break agreements it signed, that it would seek to impose its will on other countries and that it was domestically illegitimate. Members of the Administration spoke openly of undermining Soviet control of eastern Europe as well as of the republics of the USSR itself. This confrontationalist logic may well have been restricted to words (thereby changing the infamous comment that the USA should 'talk softly and carry a big stick' to 'talk stickly and carry a big soft'!), but these words caused considerable worry in European countries (as well as, no doubt, in the USSR). The attack on Soviet legitimacy combined with the Reagan Administration's assessment of the Soviet threat lead to a division between the USA and the European members of the Alliance: even conservatives such as British Prime Minister Margaret Thatcher did not go as far as did President Reagan in criticising the USSR. Later, of course, the harsh rhetoric was mollified.

THE RESURGENCE OF AMERICAN POWER

Related to the emergence of a second Cold War and the assessment of the Soviet threat accepted by the Reagan Administration was a much more confrontationalist American foreign and defence policy. The Reagan Administration, having identified the nature of the threat facing American interests, advanced a much more bipolar view of the world than its immediate predecessors. Whereas President Carter stressed the essentially problematic, multicausal nature of world events, with change occurring for predominantly domestic and social reasons, and with military power being of lower utility in managing the inherent complexity of world politics, President Reagan instead stressed a very simple view of the world problems. Behind the unrest, in Nicaragua or Libya, was the USSR; not only were world problems relatively clear-cut but also the cause of the major threats to American interests was the USSR. Managing this environment simply needed more power, especially military power. The decline of American influence in the 1970s had largely resulted from a decline in American power *vis-à-vis* the USSR.

As a result of this change of world view, the Reagan Administration attempted to restore American power and to reassert American interests in all parts of the world. The American leadership viewed the world through bipolar glasses, and became concerned to be able to project American power in any theatre of the world in which Soviet influence seemed to be spreading. This led to a set of actions in Central America and the Middle East that caused serious problems for the Europeans. Whilst NATO could not become involved as an organisation in out-of-area operations, the individual countries felt considerable pressure to support American actions in the Lebanon, Grenada, Libya and the Gulf. When such suppport was not forthcoming, the result was tension in US–European relations; when it did come from governments it led to sizeable public opposition within European countries. To the extent that the USA adopts a more bipolar view of the world and assumes a hegemonic position within the Alliance, it becomes more difficult for intergovernmental and intrasocietal consensus on defence to be maintained; reverse linkage rears its head.

THE DECLINE OF ARMS CONTROL AND THE ARMS BUILD-UP

The Reagan Administration came to power with an explicit mandate to rebuild American military strength. Indeed, although the crucial shifts in arms expenditure occurred in the last two years of the Carter Administration, Reagan's arms build-up in the early 1980s was unprecedented in peacetime. This came to symbolise the second Cold War. Not only did the Reagan Administration increase the defence budget in real terms by about 7 per cent a year, but decisions were made to introduce a whole new range of strategic systems. When combined with the drift in American nuclear strategy from a policy of countervailing (as in Carter's PD 59) to one of prevailing (as was rumoured to be contained in the classified NSDD13), this led to exaggerated claims that the USA was planning to achieve a nuclear war-winning capability. This became a common image in Europe, and like many common images it was seriously misleading. The USA has not achieved a pre-emptive nuclear capability, nor will it do so in the medium-term future; it simply does not have the force structure for such a posture. What the USA has been developing, however, is a capability to fight through a nuclear war. The problem, of course, is that the kinds of technologies needed for such a capability are exactly those needed (albeit in different proportions) for launching a strategic attack. Again, the intentions are secondary; what is central is how this arms build-up and shift in nuclear strategy were seen in Europe and in the USSR.

The other side of this particular coin was that the Reagan Administration was essentially uninterested in arms control. This is a bald statement, especially when the USA did make a number of proposals to the START and Geneva talks on strategic arms. However, a detailed evaluation of these proposals,[5] as well as analyses of the internal debates within the American arms control community,[6] supports the conclusion that the Reagan Administration never wanted a strategic arms agreement unless it was on terms that no Soviet leader could (or should) accept. At the START talks, American efforts were concentrated on making the Soviets cut back their SS18 force, at the same time as allowing unlimited cruise missiles (in which the USA had a clear lead); at Geneva, from the start of the talks onwards, the USA refused to link agreement on strategic forces to agreement on defensive systems and, although the two sides had roughly similar numerical proposals, they disagreed again over the size of the Soviet ICBM force. The real role of strategic arms control talks during the Reagan Administration seems to have been to protect the American modernisation of its strategic forces; this is certainly how the MX missile continued to survive. The Reagan Administration had never really wanted an agreement to limit strategic systems, as the breakdown of the summit at Reykjavik in October 1986 indicated. The reason for this is simply that the key decision-makers in the Administration felt that arms control had harmed American interests during the 1970s. The result of such a view, which prefers managing the strategic relationship with the Soviets by arms build-up rather than by arms control, was seen in the Administration's violation of the SALT II Treaty in December 1986 and by its attempt to move towards a completely unprecedented interpretation of the ABM Treaty from October 1985 onwards.

The Reagan Administration's attitude to arms control and its preferred alternative of building up strategic systems stands in marked contrast to the preferences of virtually every European government. Indeed leaders such as Chancellor Kohl and Mrs Margaret Thatcher were open in their attempts to push President Reagan towards an arms control agreement with the Soviets and in reversing the trend of undermining those arms control agreements that existed. This issue was not particularly problematic within NATO because the talks and agreements concerned were bilateral US–Soviet ones, but it nonetheless led to considerable protest within European countries. The Reagan Administration's position on arms control, combined with the reassertion of its military power into many regions of the world, led to an attitude in European public opinion that American hawks have characterised as 'moral equivalence'. According to such a view, both superpowers are as bad as each other, there being little difference in their activities despite the rather different justifications given. The coming to power of Secretary, later President, Gorbachev saw the public relations battle begin to shift against the USA in this regard, with the low point of America's popularity in Europe being reached after the American raid on Libya in April 1986.

THE STRATEGIC DEFENSE INITIATIVE

President Reagan's speech launching SDI, on 23 March 1983, came as a shock to European leaders: only a very small group of advisers in Washington knew about SDI. Nonetheless, this issue caused a major problem for the Alliance, although it must be noted that the problem was one that led to opposite conclusions. For some, SDI symbolised American concern to defend itself, making alliances unnecessary. For adherents to this view, SDI represented a decidedly unilateralist strand in American defence policy and, accordingly, the European theatre seemed less important for the USA since it could defend itself without entangling (and costly) alliances. SDI therefore threatened to lessen the American commitment to Europe; the USA did not need Europe for its defence. The opposite position saw SDI as making Europe much less stable since the USA could use Europe as an arena to pressurise the USSR without fearing a response on its own territory; to many in the European peace movements, SDI therefore was related to an American desire to use a defensive capability to further the undermining of Soviet control. Both of these reactions were admittedly simplistic, but each found many supporters in the period after the speech.

There is no need to review the complex technical background or history of SDI as there are already many good summaries available.[7] However, it is useful to note that SDI conceived in the USA by the time of President Bush's inauguration was a very different animal than was originally portrayed after Reagan's speech; it was also likely to have strategic consequences far removed from those assumed by the two European reactions cited above. This is because it is now abundantly clear that SDI will not radically alter the US–Soviet strategic relationship; it will not be able to offer a defensive shield for the USA, let alone for its allies as well. Yet, of course, this is the public image of SDI – space-based, directed-energy weapons providing a kind of 'Star Wars' defensive astrodome. President Reagan's original proposal was for American scientists to provide the means to render Soviet nuclear weapons 'impotent and obsolete', that is to say that the goal was to replace (as distinct from enhance) deterrence; moreover, this capability was to be extended so as to cover American allies.

Virtually no-one accepted this view of SDI; even those working in the Strategic Defense Initiative Organisation (SDIO) in Washington were not optimistic about the possibility of achieving area defence. By the autumn of 1987 the SDI debate had moved through a number of phases: an initial one claiming that the hardware would not work;[8] then a debate over the software problems;[9] finally a discussion of the virtues of early deployment.[10] We do not need to evaluate these debates in order to be able to hint at the likely nature of any SDI that might be deployed early. Such a defensive system would, in contrast with almost all the public imagery associated with SDI, consist primarily of a set of ground-based kinetic energy systems. Whereas the popular image of SDI involves space-based directed-energy weapons, the current budgetary trends indicate that these types of systems are being massively downgraded within the SDI research proposal. Certainly the kinds of system discussed by Pentagon officials as suitable for early deployment (Space-Based Kinetic Kill Vehicles – SBKKVs – Exoatmospheric Reentry Vehicle Interception System – ERIS – and the High Endoatmospheric Defense Interceptor – HEDI) are kinetic energy systems; of these only the SBKKVs are to be based in space, with ERIS and HEDI being ground-based. The role for directed energy technologies will be that of discriminating decoys from warheads in the mid-course phase of the ballistic trajectory.

What is crucial about such an SDI, and we should bear in mind that it appears to be completely non-negotiable in the sense of being a bargaining chip at Geneva, is that it is likely to be very ineffective indeed, and we can certainly rule out any prospect of it being able to provide area defence for the USA. A report for Senators William Proxmire and J. Bennett Johnston, released in April 1987, concluded that such an architecture would be able to destroy no more than 16 per cent of Soviet ballistic missile warheads.[11] A study by physicists at the Lawrence Livermore National Laboratory found that at least 70 per cent of Soviet warheads would get through the defensive shield, without any Soviet attacks on the space-based components.[12] Meanwhile the American Physical Society reported in April 1987 that directed energy defences would be decades away.[13]

While such conclusions give little support to the proponents of either of the two European reactions to SDI cited previously, a number of problems remain for NATO. The most obvious of these is the effect of American deployment on arms control, on US–Soviet (and East–West) relations, on the credibility of the American guarantee to Europe and on the opportunity costs of SDI for the conventional or nuclear defence of Europe. But more important than these is the concern that the USA is drifting away from entangling alliances towards unilateral mechanisms for defence. At the strategic level, early deployment, especially if at the cost of strategic arms control, threatens to usher in a period of strategic instability as the deployment of a leaky defensive system is accompanied by a proliferation of offensive forces to swamp the other side's defences (and the American manoeuvrable warhead – MARV – is already being justified on the grounds of the need to overcome any Soviet defensive shield). At worst such a mixture of offensive and defensive forces might encourage thoughts that it might be better to attack first than to attack second; at best it is very difficult to believe that the transition towards a mixed offence-defence orientation will be managed smoothly, thereby leading to a period of considerable instability as the defensive systems are being built. One does not have to impute aggressive intentions to American or Soviet leaders to accept that such a transition phase opens up the prospect of serious misunderstandings. Given the probability that SDI will be introduced in an environment that has little arms control, then the likely result is enhanced Soviet fears of American intentions; Soviet deployment of its own defensive systems will produce exactly the same worries in the USA. Added to this is the obvious problem that SDI will cause for any space-based assets, with the result that the arms race gets extended into another dimension thereby threatening the systems of both sides that serve to provide critical communications and warning functions.

The problem that SDI has caused the European members of the Alliance is therefore rather difficult to define, because SDI is still at such an early stage of research that there is little agreement on what it will look like eventually, and with what capabilities. In the short term, European governments have been concerned to get on the SDI research bandwagon, at the same time as being worried by the technological lead that the programme might give the USA. However, there remains a very serious worry, certainly in the governments of the UK and West Germany, that SDI deployment is fraught with problems. The Europeans seemed much more concerned to retain those arms control agreements that had survived thus far than was the Reagan Administration given the considerable scepticism over the wisdom of changing the strategic environment by introducing SDI. So, whilst there has not been a uniform European reaction to SDI, let alone a US–European crisis over it, it remains the case that SDI looks like being one of the most problematic issues for the Alliance to deal with in the future. This is because it threatens to alter the predictable nature of East–West relations in Europe and introduces a cause for tension, as well as an obstacle for arms control, in US–Soviet relations, at the same time as unsettling the strategic environment. Towering over all of this is the worry that SDI must result in a reassessment of the USA's need for alliances, as well as opening up the reverse side of the European–US linkage. After all, if NATO continues despite SDI's deployment, it must worry European leaders that the relatively less well-defended European part of the Alliance is open to Soviet influence in a crisis in a way that will apply less obviously to the USA. This is to say that the Soviets might put pressure on the Europeans as a way of trying to influence the USA; if deterrence fails, where might Soviet retaliation take place? The Alliance has always needed relatively equal levels of vulnerability for the USA and the European members, and SDI makes the Europeans a little more vulnerable than the USA. Of course this is not a statement about actual vulnerability if conflict broke out, but about intra-alliance perceptions of that vulnerability. This will make consensus very difficult to achieve between governments, and within European states will raise the spectre of the dangers of being in an alliance with the USA.

AMERICAN INF IN EUROPE

The issue of American INF in Europe has been the most troublesome dispute in US–European relations during the Reagan era, and the US–Soviet INF double zero agreement represents a classic example of a public relations triumph masking a serious problem for the Alliance. The reason for the problem is relatively simple: European leaders (especially the UK and West German governments) called for American INF modernisation in the late 1970s as a way of strengthening linkage.[14] Although publicly justified by the Soviet deployment of the SS20 this was never a major reason for the deployment. Even the announcement of the decision on 12 December 1979 masked the reasons for deployment by putting arms control as the priority; if, and only if, this failed would deployment of Cruise and Pershing II go ahead. Again, this was only done for public relations reasons: deployment was needed regardless of the Soviet levels of INF. Thus, even if the Soviets had not deployed the SS20 there would have still been very strong reasons for deploying Cruise and Pershing II. This is because American INF in Europe are not there to match Soviet INF; they are there to do two things. First, to match a Soviet conventional superiority – hence NATO's reliance on nuclear weapons since its failure to reach the Lisbon Force Goals back in the mid-1950s – by the threat of first nuclear use; second, to link conflict in Europe to the American strategic nuclear arsenal. This spurious linkage between American and Soviet INF became the centrepiece of the rationale for President Reagan's 1981 proposal for a 'zero option', the logic of which was that since NATO's preferred solution was for zero INF on both sides, then there was a clear strategic relationship between American and Soviet levels of INF in Europe.

Of course, by late 1987 this zero option had become the double zero option with European leaders putting a brave face on events, claiming (erroneously) that the reasons behind the INF deployment decision had been vindicated, as if NATO took the decision to get the SS20s removed. Even the way in which the double zero emerged, as a result of Gorbachev accepting a hastily announced European objection that a zero option would leave an imbalance in short range nuclear systems, indicated a real lack of any sense of direction on this issue within Europe. The zero option was never really meant to be taken seriously, as Alexander Haig's memoirs have made clear: it was only ever proposed for propaganda purposes. But by 1987 President Reagan needed an arms control deal for domestic reasons. When the Soviets called the West's bluff on the stumbling block issue of verification, the USA had to retreat and withdraw its proposals for intrusive on-site inspection; this and the Soviet acceptance of double zero had led to an INF agreement almost by accident. This is not to deny that many European politicians are happy that levels of INF and SRINF have been reduced, but the INF episode can hardly be called a success for NATO. Not only have Alliance countries had to go through very serious internal disruptions because of the opposition to the deployments, but there has been an evident growth in dissatisfaction with the linkage with the USA. Public opinion polls show a clear trend of opposition to American nuclear bases remaining in most European countries. Furthermore, the Alliance has now agreed to remove American INF without dealing with the issue of why they were needed in the first place.

In one regard the double zero agreement can be presented as a public relations success, and it does support the claims of European governments that they have lowered the numbers of Soviet nuclear forces facing Europe, thereby achieving something that the peace groups could not. For this reason perhaps the problems involved in getting the missiles into Europe have been worth it, but at the cost of ignoring the reasons why the deployment decision was taken in the first place. It would be naïve to accept the fears of some European politicians that the agreement leads to the denuclearisation of Europe (there are still some 4,000 American nuclear warheads in Europe), but the logic of the double zero option does extend down to a complete removal of nuclear weapons, and one can be sure that the Soviets will press this in the future. In this regard, even the victory of governments over peace groups may be rather temporary, as the double zero logic impels proposals for cuts in remaining forces. But what is really called into question by the agreement is the structural issue of how to ensure linkage. That was the driving force behind deployment, and the agreement does nothing to solve the dilemma. The Reagan Administration's wish for an INF agreement seems to have led NATO to accept a proposal it never meant to be taken seriously, the logic of which omits completely, indeed distorts, the original reasons behind the deployment. This looks like a classic case of short-term political advantages outweighing long-term concerns; the INF agreement does nothing to calm European worries about the American commitment and, when combined with American proposals to eliminate ballistic missiles (made at Reykjavik, but later dropped by President Reagan), may heighten worries that the USA is drifting away from NATO. This looks likely to be a particularly salient issue for the next decade or so.

RAISING THE NUCLEAR THRESHOLD

The final issue that has risen to prominence during the Reagan era is that of how to raise the nuclear threshold in Europe. There have been a number of proposals as to how to achieve this, ranging from calls for NATO's acceptance of a proposal for 'No First Use' (NFU) of nuclear weapons, to plans for increasing the role of conventional forces in NATO strategy, either through numbers or through relying on emerging technologies (ET) (what might be termed no early first use).[15] There have also been a number of proposals for a change in strategy, such as SACEUR's proposal for follow-on-forces-attack (FOFA) and the US Army's concept of Air-Land Battle (ALB).[16] Again, we do not need to review any of these in detail, since what is of concern in this chapter is the problems that these cause NATO. Of course, these discussions are of renewed importance given the signing of the double zero INF agreement.

Essentially, proposals to raise the nuclear threshold raise two main problems within NATO. The first is cost; nuclear weapons are relatively inexpensive when compared to conventional forces, and certainly if NATO felt it necessary to match Soviet forces troop for troop then this would involve a major increase in defence expenditure. Such a requirement is unnecessary but, even then, any proposal that increases conventional forces, either by numerical level or by quality of equipment, will involve additional expenditure, and the European members of the Alliance are very unlikely to be willing, or able, to meet that expenditure. Not only this, but to the extent that increasing the role of conventional forces involves increasing the role played by high technology (especially ET), then this equipment is basically manufactured in the USA, so that were NATO to purchase it, it would worsen the one-way nature of the two-way street. The European members of NATO have already been unable to keep up with the 3 per cent increase in defence expenditure agreed in 1977. What this does is to raise the thorny old problem of burden-sharing, with the politically explosive issue of the drain on American resources of its commitment to Europe waiting in the wings.

The second main problem is that of the commitment to forward defence. Here the difficulty is that whilst FOFA/ALB/ET and No-First-Use may make considerable sense when looking at the conflict from a European (or especially an American) perspective, such a view is not shared by West Germans. After all, the defence requirement for West Germany is to prevent conflict *per se;* it will matter whether such a conflict goes nuclear or not, and it will obviously be impossible to hold WTO forces at the border; but any conflict that occurs is going to be fought on German territory, and conventional weapons are perfectly capable of reducing that territory to a smouldering wasteland. Furthermore, FOFA and ALB actually encourage a war of manoeuvre, and this really is difficult for West German leaders to accept. For this reason any shift away from a stated willingness to use nuclear weapons first and a commitment to Forward Defence will prove especially divisive within NATO (and within West Germany itself). An example of the problems to be faced is the length of time it took to persuade the West German government to agree to the scrapping of its 72 Pershing 1As.

When the issue of how to raise the nuclear threshold is combined with the agreement to remove American INF it becomes clear that the underlying concern for European leaders will be that of the reliability of the American commitment to Europe. For, if American INF are removed at the same time as NATO has to increase its conventional forces, can the Europeans rely on the USA to increase its commitment to the defence of Europe, especially given the pressure on the defence budget as a result of the American budget deficit?

CONCLUSION

These events during the Reagan era have, as was noted earlier, caused problems for NATO for two main reasons: they either involve too great a pace of change, thereby threatening the tenuous consensus that exists within and between NATO countries over defence issues; or they appear to undermine the linkage between the defence of Europe and the American strategic nuclear arsenal. Underlying these contemporary problems is the structural *problématique* discussed at the beginning of this chapter, and this is a structural factor that is inherent in the nature of the NATO Alliance. What we may be witnessing is a historical coincidence, whereby the problems faced by NATO during the Reagan years compound the structural tensions within the Alliance because the resolution of the problems requires an explicit discussion of precisely those ambiguous mechanisms whereby consensus was maintained until then.

The structural *problématique* has historically resulted in at least three features that the events of the Reagan years have brought into the open. First, European leaders have always tended to rely on an uninterested, and essentially bipartisan, domestic environment, one that enables those leaders to say one thing in public and another in private. This was reflected in calls for arms control in public, with plans for modernisation continuing in private. The Cruise/Pershing II *débâcle* brought this ambiguity into the open. Eventually, European leaders were hoist by their own petard and had to accept their own public rationale for deployment, although that was, as has been pointed out above, definitely not the reason for the original decision. Second, what makes European leaders happy tends to worry the European public. Historically, European leaders felt secure in the knowledge that the American nuclear guarantee to Europe meant first use of nuclear systems by NATO; it was this guarantee that cemented linkage and (so the argument went) deterred the Soviets. Yet when this was brought into the open, as it was by the INF modernisation decision, the logic of it being in the USA's interests to keep the war limited to Europe led to enormous public disquiet. The point is that this was never a problem for European leaders because their concern had to be with the credibility of deterrence, not with the nature of any conflict that would result if it failed. Also, the American commitment was designed to influence Soviet perceptions, and thereby their decisions on whether to commence hostility, rather than make European people feel secure if that policy failed. Finally, European leaders have always wanted American leadership of the Alliance, but not American dominance. Leadership from Washington strengthened the commitment to Europe in the eyes of the European leaders, yet dominance by Washington worried them at the same time as reminding European people of the dangers of reverse linkage. Thus, European leaders were alarmed at the 'weakness' of the Carter presidency, and Europeans were worried by the 'strength' of the first few years of Reagan's leadership. Walking the line between leadership and dominance became more difficult, as the Reagan Administration's 'strength' was directed in a way that many Europeans found rather threatening.

The Reagan years have, therefore, seen the emergence of a series of issues that have opened up the structural tensions in the Alliance. Of the six described above, the rise of a second Cold War and the resurgence of American power made explicit the dangers of being in a hierarchical alliance in the nuclear age; the decline of arms control and the pursuance of SDI threatened to change dramatically the strategic environment, and in doing so make consensus in NATO difficult to maintain; and the INF deal and the attempts to raise the nuclear threshold opened up the ambiguities of Flexible Response and Forward Defence. The problem for the remainder of this century is whether NATO can withstand the challenge of all these changes occurring together. Again, this is especially difficult since the ways in which intergovernmental consensus is best attained is by means that make consensus on defence harder to achieve within European NATO countries. It is for this reason that the Reagan years have led to a potential crisis for US–European relations that is different in kind to those that have gone before.

Where the contemporary issues of the Reagan era and the structural problematique of US–European relations came together was that the Reagan Administration reasserted the bipolar nature of post-war international relations. In marked contrast to its predecessor, the Reagan Administration had seen the world through decidedly bipolar glasses. Viewed in this way, the USSR was a threat in a way that simply could not be seen from Europe. From Europe, the USSR looked like a neighbour which, however menacing, had to be lived with; there might be no alternative to detente. Thus, whereas the Reagan Administration's foreign and defence policies were based on the global bipolar conflict with the USSR, those of European countries saw the USSR almost entirely as that country behaved within Europe. In this light, the USSR looked more like a country wanting predictability and stability in its relations with western European states than one set on an expansionist course.[17] For European people, and maybe for European governments, it was difficult to substantiate the view that the USSR was expansionist in Europe, yet it was exactly this logic which informed the Reagan Administration's assessment of the global Soviet threat. And it is here that the structural factor assumes its greatest importance, since Europe is only one theatre for the USA's global power struggle with the USSR, whereas it is, of course, *the* theatre for Europeans. Within that theatre the rationale underlying the Reagan Administration's view of the USSR was difficult to accept.

The implication of this for the future is clear: if the Bush Administration shares the Reagan Administration's bipolar conception of the Soviet threat, then consensus between the American and European governments will be difficult to achieve. Thus, although the Alliance has got through the Reagan years with some short-run successes, the legacy of the Reagan Administration is rather different, for those years have seen the emergence of a set of issues on which it is difficult at the best of times to maintain consensus. The bipolarisation of international relations during the Reagan years does not translate well to the Europeans, and these differing perceptions of the threat imply different ways of dealing with the Soviets. The Alliance historically has dealt with differing perceptions and prescriptions by a combination of a quiescent domestic setting and a set of ambiguous strategic formulations and understandings. Precisely because the Reagan years brought into the open these ambiguities and broke the bipartisan nature of defence policy within European countries, the structural *problématique* seemed particularly acute as the Reagan years came to an end. And certainly if the next decade sees American attempts to confront the USSR globally, if it sees plans for rapid change in the strategic environment at the same time as NATO has to re-examine linkage, then this will surely be a period of considerable instability in US–European relations. Indeed, if the trends of the Reagan years continue, future historians may look back upon these years as the beginning of the end of the NATO Alliance.

NOTES

1. For very good discussions of NATO's nuclear strategy see David Schwartz, *NATO's Nuclear Dilemmas* (Washington DC, Brookings, 1983) and Leon Sigal, *Nuclear Forces in Europe* (Washington DC, Brookings, 1984).
2. The development of MC14/3 is very clearly outlined in Schwartz *op. cit.,* pp. 136–92.
3. These are discussed in Steve Smith, 'The Myth of the Soviet Threat', *RUSI Journal*, vol. 127(2), June 1982, pp. 41–8.
4. See, for example, the interviews in Robert Scheer, *With Enough Shovels* (updated edition, New York, Vintage Books, 1983).
5. See Steve Smith, 'US–Soviet Strategic Nuclear Arms Control: From SALT to START to Stop', *Arms Control*, vol. 5(3), 1984, pp. 50–74.
6. See, for example, Strobe Talbott, *Deadly Gambits* (New York, Knopf, 1984).
7. For an overview of SDI a good starting point is Rip Bulkeley and Graham Spinardi, *Space Weapons* (Cambridge, Polity Press, 1986). See also Office of Technology Assessment, *Strategic Defenses* (Princeton NJ, Princeton University Press, 1986). For a discussion of SDI and contemporary US–Soviet relations, see Steve Smith, 'SDI and the New Cold War' in Richard Crockatt and Steve Smith (eds) *The Cold War Past and Present* (London, Allen & Unwin, 1987), pp. 149–70.
8. For examples of this kind of attack on SDI see John Tirman (ed.) *The Fallacy of Star Wars* (New York, Vintage, 1984); John Tirman (ed.) *Empty Promise* (Boston, Beacon Press, 1986); and A. Carter, *Directed Energy Missile Defense in Space* (Washington DC, Office of Technology Assessment, 1984).
9. See for example H. Lin, 'The development of software for ballistic-missile defense', *Scientific American*, vol. 253(6), 1985, pp. 32–9.
10. See Richard Ruquist, 'SDI: Early Deployed, Early Destroyed', *Arms Control Today*, vol. 17(6), 1987, pp. 18–19.
11. Douglas Walter and James Bruce, 'SDI: Progress and Challenges Part Two',

(unpublished report to Senators William Proxmire and J. Bennett Johnston, 8 April 1987), p. ii.
12. *International Herald Tribune*, 13 August 1987.
13. The report is summarised in Kurt Gottfried 'The Physicists Size up SDI', *Arms Control Today*, vol. 17(6), 1987, pp. 28–32.
14. For an excellent discussion of the deployment decision see Simon Lunn, 'INF and Political Cohesion in NATO' in Hans-Henrik Holm and Nikolaj Petersen (eds) *The European Missile Crisis: Nuclear Weapons and Security Policy* (London, Frances Pinter, 1983), pp. 208–24. See also Schwartz *op. cit.*, pp. 193–251 and Steve Smith, 'Theatre Nuclear Forces and the NATO Alliance' in Walter Goldstein (ed.) *Fighting Allies* (London, Brassey's, 1986), pp. 39–54.
15. For a good collection of papers dealing with this issue see John Steinbruner and Leon Sigal (eds) *Alliance Security: NATO and the No-First-Use Question* (Washington DC, Brookings, 1983) and Frank Blackaby, Jozef Goldblat and Sverre Lodgaard (eds) *No-First-Use* (London, Taylor and Francis, 1984).
16. See, for example, Report of the European Security Study, *Strengthening Conventional Deterrence in Europe: Proposals for the 1980s* (New York, St Martin's Press, 1983). A very good survey of FOFA and ALB can be found in D. Boyd *et al.*, 'Deep attack Concepts and the Defence of Central Europe', *Survival*, vol. 26(2), 1984, pp. 50–70.
17. For an excellent treatment of the changes in Soviet military objectives see Michael McGuire, *Military Objectives in Soviet Foreign Policy* (Washington DC, Brookings, 1987).

9 · THE STRATEGIC DEFENSE INITIATIVE AND THE EUROPEAN RESPONSE IN HIGH-TECHNOLOGY RESEARCH AND DEVELOPMENT
The Military–Civilian Dilemma for Western Europe

Michael Lucas

Since its announcement in March 1983, the Strategic Defense Initiative (SDI) has posed a set of strategic, technological and political challenges which have continued to dominate the Western security debate. SDI reintroduced the highly controversial notion of defending the American population against nuclear attack by ballistic missile defences – an approach that had been shelved by the Anti-Ballistic Missile (ABM) Treaty of 1972 because of its immense strategic, technological and financial problems. With SDI the USA, without consultation with its allies, now proposed a highly ambitious long-term research and development programme aimed at altering the very foundation of Western security. Nuclear deterrence and the doctrine of Mutual Assured Destruction (MAD) would be replaced by ballistic missile defence through the development of futuristic technologies, including space-based kinetic and directed energy weapons, surveillance and battle management systems. In addition, the innovations associated with SDI would also constitute, according to its sponsors, an historically unprecedented technological revolution.

The USA's allies considered SDI a serious military–political challenge to the stability of the traditional NATO security framework of nuclear deterrence and flexible response. Fears of unequal zones of security, of denuclearisation, of the effects of SDI on commercial European space programmes and on the ABM Treaty were important elements of Europe's initial response.[1] The criticisms of the USA's allies crystallised in the four points that emerged at the conclusion of British Prime Minister Thatcher's meeting with President Reagan at Camp David in December 1984. These were:

1. The West's aim is not to achieve superiority but to maintain balance, taking account of Soviet developments.

2. SDI-related deployment would, in view of treaty obligations, have to be a matter of negotiation.
3. The overall aim is to enhance, not undercut, deterrence.
4. East–West negotiations should aim to achieve security with reduced levels of offensive systems on both sides.[2]

In March 1985 the UK made clear its rejection of SDI as a replacement for deterrence and as a programme going unilaterally beyond research.[3] Echoing the position of other western European governments, British Foreign Secretary Sir Geoffrey Howe expressed support for SDI as a tentative research programme tightly circumscribed by the ABM Treaty and the existing regime of deterrence and Mutual Assured Destruction.[4] Similarly, West German Chancellor Helmut Kohl, whose speeches had been interpreted by some as broadly endorsing SDI, demanded that 'NATO's strategy of flexible response must remain fully valid'; that arms control, particularly, 'the observance of the ABM Treaty, have priority' over the political and strategic aspects of SDI; that the USA and the USSR work together to maintain and where possible improve strategic stability and to dramatically reduce nuclear offence forces; and that any decision to go beyond research be negotiated with Bonn and other NATO governments.[5]

Faced with this European consensus, the Reagan Administration realised that if it wanted alliance support it would have to change tactics. Washington subsequently began to de-emphasise SDI as a space-based weapons system and emphasise SDI as a 'research programme' that would yield substantial benefits for the civilian as well as military sectors of the economy.[6]

As part of this change in focus, Lt. General James Abrahamson, the director of the Strategic Defense Initiative Organisation (SDIO) announced, in Congressional testimony, later widely circulated to foreign officials, that Mrs Thatcher's four points were now goals of SDI. In addition, he spoke enthusiastically about the technological spin-offs that could be expected from SDI, which in his opinion would be considerable, 'for all facets of our economy and society'.[7] In this and subsequent statements from the newly created Office of Innovative Science and Technology, SDIO officials not so subtly let Europe know that the 'new product types and entirely new industries' that would be allegedly spawned by SDI would provide the USA 'with a competitive edge in international markets'.[8] At the same time, US Administration officials stressed that European firms could share in the technological bonanza. In trips to Europe during and after late 1985, Secretary of Defense Caspar Weinberger emphasised to allied leaders that billions of dollars worth of SDI contracts could be allotted to European firms.[9]

SDI AND THE EUROPEAN RESPONSE   181

As the Administration's tactics for selling SDI shifted, so did the official debate in Europe. This became increasingly concerned with political and economic questions. Much discussion centred on the merits of the claim that SDI would bring about a technological revolution. One exponent of this claim was Konrad Seitz, the director of planning in the West German Foreign Office. Seitz suggested that SDI research could cause the American economy to make a quantum jump into the twenty-first century.[10] He emphasised the future importance of certain technologies being developed in the SDI, such as lasers, sensors, very high speed integrated circuits (VHSICs), fifth-generation computers and artificial intelligence.[11]

Seitz's optimistic belief that SDI would yield monumental civilian spin-offs was not, however, shared by many West German experts. The conservative newspaper *Frankfurter Allgemeine Zeitung,* for example, said in an editorial that 'to await non-military technological advances from SDI is to overestimate its civilian spin-off'.[12] Echoing a widely held view in Europe, the paper estimated that it would cost ten times as much to develop civilian innovations through military research and development (R&D) and through such military programmes, than was the case if investments were made directly into civilian projects. A similar view was expressed at a conference in Europe by the vice president and chief scientist of IBM, who asserted that SDI would be largely irrelevant for the non-military economy.[13]

West German industry was also sceptical about SDI. This was partly because of the fear that a premature rush to join the programme would lead to a unilateral transfer of West German high technology to the USA without any reciprocal flow, in effect compromising the Federal Republic's lead in key non-military technologies.[14] This concern was also linked to the larger technological context. As West German Foreign Minister Hans-Dietrich Genscher put it, Star Wars made many Europeans 'aware of something that has long been in existence, namely the technological challenge facing Europe – with or without SDI'.[15]

A specific but major European concern here related to the American practice, intensified by the Reagan Administration, of placing restrictions on export to the Soviet and eastern European economies of so-called 'dual-use' technology, that is items that can be used for civilian as well as military purposes.[16] American measures have negatively affected European east–west trade.[17] European governments interested in SDI contracts have tried to safeguard their commercial interests against too wide an embargo by the SDIO. European firms also worry that the legislative and executive weapons in the USA's expanding protectionist arsenal will be used to curtail their external trade, and their use of SDI technology. These weapons include the Arms Export Administration Act (AEAA) of 1979.

The AEAA, for example, defines export goods as including 'technical data' as well as 'dual use' civilian and military technologies. These are itemised in the Commodity Control List (CCL) and the Military Critical Technologies List (MCTL). Since 1979, the unwieldy and complex MCTL has become a major source of transatlantic controversy.[18] European firms have also been concerned about the wide applicability of the restrictions of the Co-ordinating Committee for Multilateral Export Controls (COCOM). The Reagan Administration has made considerable efforts to strengthen COCOM restrictions on Western trade with the USSR and east European economies. The result has been increasing friction between the USA and its leading trading partners. A spectacular example was the Toshiba affair, in which the Japanese firm Toshiba Machine and the Norwegian state firm Kongsberg Vappenfabbrikk exported machine tools and computers to the USSR, to be used for submarine construction.[19]

In the USA, questions have been raised concerning the long-term feasibility of current high-technology export control policies, for example in a highly critical study by the National Academy of Sciences.[20] The authors maintained that American relations with its allies had been hurt by American insistence on stricter export controls, many of which were considered to have little military value but are commercially important to western European export economies. According to another study, the Federal Republic's exports to the East declined by 7.3 per cent in 1986 and 16 per cent in the first five months of 1987 as a result of COCOM restrictions on high-technology exports.[21]

SDI RESEARCH AGREEMENTS AND CONTRACTS

The general economic and political purposes of the SDI agreements were to set up conditions for transatlantic co-operation (and rules of competition) in areas of common military–industrial concern within NATO and the Western Alliance. These included SDI-related military R&D, technology transfer, civil application of military, scientific, technological and engineering data, and general guidelines concerning protection of intellectual property rights, such as patents and research data.

The USA has signed SDI agreements with the UK, the Federal Republic of Germany, Italy, Israel and Japan. Prior to the signing of the accords with its European partners, the SDIO promised billions of dollars worth of contracts. Western European governments and the large corporations involved have now more or less accepted that these early promises will not be kept. Neither the American Administration and Congress nor the American military industry is ready to share substantial amounts of technological know-how or budgetary resources with European allies. Nevertheless, individual European corporations and research institutes, including many of the most prestigious and successful electronic and military-industrial giants in the UK, West Germany, Italy and France, have contracts and are vying for additional work from the SDI. West German firms participating in SDI have, for example, received $50 million worth of contracts.[22]

Although the agreements have been secret, important details of the British Memorandum have been aired.[23] The full text of the West German–American agreement was also leaked to a Cologne newspaper,[24] later embarrassing the Bonn government, not only because of the breach of security, but also due to the terms of the agreement. These were sharply criticised as compromising West German interests.

The American–British Memorandum of Understanding of SDI replaced a 1975 memorandum which governed defence trade between the two countries.[25] Thus, the SDI agreements can be viewed, particularly in the case of the UK, as a foundation for a modified regime of military trade within NATO. The West German defence magazine, *Wehrtechnik,* considered the American–West German agreement in a similar light, that is as an instrument for placing traditional export-import, technology transfer and other forms of American–western European defence co-operation on a firmer juridical and security basis.[26]

An important motive of western European firms' participation in SDI is their expectation that such participation will further their efforts in the development of new technologies for conventional warfare. SDI is viewed as a larger framework for weapons development, less for 'Star Wars' than for what can be designated the evolving 'battlefield of the future'.

Here we can separate different factors which are playing a role in western European interest in SDI. Though aware of American reluctance to liberalise technology transfer in the military sphere, European firms expect a *quid pro quo* in technology transfer, co-operation and access to American markets to take the risk of entering into SDI contracts. Many of the European SDI contractors have long-standing relationships with American firms that pre-date SDI, so that SDI-related contracts represent a continuation of commercial ties. However, western European firms now feel they have developed sufficient expertise in certain areas of advanced technology to hold their own with the USA. These firms have therefore insisted on (and probably received) what they would consider to be a fair deal.[27] Moreover, the Europeans' experience in such dealings with the USA has made them wiser. Western European firms and research institutes are now in a much better position today to 'go it alone' in R&D projects, and thus avoid the risks of technological dependence or unfavourable contracts.

In the American–West German SDI Memorandum of Understanding, apart from direct SDI-related co-operation relating to strategic missile defence, special attention is given to development of conventional weapons. According to the agreement, both powers 'agree to exchange know-how in those mutually agreed areas of SDI research and those considered useful for improving conventional defence, in particular, air defence'.[28] In this context *Wehrtechnik* has written that:

> ... in all the projects which will be developed in the framework of the SDI research agenda we can expect military spin-off. In particular, this will be the case in the development of sensors, information technology and lasers. Taken together, the military benefits from the SDI research program will advance conventional military technologies in such a way that new, revolutionary weapon systems will result.[29]

The author goes on to list the following areas in which West German participation in SDI research programmes could, in his view, revolutionise the conventional and dual-use (nuclear and conventional) weapons systems of NATO and the Bundeswehr:

> Sensor technology with integrated signal processing will create new standards in optics and produce a new quality in munitions and submunitions.
>
> New computer hard- and soft-ware with components characterised by very large-scale integration [VLSI] and very high-speed integrated circuits [VHSIC] complex circuit architectures, artificial intelligence, expert systems and new programming languages will make possible new forms of command, control and communication.
>
> The technologies of high-speed missiles and electro-magnetic rail-runs will endow air-defense with an ATM/ATBM [Anti-Tactical Missile/Anti-Tactical Ballistic Missile] capability.
>
> High energy laser technology will have applications for weapon systems for defence against aircraft, helicopters and guided missiles.[30]

Important in the above is the link between SDI research and development programmes and the development of air defence and ATBM defence systems for Europe. This link forms a technological and political bridge between SDI and current NATO conventional arms build-up in Europe.[31]

SDI AND THE TECHNOLOGICAL REVOLUTION

In examining SDI's impact as a catalyst on current European R&D programmes, one can begin with the following statement by the OECD's Director for Science, Technology and Industry on the nature of technological development today:

> Today we stand on the threshold of a new era – an era driven by rapidly changing technologies ... The major new technologies ... electronics, telecommunications, industrial materials, production automation, biotechnology, artificial intelligence and the more specific fields of fibre optics, composite materials, CAD/CAM, robotics ... promise to alter significantly the economies of all countries.[32]

The specific challenge to western Europe is summed up in a report of the Economic and Social Committee of the European Community (EC), as follows:

The new technologies are one of the greatest challenges of our time . . . there is, however, great and widespread concern that Europe is lagging behind and must struggle even to hold its ground in the face of its major competitors, the United States and Japan . . .
. . . there is broad agreement on the reasons for Europe's difficulties with new technologies. The main causes are identified as the lack of a large unified market, which is necessary if production costs are to be brought down; the compartmentalization of the public purchasing market; the duplication of research work; the failure to exploit research findings in processes and products; and the insufficient contribution of small firms as a result of numerous bureaucratic and economic obstacles such as the lack of risk capital and many other factors. In short, the European dimension is lacking.[33]

The example of telecommunication provides a useful overview of current European high-tech problems, which is often referred to as 'Eurosclerosis'. Jacques Danzin describes the economic problems that the EC faces in the domain of telecommunications as follows:

Marked deterioration in the trade deficit of the ten in electronics, information technologies and telecommunications: Following a small positive balance in 1979, the export-import ratios have been negative since 1980 and are expected to reach 10 to 12 billion Ecus annually from 1985 to 1987 . . .
Serious loss of jobs in a job market already plagued with under employment: In 1982 it was estimated that 2 to 4 million jobs were lost as a result of increasing inability to compete in information technology . . .
The threat of technological dependence, particularly in the domain of microelectronics and certain classes of high-speed devices: It has been pointed out by European analysts that this weakness is particularly conspicuous in the ability to design military equipment and certain classes of software . . .
An across-the-board delay in Europe in comparison to the United States and Japan in the transformation of industries, services and education as a result of the slow rate of introducing and applying information technology.[34]

These problems cannot be separated from the international economic slowing down which began in the late 1960s.[35] The end of the post-war boom has been a primary motivation in the search for new technologies which have the potential to trigger a new economic upswing. Companies and governments have looked to new technologies that would reduce the cost of labour, limit capital needs, have less hazardous effects on the environment, consume less resources and provide for more flexibility in production.[36] At the centre of this effort are families of existing and emerging technologies linked to micro-electronics and biotechnology.

While it is expected that new technologies will have a long-term positive effect on job creation, in the medium-term it is predicted that technological innovations will not significantly expand the job market. Instead, they are likely to bring about greater job destruction. In earlier periods of capitalist transition, jobs lost through rationalisation were offset by new employment in the tertiary sector. This is no longer the case today, and as such it has been estimated that the introductions of new technologies will affect

40–50 per cent of all jobs. This may result in a large drop in employment during the next few years.[37] This pessimistic scenario can be contrasted with a recent OECD investigation which highlights the job-creating effects of capital investment in information technologies.[38] In this view, the drop in employment and the economic slowing down in Europe in recent years is attributed to the lack of timely and substantial investment in information technology aimed at cutting capital costs. This dovetails with an earlier study by the EC which pointed out that the 'wrong or delayed use of technical potential may not only jeopardise existing jobs through the loss of market opportunities, but also impede or at least substantially delay the creation of new jobs'.[39] Such delay takes on critical importance given the persistent slow growth of the EC.

The success of efforts to achieve long-term economic recovery also depends on a number of political factors, including the effect of the present debate on arms control, the current NATO arms build-up and the SDI. It is not clear whether efforts at arms control will lead to significant steps in arms reductions and a long-term gradual demilitarisation of the East–West conflict. We may, in contrast, be about to see the start of a new round in the high technology arms race. Heavy investments in European conventional defence and space-related systems such as SDI could easily become serious financial and political barriers to both the current economic restructuring and the development and diffusion of technologies necessary to stimulate recovery. The Reagan Administration and NATO officials had been emphasising what they perceived as the need to offset arms reductions resulting from an INF agreement. This might include the development of new conventional systems in the framework of the NATO strategy of Follow-On Forces Attack (FOFA) and in the larger framework of SDI.[40]

A new arms race in the wake of an INF agreement would, however, severely obstruct the dismantling of the iron curtain which continues to prevent greater economic intercourse between East and West. On the other hand, the further opening of Eastern markets and the restructuring of the socialist economies may be important factors in helping to generate European and global economic recovery. It is here that a breakthrough in arms control and disarmament and the technological revolution intersect. Far-reaching arms control agreements might open the way for a second wave of detente in Europe. This would include long-term economic, political and cultural agreements that are now on the European agenda. It would also advance the further institutionalisation of existing East–West policy-making bodies, such as the Conference for Security and Co-operation in Europe (CSCE).[41]

The structural reforms now taking place in the USSR under the Gorbachev leadership could play an important role in this process – not only in Europe but also in the wider international arena. On the other hand, if this socialist renaissance turns out to be short-lived as a result of a lack of domestic or external support, the chances for sustained demilitarisation of the East–West conflict and the economic stimulation that could result will be correspondingly, if not tragically, reduced.

EUROPEAN RESEARCH AND DEVELOPMENT: COLLABORATION AND RESPONSES

While SDI has helped to catalyse greater efforts in Europe for R&D collaboration, it has been only one force among several encouraging European governments and firms in this direction.[42] Other factors include those quoted in the EC's Economic and Social Committee report referred to above. In addition, pressures have stemmed from the role of emerging technologies in accelerating economic expansion and global economic integration; deregulation and intensified competition from R&D-intensive firms from the USA and Japan; the strengthening of some COCOM controls, and European efforts to lessen dependence on the USA for supplies of military high-technology and weapons systems. European political responses relate to this complex of interrelated factors, which have stimulated technological collaboration, the creation of a regional market and an R&D infrastructure.[43]

Nonetheless, western European governments have become more interested in the SDI project, particularly in contracts with potential spin-off for European military programmes. The changing response to SDI reflects a continuing confusion and ambiguity in western European positions. While not subscribing to SDI's longer-term goals, European governments have signed SDI agreements or given national firms the green light to enter into contracts with the SDIO.

The tension is reflected in the complex interplay of the military and civilian dimensions of the European response. The examples of EUREKA, ESPRIT and RACE are useful to examine in this respect.

The European Research and Co-ordinating Agency (EUREKA)

By 1987, after approximately 20 months of existence, 19 countries were participating in EUREKA. The number of individual projects was over 100 and total funding, from both public and private sources, was US$ 4 billion.[44]

A major aim of EUREKA is to harness emerging technologies to improve macro- and micro-economic efficiency. In this sense, the programme has little in common with the approach embodied in SDI. EUREKA also has a different organisational structure. Its main thrust is civilian R&D, joint production and the creation of a transborder, high-technology infrastructure to regionalise the European economy and improve its overall productivity.[45] Towards this end, new products, systems and services are being promoted in a variety of fields, including computers, telecommunications, industrial lasers, robotics, new materials, biotechnology, environmental protection and transportation infrastructures. Other goals of EUREKA include pooling resources among European economies in order to eliminate R&D duplication and go-it-alone policies; developing computer-telecommunication networks to link research institutes and firms in different countries; and using public financing to stimulate private investment in specific high technology projects.[46] Government subsidies to participating firms are therefore gauged according to how close a particular project is to coming on stream as a marketable product.

Co-operation within the EUREKA framework will not be confined to countries belonging to the EC but open to all western European states. This is partly intended to prevent growing technological disparities between large and small, and more- and less-advanced European economies. Co-operative projects with CMEA countries are also on EUREKA's agenda.

While EUREKA is a civilian response to SDI, it could easily shift to military R&D. Prominent French and West German political and military figures have repeatedly called for such a shift, emphasising EUREKA's potential for European military programmes. One of the central questions, therefore, is whether EUREKA will be pulled into the global race for emerging military technologies, under pressure from SDI, French defence modernisation, and NATO. Given its basic structure, EUREKA could not be completely transformed into a European military counterpart of SDI, but it could be burdened with an increasing number of military projects. For example, a European Parliamentary Report noted that:

> . . . sceptics have pointed out that the French "fall silent when they are asked about the military spin-off". EUREKA's drive for fifth or sixth generation computers capable of thirty gigaflops per second, for example, is unlikely to "widen Europe's grip on world markets", since the market for such machines "will scarcely run into double figures". The main users will be the military.[47]

Other criticisms of EUREKA include the fact that the scale of the project as a whole is inadequate to achieve the major mobilisation of resources that the European technological challenge requires, and that the programmes could be better distributed between participating countries.[48]

The European Strategic Programme of Research in Information Technology (ESPRIT)

ESPRIT was created in 1983, aimed at combining basic research with development. Its domains are micro-electronics, software technology and advanced information processing, including artificial intelligence and expert systems. Its more practical, market-oriented areas are office systems and computer integrated manufacturing. Individual projects are financed by up to 50 per cent by the EC with the remainder from participating firms and research institutions.[49] Two important ground rules for assessing the projects and firms selected for participation are that the research must be carried out by teams in different EC countries and projects must combine basic research with the goal of achieving new applications of the technologies developed. ESPRIT is also attempting to establish greater commonality on standards among European firms. This could enable firms to develop systems that can be readily plugged into products of other European manufacturers. In addition, a major concern of ESPRIT is to bridge the academic world and public non-profit research facilities with the private interests of small and medium-sized firms.[50]

During the first 18 months of ESPRIT's existence, it approved 173 projects with 1700 researchers, 478 organisations, 104 universities and 81 research institutes.[51] ESPRIT's industrial advisory committee consists of major European industrial firms from France, Italy, the Netherlands, West Germany and the UK. The successful first phase of ESPRIT has been hailed by its sponsors as a demonstration that co-operation among European firms is a viable road to strengthen European technology. The national breakdown of the projects associated with the pilot phase of ESPRIT demonstrates the European dimension of the programme. Of the organisations associated with the pilot phase, 27 were located in the UK, 21 in West Germany, 10 in the Netherlands, 8 in Belgium, 4 in France and 2 in Italy.[52]

Critics of ESPRIT maintain that the programme, despite its success in getting off the ground and committing its initial funds of US$ 1.5 billion, suffers from a 'Eurocratic' manner of operating, with the result that its research grants may not add up to a 'critical mass' of scientific endeavour.[53] Implicit in this critique are the traditional problems of national particularisms, bureaucratisation within the EC, entrenched interfirm international competition, and the disparity of interests between large and small companies. These have in the past repeatedly hindered European co-operation.

While these criticisms deserve serious attention, it could be plausibly argued that they are premature, given ESPRIT's successful debut and the international forces driving current European high-technology co-operative efforts. Moreover, ESPRIT must be viewed in relation to other European R&D projects to which it is linked. Finally, being a young programme, it is capable of changing course along its learning curve.

Research in Advanced Communications in Europe (RACE)

Officially born in August 1985, RACE is an EC project aimed at promoting R&D in advanced communication technology. Its goal is to strengthen Europe's position in order to overcome the weakness of the EC *vis-à-vis* the USA and Japan in the field of new basic information technologies.[54] To achieve this aim, RACE has an ambitious agenda aimed at creating the technological base for introducing a community-wide Integrated Broadband Communications Network (IBCN). RACE projects range from creating new communication infrastructure and defining relevant R&D fields to providing better access for the less-developed regions of the EC and the advanced high-technology infrastructures and service networks which are now being developed.

By 1995, RACE backers hope to make it possible for Europe to overtake the USA by overcoming currently incompatible software standards in the transmission of data.[55] However, this is easier said than done given the present fragmentation of European standards and norms and the predominantly monopolistic form of national postal and communication systems.

Transition to a more integrated regional market also raises the question of the role of large, non-European firms such as IBM. On the one hand, European programmes such as ESPRIT, RACE and EUREKA are designed to allow western Europe to keep firms such as IBM at a distance long enough to catch up in areas where Europe is technologically weak. Moreover, besides the competitive rationale behind such efforts there is also a military-security aspect. A future US government, following the patterns set by the Reagan Administration, might exercise undue influence on European high-technology exports if European goods are manufactured with US components. On the other hand, many European firms need access to American technology and have extensive business relations with IBM and other American corporate giants. These firms are already strongly represented in Europe, and in many cases are keen on collaborating with European firms across a broad range of R&D, production and marketing activities. Such collaboration, moreover, is aimed not only at western European markets but the international economy as a whole. In this context the Europeanisation trend must be situated in the larger global process of economic integration. The advancing 'Europeanisation' of European firms and their 'globalisation' through major agreements with American and Japanese firms are two salient complementary and competing tendencies today. The survival of European firms in this complex process of transnational restructuring will depend very much on their ability, through so-called 'framework programmes', such as EUREKA, ESPRIT and RACE, to develop not only standards but also a strong 'collaboration community'.[56] These are preconditions for maintaining a strong position within a larger context of a high-technology globalised economy.

However, there are signs that the 'Europeanising' of R&D programmes is diminishing. Pressure from the UK, France and West Germany has resulted in the reduction of the European Commission's budget proposal for framework programmes in 1986 from 10.3 billion Ecus to 7.7 billion.[57] This can be explained by a number of factors, including a more selective policy being adopted by Europe's major corporations concerning which areas of high-technology they want to pursue; their greater openness to joint ventures with American and Japanese firms; and the reluctance of European governments and firms to cede too much influence over their respective R&D resources to Brussels. Another important factor has been a diminution of European fears of SDI as a military or civilian R&D programme threatening Europe's economic future.[58]

THE DANGERS OF MILITARISATION AND THE POLICY CHALLENGE

The twin processes of Europeanisation and globalisation of European firms stand in contrast to existing military–political structures of the East–West conflict and the gearing up of the USA and NATO for a new arms race, partly based on SDI and sub-strategic weapons. These structures hinder the opening of new markets for Western high technology goods and services. Such structures are, however, not strong enough to prevent the increasing, often illegal, transfer of high-technology to the East. Many major Western firms are directly or indirectly involved in circumventing current restrictions. But the 'normalisation' of this flow will require a change in the structures of global political–military relations. Such a change would need to be a negotiated, gradual process of demilitarising the East–West conflict, a goal apparently desired by the new Soviet leadership. However, western European governments and firms, though recognising their stake in a new export control regime based on greater free trade, remain ambivalent concerning to what extent their R&D policy should be geared to a new wave of economic detente or to a high-technology arms race.

This ambivalence is further fuelled by the fact that the western European high-technology programmes, while having an essential civilian thrust, cannot be neatly demarcated from current military R&D projects. Civilian programmes to develop telecommunication infrastructures or advanced computer data processing networks can be readily used by military authorities in the same way that highways and telephone lines form an integral part of national defence grids. This fact and its implications for emerging systems is already in the process of creating a new set of problems of arms control as well as for economic and security policy-making. In many cases, ensuring that new technologies are suitable for possible military end-use can make their design and construction less efficient for civil use. This is why the political and arms control processes need to be effective before such systems reach advanced stages of planning and development.

The importance of civilian high-technology innovation for military projects today is, of course, recognised by Pentagon policy-makers. Accordingly, they have increased their efforts to link up with non-military research institutes, universities and industrialists. The DARPA VHSIC programme is an example of the Pentagon's attempt to exploit civilian R&D for military applications.[59] Many of the SDI contracts with European firms should be seen in a similar light.

The example of ESPRIT illustrates how western European programmes pursued as civilian R&D projects could in the future be put to military use. Many of its basic research programmes are indispensable for weapons systems and military-related information and telecommunication infrastructures linked to the SDI and NATO's planned sub-strategic arms build-up. Indeed, many of the European projects referred to in this analysis have been designed partly with this flexibility in mind. As such, neither from a purely technological nor from an economic or a political viewpoint is it clear whether the technological revolution in western Europe will take on increasingly military attributes. While many of these risks are well-known to European firms and government ministries, the temptation and political pressures for firms to adopt this course should not be underestimated. The reduction of West German, French and British budgetary support for ESPRIT is a worrisome step in the direction of a partial re-nationalisation of R&D and European weapons projects which should also be kept in mind.

To sum up, the question of the military–civilian trade-offs of SDI and related American and European weapons programmes could critically determine the future ability to deal with the broad set of economic, technological, ecological and social problems facing western Europe. Aware of these risks, the European Parliament has formulated a set of social and economic criteria to evaluate European technology projects. These include whether or not a technology programme enhances Europe's industrial competitiveness; creates jobs; promotes the protection of the environment and is consistent with a sound management of natural resources. To these general criteria for assessing technology policy, my analysis suggests that one must add the following touchstones. Does it promote a deepening of East–West detente and make possible a further relaxation of military tensions? Can it function as an incentive to create new principles, norms and rules in East–West relations, that would help to alleviate the effects of the military–civilian dilemma that firms and government policy-makers now confront? Can the technology policy adopted contribute to economic recovery and at the same time to arms control and demilitarisation? Can it remove restrictions that are blocking a freer flow of goods, information and people across the East–West divide without prejudicing the security of other states?

The watershed Europe has reached by the late 1980s must be seen as an historic opportunity to link economic and technology policy to long-term demilitarisation. Such a link has now become indispensable for the future of Europe and the international system as a whole.

NOTES

I would like to thank Stephen Gill for editorial work and Steve Smith for comments.

1. On European positions on SDI, see 'Weapons in Space', Daedalus (1985), vol. 114, pp. 257–315; P. Gallis, M. Lowenthal, M. Smith, *The Strategic Defense Initiative and United States Alliance Strategy* (Washington DC, Congressional Research Service, 1985); D. Yost, 'European Anxieties about Ballistic Missile Defense', *Washington Quarterly* (1984), vol. 7, no. 4; E. P. Thompson (ed.), *Star Wars* (New York, Pantheon, 1985).
2. North Atlantic Council, 'Britain, Arms Control and the Strategic Defense Initiative', *British Information Services Policy Statements*, 46/85, 1 December 1985.
3. Sir Geoffrey Howe, 'Defence and Security in the Nuclear Age: the British View', *British Information Services Policy Statements*, 6/86, 15 March 1986.
4. *Ibid.*
5. 'Policy Statement by Chancellor Helmut Kohl to the Bundestag on the Strategic Defense Initiative', *Statements and Speeches of the Federal Republic of Germany*, vol. VII, no. 10, 19 April 1985.
6. J. Miller, 'Washington's Allies, Some with Doubts, Support "Star Wars"', *New York Times*, 30 December 1985.
7. *Ibid.*
8. 'Report of the *Ad Hoc* Committee on the Potential Benefits to US Industry from SDI/IST Scientific Program', *IDA Memorandum Report M–110* (Alexandria, Va., Institute for Defense Analysis, 1985), p. 9.
9. 'Weinberger Predicts Star Wars by 1990', *Washington Post*, 6 December 1985.
10. K. Seitz, 'SDI – Die technologische Herausforderung für Europa', *Europa-Archiv* (1985), no. 13.
11. *Ibid.*
12. *Frankfurter Allgemaine Zeitung*, 11 June 1985.
13. J. Newhouse, 'The Diplomatic Round', *New Yorker*, 22 July 1985.
14. *Bundestag*, Dr 9/1401, p. 2. Cited by R. Rilling, 'Konsequenzen von SDI für die Forschungspolitik', *Blatter für Deutsche und Internationale Politik*, June 1985.
15. Speech by Genscher to EUREKA meeting, Paris, 17 July 1985, *Statements and Speeches of the Federal Republic of Germany*, vol. VII, no. 22, 19 July 1985.
16. For the Reagan Administration viewpoint, see Office of the Undersecretary of Defense for Policy, *Assessing the Effect of Technology Transfer on US/*

Western Security: A Defense Perspective (Washington DC, US Government Printing Office, February 1985).
17. J. Feldman, 'Trade Policy and Foreign Policy', *Washington Quarterly* (1985), vol. 8, no. 1; see also the definitive study of American policy, National Academy of Sciences, *Balancing the National Interest, US National Security Export Controls and Global Economic Competition* (Washington DC, National Academy Press, 1987).
18. National Academy of Sciences, *op cit.*, pp. 126–9.
19. P. Bruce and S. Fleming, 'Toshiba Chiefs Quit in Dramatic Bid to Allay US Criticism', *Financial Times,* 2 July 1987.
20. National Academy of Sciences, *op. cit.*
21. 'SPD: SDI fugt Osthandel schweren Schaden zu', *Handelsblatt*, 2 July 1987.
22. S. Phillips, 'European report', in *ADIU Report*, vol. 9, no. 1, January-February 1987.
23. K. De Young, 'Britain Joins US in SDI Research', *Washington Post*, 7 December 1985.
24. *Der Kolner Express*, 18 April 1986. An English translation is in Ivo Daalder, *The SDI Challenge to Europe* (Cambridge, Mass., Ballinger, 1987), pp. 111–24.
25. P. Anderson, 'British SDI Still Shrouded in Secrecy', *END Journal of European Disarmament* (1986), no. 21. See also, 'UK Participation in the US SDI Research Programme – Guidelines', *Ministry of Defence*, prepared in unclassified form for circulation to interested parties, *mimeo.*
26. H-H. Weise, 'Das SDI-Forschungsprogramm', *Wehrtechnik*, 1986, no. 7.
27. M. Lucas, 'SDI and Europe: Militarization or Common Security?', *World Policy Journal*, spring 1986.
28. Weise, *op. cit.*
29. *Ibid.*
30. *Ibid.* See also, 'A Role NATO can play in the SDI programme', *Jane's Defence Weekly*, 5 October 1985.
31. See H. G. Brauch, *Star Wars and European Defense* (New York, St Martin's Press, 1987); G. Baechler and A. Statz, 'European Defence Initiative: Implications of Missile defence in Europe for West German Security Policy', *Hamburger beitrager zur Friedensforschung und Sicherheitspolitik*, December 1986, no. 12.
32. J. Marcum, 'High Technology and the Economy', *OECD Observer* (1984), no. 131, p. 4. Cited in B. L. R. Smith, 'A New "Technology Gap" in Europe?' *SAIS Review*, winter/spring 1986; see also M. Sharp and C. Shearman, *European Technological Collaboration* (London, Routledge for Royal Institute of International Affairs, 1987), p. 5ff.
33. European Community, Economic and Social Consultative Assembly, Economic and Social Committee, *Europe and the New Technologies, R & D Industry, Social Aspects* (Brussels, EC, 1986), p. 1.
34. A. Danzin, 'ESPRIT et les vulnérabilités de la Communauté européene', *Défense Nationale*, March 1986.
35. R. van Tulder and Gerd Jünne, *European Multinationals and Core Technologies* (Amsterdam, Internationale betrekkingen en volkenrecht, 1986), Ch. 1.
36. *Ibid.*; A. Roobeek, 'The Crisis of Fordism and the Rise of a New Technologies Paradigm', *Futures*, April 1987.
37. European Community, *op. cit.*, p. 64.
38. D. Kimbel, 'Information Technology: Increasingly the Engine of the OECD Economies', *OECD Observer*, August–September 1987.

39. European Community, *op. cit.*, p. 64.
40. D. Charles, 'NATO Looks for Arms Control Loopholes', *Bulletin of the Atomic Scientists*, September 1987.
41. On the CSCE, see N. Roper and P. Schlotter, 'Die Institutionalisierrung des KSZE-Processes', *Aus Politik und Zeitgeschichte*, no. 2, January 1987.
42. Sharp and Shearman, *op. cit.*, pp. 2–3, 17ff.
43. On French responses, see P. Lemaître, 'Le Programme EUREKA doit proposer un champs d'application civiles plus large que le projet stratégique de M. Reagan', *Le Monde*, 8 May 1985; J. Fenske, 'France and the Strategic Defense Initiative: Speeding up or Putting on the Brakes', *International Affairs*, spring 1986; Lucas, *op. cit.*
44. 'Reisenhuber: die EUREKA-Initiative zeigt eine beachtliche Dynamik', *Die welt*, 13 December 1986; Sharp and Shearman, *op. cit.*, pp. 69–74.
45. European Community, *op. cit.*, p. 132ff; Der Bundesminister für Forschung und Technologie (BmFT), *EUREKA* (Bonn, BmFT, 1986); European Parliament, Committee on Energy, Research and Technology, *Draft Report on the Proposal to Establish a European Co-ordinating Agency (EUREKA) and on Community Participation in Star Wars Research* (Brussels, European Community, 1986). Reporter Glyn Ford.
46. European Parliament, *ibid.*, p. 25.
47. *Ibid.*
48. Smith, *op. cit.*
49. European Community, *op. cit.*, p. 93.
50. Danzin, *op. cit.*
51. European Community, *op. cit.*, p. 93.
52. Sharp and Shearman, *op. cit.*, p. 51.
53. Smith, *op. cit.*
54. European Community, *op. cit.*, p. 94.
55. *Ibid.*, p. 94ff.
56. Sharp and Shearman, *op. cit.*, p. 63.
57. G. de Jonquières, 'Back to Basics', *Financial Times*, 23 July 1987.
58. *Ibid.*
59. G. Fong, 'The Potential for Industrial Policy: Lessons from the Very High Speed Integrated Circuit Programme', *Journal of Policy Analysis and Management* (1986), vol. 5, no. 1.

10 · BEYOND THE WESTERN ALLIANCE
The Politics of Post-Atlanticism

Bradley S. Klein

The chapters in this collaborative volume have focused upon major structural aspects of Atlantic relations. The primary issue has been whether contemporary dilemmas besetting the Western Alliance are but the latest manifestations of those long-recurrent conjunctural and cyclical problems that have bedevilled Atlanticist policy-makers, or whether the West today faces something more permanent that challenges prevailing assumptions in a fundamentally problematic way. In so doing, some chapters have relied upon institutional and policy critiques at the level of the major state actors; or, as, for example, in the case of Stephen Gill's and Kees van der Pijl's contributions, others have drawn upon a tradition of critical political economy to analyse changing structures of transatlantic relations.[1]

This chapter takes as its departure point a related set of concerns, but its perspective is somewhat different from, perhaps even slightly at odds with, the methods relied upon by other contributors to this volume. For this chapter raises issues about the whole of the Western Alliance. Its concerns are more ontological and epistemological, rather than, as are the other chapters, empirically oriented. This chapter analyses Atlantic relations at a somewhat unconventional level, in terms of a set of political practices that have, under the auspices of a hegemonic framework, established the general terms of a discursive practice sustaining a whole way of life. That way of life, I argue, has been to articulate post-war Atlantic relations as a natural, rational and logical culmination of a universal historical project.

The chapter extends debates about the Alliance to the very strategy of the West in having granted privileged status to but one version of possible transatlantic relations. As such, it questions how the very categories of Western strategy have secured the cultural modernism of the West and of the whole world. For what we call the Western Alliance, and what many call for *as* the Western Alliance, is but the most ambitious contemporary example we have of constructing modern, technocratic industrial capitalist life as the norm for global civilisation. In its attempt to co-ordinate foreign, economic and military policy among the world's most powerful societies, the Alliance stands as the source behind the whole thrust of 'progress', development and modernisation. Indeed, if I may be permitted a certain freedom of expression, we can say that the Western Alliance is but the highest stage of modernism.

The point of a critique of that Western project is, quite simply, to render that construction problematic: to 'de-naturalise' the quality of its existence via a radical historicism of its emergence, and to politicise transatlantic relations in ways that transcend the approaches conventionally relied upon when examining contemporary crises of Western politics.[2]

It is, of course, always problematic to talk about 'modernism'. The term has no singular, locked-in meaning and functions rather as a kind of open-ended concept capable of accommodating a range of cultural concerns. But is is precisely this feature of the term that is so important for contemporary criticism, for it is not possible to fix as immutable and beyond question the meaning of those crucial categories that inform our most interesting political debates. Instead, we draw upon the essential contestability of this and other key terms – such as 'power', 'interests', 'class' and 'deterrence' – to capture the ambiguous quality of political life. Debates about these concepts are themselves part of larger processes of political contestation. But in relying upon crucial concepts, it isn't as if 'anything goes' and we can say what we want at will. The term has to be articulated within some range of recognition shared by those competing political constituencies. And here I would argue that the term 'modernism' refers precisely to the quality of foreclosing debate and politics: of imposing order, of domesticating the shape of particular bodies and constituting the identities of participants so that they conform to rules of organisation. To talk about 'modernism', then, is to talk about those strategies of power which impose definitive form upon matter, rendering it consistent with a master narrative which is accorded priority and privilege.[3]

In this sense, the Western Alliance adheres to a strategy of 'modernising'. To explore that project is to render problematic and inherently contestable the ensuing geopolitical and cultural formation commonly referred to as the Atlantic Alliance and the West.

This chapter explores the strategies by which the Western Alliance has pursued this undertaking. I begin with a critique of the idea of strategy; move to an account of the meaning of the Western civilisational project; and then articulate the post-modern challenge to the politics of Atlanticism.

STRATEGY

It has been the crippling legacy of the whole field of strategic studies to have abstracted questions of war and peace from their embeddedness in historically-produced relations of social movements, political economy and culture. The units of analysis – states and security alliances – are presumed to have been there from the start. And the rules of their interaction are likewise posited as consistent with the laws of a state system present since at least the days of Thucydides.

There is, curiously enough, a certain sensibility to these assumptions insofar as the only global actors able to undertake military strategy have been states that have constituted themselves as domestically-legitimate entities. But it has never been a simple matter to create a state: to create, in Max Weber's terms, that 'human community that (successfully) claims the monopoly of the legitimate use of physical force within a given community'.[4] Within a realist tradition anticipated by Machiavelli's *The Prince* and first fully envisioned in Hobbes' *Leviathan*, this state stands above its people, its economy and its culture to protect them and offer them leadership.

Strategy, then, or more precisely political–military strategy, is only possible on these terms of having erected a state apparatus which co-ordinates political life and which is responsible for meeting the challenges of an invariably conflictual world of like-structured legitimate entities.

From this standpoint, war and peace present themselves as challenges to the state. Thus there is some good reason, though unavoidably a myopic one, that the evolution of strategic thinking should be part and parcel of states within a state system. In early modern Europe these concerns gave rise to a balance of power politics, where the object of strategy was to ensure that no single state became dominant – dominance *here* understood in traditional realist terms of the actions of a particular hegemon. The means of strategy involved a whole panoply of political–military instruments ranging from limited warfare to diplomacy in the name of protecting civil society from incursions from without. That state would prevail which had a preponderance of the elements of national power: power, according to this point of view, in terms of material sources of economic strength, military firepower and the ability of national leadership to harness its populace.

This realist understanding always took – and still takes – place against an unexamined background of legitimately constituted states. The only significant question for international relations theorists thereby becomes which state(s) shall prevail, how, and with what means. This is the issue of realist hegemony, of dominance, of being able to prevail and to set the terms of order globally so that some other power itself should not prevail instead. In this classical parlance, then, the issue is of relative competition and stability among the leading states, only one of which can use its dominance to help preserve world order. And simply stated, the problem today of world politics in general and of the Western Alliance in particular, is that the USA seems to have lost much of its once-unquestioned leadership across the whole spectrum of dominance, whether military, economic and/or political.[5]

This conception of hegemony, a conception prevalent among those concerned with the USA's place in the Alliance, presupposes a radical distinction between the rules of domestic society and the rules of international society. The former, the realm of politics within states, is construed as relatively unproblematic, unitary and consensual, that is the realm of the national interest. Outside the state's borders, however, beyond the water's edge, in that formally anarchic realm of international life there reigns, by contrast, chaos and unrest. Security dilemmas impeding co-operation abound. Insecurity is everywhere. Each state is on its own. And only the efforts of cultivating ties of state interdependence can mitigate the ensuing harshness of a tough state system.

Such, at any rate, is the realist view of things. And out of this view of statist hegemony there arises the need for certain states to call upon allies discriminately in arranging for their mutual security. This effort was no more heroically undertaken than among the leaders of the Western Alliance in the aftermath of World War II.

Another view of hegemony is available to us, however, one that does not rely as realism does upon rigid dichotomies between internal and external, domestic and foreign, the state and the state system. This is a perspective informed by the critical Marxism of Antonio Gramsci, and its central concern is with the political production of relations of dominance by which rule over people becomes normalised and 'seen' as legitimate.[6] For Gramsci, the location of the state over civil society is not some timeless universal given but a particular historical achievement, characteristic of modern class rule by which a culturally and intellectually sophisticated bourgeoisie has sought to integrate subordinate classes, and to do so along lines that are more nearly consensual than coercive. From this standpoint hegemony concerns the production of legitimacy. And for recent students of international relations, this conception enables one to focus on the global production of legitimacy as well: on the power relations of particular regimes and classes which are able to generate ideas and practices that gain the normalising status of common currency.

We can illustrate this normalising function of hegemony in terms of Western military strategy. From a classical realist position, the state stands over the political economy and meets external threats to the national interest or to the vital interests of the West. Strategy responds to a variety of changed circumstances regarding technology and the threat posed by agressor nations. But the whole scientific practice of strategy as a particular discourse of power must itself be seen in the equation. For it is not until the post-World War II era that strategy became defined as a distinct discipline of international relations, to be known as strategic studies. Classical questions of offence and defence became in the nuclear age issues of deterrence and security. In the immediate post-war era there arose a panoply of institutions – RAND, the MIT Lincoln Laboratory, the Aerospace Corporation, the MITRE Corporation, the Airpower Research Institute, the Washington-based Institute for Defense Analyses and Georgetown University's Center for Strategic and International Studies – devoted to researching these issues. These think tanks, centres for strategic studies and university graduate programmes cultivated strategic intellectuals whose new-found organised knowledge was to underpin the whole enterprise of extended deterrence. The affinity between nuclear deterrence and strategic/security studies can be clearly seen in the fact that no journal, think tank or research centre devoted to the study of strategy and security appears in any Western country before it either 'went nuclear directly' (the London-based International Institute of Strategic Studies, for instance, first appeared in 1958) or fell under the protective graces of American strategic projection in the form of extended deterrence.[7]

Students of strategic studies explain the discipline as an enlightened, mature adaption of classical realist principles to the new challenges of the nuclear revolution: to the fact that the absolute triumph of nuclear offence over defence renders outmoded traditional war-fighting options which had, in good Clausewitzian fashion, emphasised protracted defensive battles. In Bernard Brodie's resonant words of 1946, 'thus far the chief purpose of our military establishment has been to win wars. From now on its chief purpose must be to avert them.' Thus arose a concern for the political strategy of deterrence, and to bolster this, strategic studies.[8]

Yet such an account of the birth of strategic studies removes questions of policy from their global context and constitutes itself as a self-referential discourse of techno-strategy, of managing the instrumentalities of violence – all in the name of these weapons never having to be used. But knowledge, and more specifically here, the systematic organisation of knowledge as a form of power, occurs in a context of political relations, of state and interests and of the will to power manifested by those with public responsibility. To organise knowledge as a form of strategic power is to constitute the world in particular ways and to construct standardised rules of interpretation that are to serve as a guide to action. This is what is meant by a discourse, a practice of organised knowledge that informs relations of power. Just as the whole field of international relations was developed in the wake of World War I and the face of the challenges posed by both imperialist rivalries and by the socialist *problématique* of imperialism – thus were born, for instance, the London-based Royal Institute of International Affairs and the New York-based Council on Foreign Relations[9] – so, too, was strategic studies part of a larger enterprise, undertaken by the West, to reconstruct a war-torn continent and to establish a global regime of stabilised relations. Thus a modicum of world order could prevail, an order underpinned by the Western powers in general and by the USA in particular.

Within this framework, the function of strategic studies is to make the discourse of deterrence appear normal or natural and to give nuclear weapons a privileged status in preserving a world military order. The privileged status of nuclear weapons, and of a nuclear balance between the USA and the USSR, is nowhere clearer than in the rendering of these weapons as essential to life and as sources of security in the modern world. Like the television advertisement run a few years ago in the USA by a company that proclaimed that 'without chemicals, there wouldn't be life itself', nuclear weapons under the guiding hands of strategists are proclaimed so vital that without them we would be naked, insecure and without protection. After Reykjavik this claim has been renewed. Thus 'living with nuclear weapons' becomes a matter of adjusting ourselves to another advance of technology which is to make our life safe and therefore better.[10] Those who have questioned this reversal – a reversal whereby we are to see nuclear strategy as a necessity of life – become construed as a threat, a danger to public safety. Peace movements endanger our security. Nuclear weapons enhance it. And by defining security in these terms, in terms of the absence of a continental war, the avoidance of general nuclear war, and in terms of the presence of that which deters them, any challenges to the prevailing strategic discourse become construed as irresponsible by those acting 'responsibly' in positions of power. In this manner, of course, strategy deters not only foreign aggression but domestic politics as well. It seems the normal thing to do, or in the parlance of both the Spanish Socialists and the British Labour Party in their *encomia* on behalf of Alliance strategy, it is the 'modern' thing to do: to rely upon nuclear weapons, to adhere to commitments to NATO.

THE WESTERN ALLIANCE AS A PROJECT

Deterrence, security, nuclear weapons, indeed, the whole post-war network of military bases, alliance-building and security assistance were part of an ambitious attempt to erect a globally stable framework for multilateral trade that would circumvent the venal protectionism and competitiveness of inter-war rivalries. A whole host of institutions were crucial to this undertaking: the IMF, the World Bank, GATT, NATO, ANZUS and the like. This is what we call the Western System. Its focal point was the transatlantic network embodied – and consolidated – under the protective umbrella of the North Atlantic Treaty Organisation.

NATO, then, is more than NATO. It is one particular manifestation of a larger and more ambitious set of political and cultural relations that, briefly stated, while concentrated in western Europe and the North Atlantic, have as their aim the reconstruction, intensification and perpetuation of a post-war world order at both its core and its periphery.

At the core this entailed the emergence of more or less stable capitalist political economies, with the transcendence of extreme right-wing and left-wing forces leaving the field clear for the narrower terms of 'debate' and electoral contestation between somewhat more conservative and somewhat more social-democratically oriented parties occupying the mainstream of the political spectrum. In recalling this production of relative consensus one cannot overlook the difficulty of effecting it: McCarthyite tactics, the covert subversion of trade unions, the electoral propagandising and red-baiting of critics. Were it not for the general economic growth enjoyed by these countries it is unlikely that hegemony would ever have been created. In the USA the outcome was heralded as 'the end of ideology'.[11] In the west European countries we saw a similar – though never so fully consolidated – consensus in terms of social welfare states, efforts at co-determination of labour policy and grand coalition-type governments.

The global consequences of these domestic Atlantic consolidations involved the rise of multilateral co-operative efforts in the form of security alliances, trade regimes and international organisations, all designed to deepen the ties that bound not only the West but also the West to the post-colonial states of the Third World. Thus arose the dual strategies of security assistance and 'development'.[12] The two went hand in hand, not so much to prevent regional Third World conflicts – nor, as announced by the Truman Doctrine, to fend off armed aggression by outside forces – but rather to stabilise often shaky paramilitary regimes from their own domestic opposition: opposition overwhelmingly from the Left, as in Greece, Indo-China, Malaysia, the Philippines, Iran (in 1953) and Guatemala.

In Europe this dual strategy entailed military assistance and economic reconstruction. In the Third World this meant security assistance and 'modernisation'. No better proof of this connection is to be found than in the work of W. W. Rostow, the chief celebrant of the whole school of development, who, having idolised the Atlantic path of national industrialisation, sought to bring it to the newly-independent state; and who, after arguing that Communism is 'a disease of the transition' from traditional to modern society and that Communists 'are the scavengers of the modernisation process', as John F. Kennedy's security advisor, went on to develop blue-prints for counter-insurgency operations and the Vietnam War.[13]

Thoughtful strategists, particularly those concerned with the Western Alliance, were more cautious in their formulations. It is not consistent with liberal hegemony to call openly for the militarisation of world politics.

Certain standards of enlightened 'business pacifism', of an internationalist, classically liberal suspicion of a military-industrial complex, play at least a moderating role in post-war Western states. Moreover, the accumulated infrastructure and ideologies of advanced Western industrialisation were already so fully adumbrated even in the immediate aftermath of World War II that far more modest efforts were required. Reconstruction, by definition, is less ambitious than enforced modernisation. Still, capital resources and state planning were called upon, and as foresighted policy-makers understood, these would be more important to western Europe than military programmes. Back in 1947, for instance, when George F. Kennan realised that strategists in Washington were taking his 'X' article literally, he began dissenting from that version of containment and to call for post-war reconstruction primarily on economic and psychological terms, not military terms. Far better than the techno-strategic architects of deterrence, tactical war-fighting and escalation options, Kennan has always appreciated, though perhaps in quaint ways, the interconnectedness of Alliance strategy. And he has always understood this as part of a larger cultural undertaking, which the West ought to lead, and proudly so, on behalf of all the world's people. Writing in 1948, for example, in the context of debates about the European Recovery Plan, the ERP, Kennan argued that:

> This is the significance of the ERP, the idea of European Union, and the cultivation of a closer association with the UK and Canada. For a truly stable world order can proceed, within our lifetime, only from the older, mellower and more advanced nations of the world – nations for which the concept of order, as opposed to power, has value and meaning. If these nations do not have the strength to seize and hold real leadership in world affairs today, through that combination of political greatness and wise restraint which goes only with a ripe and settled civilization, then as Plato once remarked: '. . . cities will never have rest from their evils – no, nor the human race, as I believe'.[14]

To reappropriate these elements today, nearly 40 years later, is no easy matter. For this requires an explicit recounting of the promise of Western culture, a promise or master narrative of international political life that is increasingly more difficult to sustain. Helmut Schmidt, for example, in recently acknowledging the interconnectedness of Western policy spheres, has issued the call for what he calls a 'grand strategy', a formal explication of foreign policy, military strategy and economic policy among the Western states. For Schmidt, there are serious problems confronting the West which are best overcome by transcending national rivalries, by putting an end to long-standing American dominance and its overextension. Western Europe needs to play a greater role, especially along the lines of enhanced Franco–German policy co-ordination. The point of Schmidt's inquiry is that no profound structural crisis of dissolution is at hand and that contemporary dilemmas, while more serious than past ones, are not beyond repair.[15]

But what are we repairing? What is it we would be saving? Indeed, what really is 'the West', for whom a grand strategy is needed? On this vital issue Schmidt is silent, doubtless because the answer is so obvious. Yet it is precisely the familiar which we need to examine if we are to understand where we are. Only that which has been so fully produced and replicated that its existence becomes second nature and therefore self-evident: precisely here, beyond the dilemmas of arms control policy, interest rates and security co-operation is where the most important politics of all needs to be rescued from the oblivion of silence.

NATO and the whole Western Alliance are part of the attempt to construct a particular form of political identity. By 'identity' here, I do not mean some inner sense of the self as may be found in popular forms of ego psychology. Rather, I refer to the making of a whole way of life, a distinct civilisational project, which makes both promises to and claims upon its people. The kind of political identity discussed here, then, is part of a larger set of relations by which a culture and ways of thinking about it – including ways of living in it – are produced and reproduced.

Institutions and political practices that are hegemonic in the Gramscian sense construct relations of power that are construed as legitimate. These relations thereby privilege certain arrangements while depoliticising and disabling other, alternative arrangements. But what is characteristic of the whole Western project is the ruthlessness of its modernist impulse, its tendency to transform the landscape, to revamp economies, to make over traditional values, and to appropriate the culture and identities of the world's peoples. A cheap kind of anti-Americanism, the kind prevalent amongst European cultural conservatives and also relied upon by condemnatory leftists, might attribute this redrawing of the map to the machinations of US-based institutions. But in doing they exclude themselves from any implications, as if the problem with world politics were that Europeans had lost influence to the Americans, without questioning how Europe had achieved its once-prominent position in the world, or whether the transatlantic and global ties of economic and military power enable one so readily and so neatly to exclude European states and European capital from these processes.

In this sense, the play of internal Alliance politics becomes important, for just as the problem cannot be dumped solely on the doorstep of the Americans, nor should we succumb to the claim that modernism as some autonomous, unitary force were driving on the whole world. Indeed, I would argue, it is precisely the convergence of three complementary dimensions of conflict that has nurtured a general tendency of modernisation on a world scale and that returns in the form of dilemmas to overburden the managers of Western strategy and policy.

The first dimension has to do with the development in the West of productive forces whose ability to absorb the labour and resources of the world's peoples has been unparalleled in human history. The particular terms of the emergence of capitalism as a regional and global force are less important here than the scope of the ensuing incorporation on a world scale – a process which has if not triumphed in the form of a singular world-system has certainly generated the prevailing terms of conflict between the modernising forces of capitalist production on the one hand and traditional, agrarian, subsistence and barter modes of existence on the other.[16]

The second, based upon the first, involves a tension between national and international sectors of capital. In the nineteenth century this was celebrated as a global division of labour. Its historical effect was the commodification of the world. During this century the tension between national and international sectors has been consolidated in the West so as to favour neo-classical economic policy management and the accompanying multilateralisation of Fordism.[17] In the Third World the state has played the role of securing post-colonial dependency upon the ownership, technology, extractive ability, financial strength and marketing power of advanced industrial societies and their international representatives. Thus multinational agribusiness co-ordinates the geopolitics of protein, such that the country of Senegal is transformed into a giant peanut farm while Costa Rica becomes a vital link in the 'hamburger connection' to Burger King.[18] Back home in the core we all (almost all) become voracious consumers living on credit as the working class enjoys levels of life and leisure unimaginable three decades earlier.

The third dimension, a military–strategic one, overlays the other two. It has involved American dominance of the Alliance and prompted, in strategic terms, a techno-culture of instrumental power projection at odds with classical continental modes of political–military relations. The chief manifestation of this intra-Alliance tension is a tendency for NATO to acquiesce in American-sponsored military solutions to what are, in essence, political–economic problems. In other words, tactical war-fighting rather than the Rapacki Plan; SDI rather than arms control; a Rapid Deployment Force and AWACS aircraft to the Middle East and war upon Libya. But even here we can see that the west Europeans are not innocent victims in this process of militarisation, for part of the post-war domestic consensus was to accept American leadership – replete with nuclear weapons – in an attempt to save domestic capital for investment that would otherwise have been spent on conventional armaments. And the same consensualists, Christian Democratic and Social Democratic alike, have agreed on the necessity of strategic protection afforded by the USA in the form of globally-extended deterrence and counter-insurgency operations in the Third World. If of late these tensions have mounted, and they have within the Alliance, it is simply because the reliance upon American strategy has exacerbated rather than, as was hoped, stabilised global order. This exacerbation is due, in part, to the persistence of the USSR and the Warsaw Pact in countering with their own levels of militarisation in response. And most dramatically, in terms of the sheer number of wars since World War II, the problem in the Third World is that the social conflicts which were supposed to be forestalled thanks to the promise of modernisation and development have for the most part not materialised, leaving peasants and students with little recourse for a decent existence but to build their own societies with their own hands.[19]

The dilemma now facing the Alliance is that it is increasingly difficult to sustain the basic course of the Western project. There are inherent limits which today confront the West. The global project of Alliance politics is beginning to fold back in upon itself in a kind of involutionary process. On a military level, the historic intensification of power projection has been driven on to the point where it has to resort to competitive arms trading abroad in order to fill up the surplus capacity of an overdeveloped domestic arms manufacturing sector.[20] This creates pressures for stepped-up searches for new, breakthrough technologies at home that might lead to yet further appropriations and deployments. Yet this induces global crises of increased military expenditures, overburdened national economies, the militarisation of regional conflicts, social underdevelopment, domestic repression, a loss of the long-standing legitimacy of so-called 'deterrence' and, ultimately, to a wide range of proposals and popular calls not just for arms control but also for disarmament.

On an economic level, it is increasingly difficult to generate a social surplus. Growth rates have slowed down markedly. Labour inputs have risen in the advanced industrial countries, and unemployment mounts there as wage work is increasingly relegated to those at the margin, whether as 'guest workers' or abroad, to such newly industrialising countries as South Korea and Taiwan. The inexpensive fuels so vital to earlier phases of spectacular growth rates are no longer quite so readily available. Currency stability under American aegis has been displaced to a global market at once more volatile and impervious to national economic control. Industrial manufacturing is giving way to capital-intensive technologies as the leading economic sectors. State-sponsored sectors are overloaded, and neo-conservatives call for fiscal cut-backs precisely when there is emerging heightened social conflict between the indigenous labour force and those who have migrated from the periphery in search of opportunity in the core. Thus we find increased racial and xenophobic conflicts, whether in the form of American legislation aimed at preventing Mexican refugees from crossing the border, 'Paki-bashing' in London, or the dispatch of Turkish workers out of West Berlin. The point here, though, is not to catalogue Western economic and social woes but to suggest that their emergence is part of a more organic rupture in the basic flow of Western industrial life, a life denoted by commitments to productivity, growth and material wealth which are proving increasingly difficult to sustain. And it is the simultaneity of these developments, in the military and economic realms, that manifests itself in the proliferation of alternative movements that array themselves from within the West and from without the West against it.

THE POLITICS OF POST-ATLANTICISM

The task of a politics of post-Atlanticism is to engage in the de-naturalising of the Western project and thereby to render it as something constructed, provisional and subject to contestation. This task has already begun at the level of various peace movements, insofar as over the past few years there have arisen alternatives to the techno-strategies of nuclear deterrence: alternatives in the form of a critical peace research literature and its accompanying discussions of transitional political-military arrangements. In terms of language alone, these debates have opened up the whole discussion of strategy and infused it with moral discourses drawn from just war and pacifist teachings, with nurturant and emotive discourses drawn from feminist circles, with populist discourses drawn from counter-cultural circles, with environmentalist discourses derived from ecology and anti-nuclear movements. The importance of these critical debates is that they have seized the very terms of strategy from the strategists and displaced – if only partially – the technical arms control community which for years had been the source of in-house criticism from an essentially liberal, reformist point of view. The significance of this discursive shift is that the critique of strategy is no longer a friendly debate within the defence community between what might be called the 'minimalist' and 'maximalist' positions – the former advocating restraint, arms control negotiations and assured destruction, the latter advocating 'bargaining chips', strategic modernisation and the need to recapture strategic superiority. The new debates, by contrast, have shown that the mainstream strategic debates have largely taken place within a community of shared assumptions regarding the structure of the state system and of the hope that violence could be centrally co-ordinated in order to manage that world.

The political movements critical of the normalising function of strategic discourse are unavoidably engaged in a counter-hegemonic struggle, a struggle that seeks to displace the modernist logic of strategy and to rebuild politics along lines that are not centrally co-ordinated by states and alliances of states. Thus this kind of struggle is somewhat at odds with traditional revolutionary activity, where counter-hegemonic efforts sought to organise a working class in opposition to the ruling class of the Western system. Such political and economic movements have been active since the first articulations of industrial capitalism and were crucial to the first assault on that global system via a critique of imperialism. Yet this classical tradition, as a counter-hegemonic one, has also always been counter-modernist in orientation, and this tendency, to 'counter' modernism, has not challenged but actually replicated the prevailing terms of contemporary life. By counter-modernist I mean that it has accepted as inevitable, indeed as necessary and good, the basic parameters of modern industrial culture and would not repudiate that mode of life but rather generalise its benefits so as to redound to the benefit of the vast majority of the world's population. This has involved these alternative movements in struggles which have sanctioned the state's claims to resources in the name of meeting the needs of the whole of civil society. Thus the revolutionary tradition, in challenging the Western system of capitalism, has replicated the modernism in the name of a new form of hegemony, socialist hegemony. In this manner a revolutionary socialist tradition has triumphed against enormous historical obstacles to create in practice industrial statisms deficient in democratic representation and committed instead to paths of bureaucratically-centred productivism.

This is an ambiguous achievement, an ambiguity manifest in the counter-militarisation of the Warsaw Pact. Without in any way equating to the Warsaw Pact the degree of global militarisation undertaken by the Western System, we can see that this particular counter-hegemonic alternative is but a counter-modernism that has itself succumbed to a profound impasse. It is less a break with modernism than an attempt to reorganise it in the name of the working class.

This is not to denigrate the socialist critique of the West. It is merely to suggest that more than counter-hegemonic and counter-modernist impulses will be needed to overcome the crises of militarisation, repression and economic stagnation that now confront the world.

These alternatives are to be found in broader circles of opposition.[21] We find them in anti-modernist environmental struggles. And we find them in the post-modernist struggles of feminism, pacifism, regionalism and self-reliance. These have proliferated in the past two decades to the point where they pose a broad basis of cultural opposition to the general discourse of modernism and to those hegemonic institutions of the Western Alliance which have sought in the post-war world to organise that mode of identity.

Such oppositional discourses are part of larger crises in the ability of the West to maintain the military and economic hegemony which for years had underpinned Alliance politics. They reflect a subtle erosion in the self-evident rationality of post-war arrangements – an erosion in the ability of the West to sustain its hegemony; an erosion in the quality of that life; an erosion in the confidence that when push comes to shove the Americans will be able to come to the rescue; a sense of unease with the general thrust of militarisation and with the palpable failures of Third World development. They represent a sense that questions of war and peace are intimately connected to those of political economy, and that as the whole culture of modernism seeks to extend itself and to organise the world on its terms this will induce yet greater imperatives for Western responses to crises: that it will have been precisely the whole project of instrumental, commodity-laden productivist Atlanticism that really since the sixteenth century has been domesticating the world's 'otherness' and has either co-opted it as part of its own celebratory self or condemned it to the various netherworlds of counter-Western identity, whether in the guise of 'Orientalism', 'terrorism', 'Luddism' or 'the Soviet threat'.

To participate in this kind of politics of post-Atlanticism is to call to mind those who paid with their lives in the making of the West. It is to recall that beneath the waters of the Atlantic Ocean there remain the bloated corpses of African slave labourers. It is to recall the role of violence perpetrated against Scottish Highlanders and Irish peasants in the making of the United Kingdom. And it is to reappropriate the subjugated knowledges of villagers and local craftsmen whose skills and identities were overtaken by the organised industry of development and modernisation.

This kind of politics is inescapably post-modern in outlook insofar as it seeks to build new structures of power and identity at levels both below and beyond those of the modern state: to transcend those classes and institutions which have been co-ordinated within the imperatives of the Western Alliance in the name of building a consensualist civilisation. This will require affinities and meaningful alliances that are not bound by their geographic location in a transatlantic space. It will require, instead, the reconstitution and empowerment of radical subjectivities and suppressed forms of being in the world – subjectivities and modes of being until now relegated to the margins and subterranean undercurrents of that ambiguous historical construction which has been bequeathed to us and which the managers of Atlantic policy would prefer to handle on their own.

NOTES

Research for this paper was funded by the German Academic Exchange Service and the Dean's Office of St Lawrence University. I am grateful to David Brown, Stephen Gill, Fred Halliday, Steve Smith and Frank Unger for their trenchant criticisms of earlier drafts.

1. See Chapters 2 and 4 of this volume.
2. The theoretical framework for this paper is derived from recent theories of discourse analysis. See Michel Foucault, 'The Discourse on Language', in *The Archaeology of Knowledge and The Discourse on Language,* trans. A. M.

Sheridan Smith (New York, Pantheon, 1972), pp. 215–37; Michael Shapiro (ed.) *Language and Politics* (New York, New York University Press, 1984); William E. Connolly, *The Terms of Political Discourse*, 2nd edn (Princeton, Princeton University Press, 1984); Richard K. Ashley, 'The Geopolitics of Geopolitical Space: Towards a Critical Social Theory of International Politics', *Alternatives*, vol. XII (1987); R. B. J. Walker, 'Realism, Change, and International Political Theory', *International Studies Quarterly*, vol. 31 (1987), pp. 65–86.
3. See the account of post-modernism as 'incredulity toward metanarratives' in Jean-François Lyotard, *The Postmodern Condition: A Report on Knowledge* (Minneapolis, University of Minnesota Press, 1984), p. xxiv.
4. Max Weber, 'Politics as a Vocation', in Hans Gerth and C. Wright Mills (eds and translators) *From Max Weber* (New York, Oxford University Press, 1946), p. 78.
5. The best statement on realist hegemony is Robert Gilpin, *War and Change in World Politics* (Princeton, Princeton University Press, 1981). Robert O. Keohane, *After Hegemony* (Princeton, Princeton University Press, 1984), assays the dilemma of world co-operation in an era of waning American dominance.
6. The Gramscian conception of hegemony derives from Antonio Gramsci, in Quintin Hoare and Geoffrey Nowell Smith (eds and translators) *Selections from the Prison Notebooks* (New York, International Publishers, 1971), pp. 210–76. The case for the superior explanatory power of the Gramscian conception of hegemony can be found in Robert W. Cox, 'Social Forces, States and World Orders: Beyond International Relations Theory', *Millennium*, vol. 10 (1981), pp. 126–55; 'Gramsci, Hegemony and International Relations: An Essay in Method', *Millennium*, vol. 12 (1982), pp. 162–75; and Richard K. Ashley, 'Theory as War: Antonio Gramsci and the War of Positions', paper presented at the 1984 Annual Meeting of the American Political Science Association, Washington DC. For a comparison of the realist and Gramscian conceptions of hegemony as applied to the Trilateral Commission, see Stephen Gill, 'Hegemony, consensus and Trilateralism', *Review of International Studies*, vol. 12 (1986), pp. 205–21.
7. This paragraph summarizes the argument of Bradley S. Klein, *Strategic Discourse*, Center on Violence and Human Survival Occasional Paper no. 3 (New York, John Jay College of Criminal Justice, 1987).
8. Bernard Brodie, 'Implications for Military Policy', in Bernard Brodie (ed.) *The Absolute Weapon* (New Haven, Harcourt, Brace and Co. for the Yale Institute of International Studies, 1946), p. 76.
9. A fascinating sociology of knowledge of the international relations discipline is offered by Ekkehart Krippendorff, *Internationale Beziehungen als Wissenschaft: Einfuehrung 2* (Frankfurt, Campus Verlag, 1977), pp. 24–39. The most influential volume published by the Royal Institute of International Affairs reiterates the theme of international relations as a young discipline. See E. H. Carr, *The Twenty Years Crisis, 1919–1939: An Introduction to the Study of International Relations* (London, Macmillan, 1940).
10. The phrase 'living with nuclear weapons' refers to a popular paperback written by a group of Harvard University political science professors in the midst of the rise of the recent American peace movements. The point of the volume was to present a moderate position against the more radical claims of disarmers. The effect was to normalise the system of nuclear deterrence. See The Harvard Nuclear Study Group, *Living with Nuclear Weapons* (New York, Bantam,

1982). For a devastating critique of their thinking, see Carol Cohn, 'Sex and Death in the Rational World of Defense Intellectuals', *Signs,* vol. 12 (1987).
11. Daniel Bell, *The End of Ideology* (Glencoe, Il., The Free Press, 1960).
12. The relationship between security assistance and development/modernisation is discussed by Bradley S. Klein and Frank Unger, 'Die Politik den USA gegenueber Militaerregimen der Dritten Welt', in Reinar Steinweg (ed.) *Friedensanalysen, Bnd. 22: Militaerregimen der Dritten Welt* (Frankfurt, Suhrkamp, 1988).
13. The first citation is from W. W. Rostow, *The Stages of Economic Growth: A Non-Communist Manifesto* (Cambridge, Cambridge University Press, 1960), p. 162. The second citation, from his 'Guerrilla Warfare in the Underdeveloped Areas', *Department of State Bulletin,* 7 August 1961, p. 234, was part of Rostow's address at the graduation ceremonies of the US Army Special Warfare School, Fort Bragg, North Carolina, 28 June 1961.
14. From Kennan's 'PPS: 13, Résumé of World Situation, November 6, 1947', in Thomas H. Etzold and John Lewis Gaddis (eds) *Containment: Documents on American Policy and Strategy, 1945–1950* (New York, Columbia University Press, 1979), p. 100. This collection of documents contains many of Kennan's previously classified memoranda written while at the State Department's Policy Planning Staff during and immediately after the publication of his famous 'X' article, 'The Sources of Soviet Conduct', *Foreign Affairs,* vol. 25 (1947), pp. 566–82.
15. Helmut Schmidt, *A Grand Strategy for the West: The Anachronism of National Strategies in an Interdependent World* (New Haven, Yale University Press, 1985).
16. Eric R. Wolfe, *Europe and the People Without History* (Berkeley, University of California Press, 1982).
17. The claim about the multilateralisation of Fordism as one definitive characteristic of recent Western strategy is masterfully dealt with by Mary Kaldor, 'The Global Political Economy', *Alternatives,* vol. XI (1986), pp. 431–60.
18. See Malcolm Caldwell, *The Wealth of Some Nations* (London, Zed Press, 1977) for a dramatic account of the 'protein imperialism' by which the 'overdeveloped' industrial countries engage in the 'development of underdevelopment'.
19. Istvan Kende, 'Local Wars 1945–76', in Asbjorn Eide and Marek Thee (eds) *Problems of Contemporary Militarism* (New York, St Martin's Press, 1980), pp. 261–85. Kende analyses 120 regional wars since 1945, the overwhelming majority of which took place in the Third World. Also see Ruth Leger Sivard, *World Military and Social Expenditures 1986* (Washington DC, World Priorities, 1986).
20. Mary Kaldor, *The Baroque Arsenal* (New York, Hill & Wang, 1981).
21. A variety of critical social movements are assessed in Saul H. Mendlovitz and R. B. J. Walker (eds), *Towards a Just World Peace* (Guildford, Butterworths, 1987).

INDEX

This index can also be used as a key to abbreviations used in the book.

ABM Treaty (Anti-Ballistic Missile), 97, 168, 179
Abrahamson, Lt. General James, 180
Adomeit, H., 49, 59, 60
AEAA (Arms Export Administration Act, USA), 181
  Commodity Control List, 182
Aerospace Corporation (USA), 199
Afferica, J., 61
Afghanistan, 25, 74, 92, 104, 165
  Soviet invasion of, 22
  'freedom fighters', 30
AFL–CIO (American Federation of Labor–Council of Industrial Organisations), 17
Africa, starvation in, 72
Agnelli, G., 85
Agricultural Adjustment Act (USA), 121
AIDS, 72
Airpower Research Institute (USA), 200
ALB (Air-Land Battle), 156, 173, 174
Allen, D., 30, 88, 109–10
Allen, R., 75
Allum, P., 85
Altvater, E., 84–5
AMC (American Motors Corporation), 79
American Chamber of Commerce, 81
American Physical Society, 170
Amin, S., 134
Anderson, P., 193
Andropov, Y., 41
Anglophobia, 113
anti-Americanism, 55, 204
anti-Sovietism, 9, 40, 45
  West European integration as moderating influence on, 49
ANZUS (Australia–New Zealand–US defence pact), 201

Arab–Israeli conflict, 99–100
  October War, 23, 139, 165
Araskog, R., 84
Arbatov, G., 60
Argentina, 30, 67, 104
  Italian Masonic connection, 67
Arias Plan, 105
arms control, 94, 167
  and technological revolution, 186
Aron, R., 44, 58
Aronson, J. D., 137
Arrighi, G., 134
artificial intelligence, 181
Astre, G. A., 87
Ashley, R. K., 210
ATBM (Anti-Tactical Ballistic Missile), 184
Atlanticism, xi ff., 1, 36–7, 112–13
  anachronism of, 12
  basic questions, 1–2
  contradictions, 115
  crisis of, 7, 12
  cycles of history, 4–5
  denaturalised, 197
  eroding socio-cultural base of, 113
  hegemonic concepts, 10
  as 'highest stage of modernism', 197
  ideology, 19
  inertial power of, 48
  main changes in, 7
  minimal consensus in, 36
  post-, 196 ff.
  public opinion in USA, 15, 26
    in Europe, 161, 171 ff., 207–8
  structural trends, 1
    international, 90
  'two pillars' concept, 20
  universal historical project of, 196 ff.
  and views of USSR, 18

Atlantic Alliance, 156
  interests, convergence of, 18
  involution of, 206
  see also Atlanticism; Atlantic relations; NATO
Atlantic Charter, 22
Atlantic Council of United States, 16
Atlantic Institute (Paris), 16
Atlantic partnership concept, 89
Atlantic relations, trans-
  arms control, 94
  balance of forces, 50, 51
  breakdown of consensus, 89
  centrifugal forces, 1, 7, 42, 44, 47, 49, 52, 56, 112
  centripetal forces, 1, 7, 42, 44, 47–9, 52, 56
  as civilisational project, 10
  class formations, 8
  consensus on social policy, 12
  and East–West relations, 11, 91–2
  harmony and crisis, 89
  and Middle East, 99–102
  normal politics of, xi ff.
  and Persian Gulf, 102–3
  ruling class, restructuring of, 62
  as a system, 88
  theorising change in, 4
  two stories of, xii
  and Western Hemisphere, 104
  see also Atlantic Alliance; Atlanticism; NATO
'Atlantic to Urals' concept, 41
Atlantic Union concept, 112
ATT Corporation (USA), 48, 73, 127
ATT–Phillips (USA–Netherlands) (joint venture), 137
AWACS (Advanced Warning Airborne Control Systems), 205
Axis powers, 18

Baechler, G., 194
Baker, J. III, 75, 83, 138–9, 153
Baker Initiatives, 33, 138 ff.
  and 'market-place magic', 142
  and structural economic change, 140
Baldridge, M., 75, 76
bankruptcy of US farmers, 123
banks, 143–9
  government-private banks in co-operation, 145
  International Banking Facilities (IBFs), 82–3
  liberalisation, 82
  offshore, 83
  renewed importance of, 70 ff.
  see also capital; debt; money; neo-liberalism
Barraclough, G., 4, 12

Barre, R., 68
Barry Jones, R. J., 108
BDI (West German Employers' Association), 68
Beggs, J., 81
Beletsky, V., 60
Belgium, 73, 77
Bell, D., 211
Bell Telephone Inc. (USA), 128
Benetton Corporation (Italy), 73
BENS (Business Executives for National Security, USA), 81
Bergsten, C. F., 23, 25, 32, 34, 39
Berlin (Four Power) Agreement, 160
Berlusconi, S., 73
Berufsverbote, 68
Bialer, S., 61
Bilderberg Meetings, 16, 48
Billing, R., 193
biotechnology, 54, 184–5, 188
Blackaby, F., 178
Blanchard, O., 135
Blumenthal, S., 39
Bluth, C., 109
BMD (Ballistic missile defence), 179
Bode, R., 84
Boeing Corporation (USA), 80
Boesky, I., 10
Bogdanov, A., 60
Bokassa diamonds, 68
bomb culture, 6
Borodaevsky, A., 59
Boulin, R., suicide of, 68
Bovin, A., 61
Boyd, D., 178
Brainard, W. C., 135
Brandt, W., 23
Brauch, H.-G., 193
Brazil, 145
Brett, E. A., 135
Bretton Woods, 140
  breakdown of, 152
British International Studies Association, xiv, 1
British Telecom Plc, 128
Brock, W. R. III, 76
Brodie, B., 200, 210
Brookings Institution, 16
Brown, A., 58
Brown, D., 209
Brownstein, R., 86
Bruce, J., 177
Bruce, P., 193
Bruxelles-Lambert Bank (Belgium), 73
Brzezinski, Z. K., 45
Buchan, A., 13
Bulkeley, R., 177
Bundy, McGeorge, 20
Bunkina, M. K., 59

Burch, P., 85
Burger King Inc. (USA), 205
Bush, G., 75, 132–3, 138–9, 153–4, 169
 as Director of CIA, 69
Bushkoff, L., 39
business pacifism, 203
Bykova, A., 59, 60

Cafruny, A. W., 28, 151
California, 2, 12, 17, 58
Caldwell, M., 211
Calleo, D. P., 13, 19, 24, 38, 108, 134, 135
Camp David Accords, 99
Canada, 122, 149, 203
Canal 5 (France), 73
CAP (Common Agricultural Policy of the EC), 120–2, 124–5, 130–1, 151
capital, 7–8, 11–12, 14, 19, 33–4, 36, 39, 42, 45, 140–2, 146–9, 151, 153, 155, 185–6
 circuits of, 62
 international, of money, 65
 financial, 14, 63–4
 global capital flows, 140
 global restructuring of, 65
 internationalisation of, 62, 65, 70
 internationally mobile, 14, 140
 money, 62
  renewed importance of banks, 70
  viewpoint of, 63
 national vs. international sectors, 205
 productive, 62
  viewpoint of, 63
 from state monopoly- to inter-state monopoly-, 47
 transnational, 14, 129
 see also banks; classes; money; production; TNCs
Carlucci, F., 75, 81
Carnegie Endowment (USA), 16
Carr, E. H., 5, 210
Carter, A., 177
Carter Administration, 1, 21, 99, 104, 105
 and CPD, 24
 economic policy, 24–5
 grain embargo, 25
 and Trilateral Commission, 24
 and Volcker Shift, 25
Carter, Jimmy, 14, 21–2, 24–7, 38, 163, 165, 166, 167, 175
 moralism of, 69
Carvalho, J., 137
Casey, W., 75
Caterpillar Tractor Corporation (USA), 76
Cathie, J., 136
Cavanagh, J., 137
CED (Committee on Economic Development, USA), 16

Central America, 53, 104–5
CFR *see* Council on Foreign Relations
Chalban-Delmas, J., 68
Chamsol, P., 84
Chargeurs Réunis (France), 73
Charles, D., 194
Chase Manhattan Bank, 69
Chile, 66
 coup d'état, 66
 economic model, 74
 mass repression, 67
China, 2, 3, 28
Chirac, J., 68
Christian Democrat coalition (West Germany), 69 ff.
Christian Democratic Party (Italy), 67
Christian Democratic Union (West Germany), seen in USSR as Atlanticist, 54
Chrysler Corporation (USA), 70
Chrysler–Mitsubishi (USA–Japan) (joint venture), 79
CIA (US Central Intelligence Agency), 75
Clark, W. P., 93
classes, 6–8, 13, 18–19, 37–8, 45, 185
 Atlantic–Pacific ruling, 64
 conflict, 45
 fractions, 62–3
 global alignments, 62
 rentier, 70–1
 see also capital; labour; money; neo-liberalism; production
Clausewitz, C. von, 200
Cleveland, H. van Buren, 13
CMEA (Council for Mutual Economic Assistance–Eastern European), 41, 188
COCOM (Co-ordinating Committee for Multilateral Export Controls), 29, 93, 182, 187
Cohen, B., 84, 153, 155
Cohn, C., 211
Cold War, xiv, 6, 10, 15, 18, 20–1, 23–6, 38, 47, 67, 52, 113, 158–9
 militarisation of Atlantic Alliance, 18
 new, 52, 69–70, 76
 phases of, 20
 second, 10, 164, 166–7, 176
 trimmed back, 81
 see also USA–USSR
Cold War Internationalism (CWI), 17, 21
Commentary, 17, 28
Commerzbank (West Germany), 68
Commission on Defense Management (USA), 81
Committee on Economic Development (CED) USA, 16
Committee on the Present Danger (USA), 17, 69, 74, 81
 members in Reagan Administration, 74

Commodities Credit Corporation (USA), 121
Communist Party of the Soviet Union (CPSU), 40–2, 56
Conference on Security Co-operation in Europe (CSCE), 97, 160, 186
Connally, J., 23
Connolly, W. E., 210
Contadora Group, 105
Containment,
  ideological, 28
  realist, 29
  'without confrontation', 30
  see also Cold War; USA–USSR
Continental Illinois Bank, failure of, 83
Cooper, R. N., 147, 154–5
Coors, Joseph, 69
Coriat, B., 85
corporate liberalism, 14, 62–3
  'liquidated by money capital', 65
  marginalised in France, 68
  and West German politics, 68–9
  see also neo-liberalism
corporatism, 113 ff.
Corral, D. de, *Rape of Europe*, 3
cosmopolitanism, 19, 48
Costa Rica, 205
Council for International Business (USA), 127
Council for Mutual Economic Assistance, 41
Council on Foreign Relations, New York (USA), 13, 16, 34, 38, 41, 49, 65, 69, 193, 200
counter-hegemony, 207–8
  see also hegemony; USA
counter-insurgency, 205
counter-modernism, 208
Cowhey, P. F., 137
Cox, Robert W., 12, 38, 39, 135, 210
CPD see Committee on the Present Danger
CPSU see Communist Party of the Soviet Union
Craxi, B., 67, 73
Crédit Lyonnais Bank (France), 78
Crédit Suisse Bank (Switzerland), 73
Crockatt, R., 177
Croft, S., 110
cruise missiles, 25, 35, 156, 158, 162, 171, 175
CSCE see Conference on Security Co-operation in Europe
CSFB-Effectenbank (West Germany–Switzerland), 73
Cuba, 105
Cuellar, P. de, 103
CWI see Cold War Internationalism

Daalder, I., 194
Dahrendorf, R., 37, 39
Dando, M., 110
Danzin, A., 193
Danzin, J., 185
Darilek, R., 110
Davignon, E., 39
Davis, M., 75, 86, 135
Davydov, Y. P., 61
Dawisha, K., 61
De Young, K., 193
debt crisis, xii, 83, 123, 140 ff.
  Africa, and European concerns, 149
  debt–equity swaps, 149
  debt-to-export ratios, 143
  government–private banks in co-operation, 145
  Latin America, 144, 148
  rescheduling of, 143
Deep Strike, 156
deflation, 33, 75–6, 145
DeLauer, J., 74, 82
demilitarisation, 186–7, 191, 193
Democratic Party (USA), 17, 27
  see also Carter; Kennedy; Truman
denuclearisation, 179
deregulation, 8, 32, 141, 151, 187
  of finance, 120
  and R&D, 187
  of telecommunications, 127, 128
  in USA, 32
  see also neo-liberalism; regulation
Destler, I. M., 109
detente, 8–9, 20, 160
  west European–Soviet, 20, 28, 40–60 *passim*
deterrence, 9, 157, 163, 179–80
  credibility of, 159
  discourse of, 201 ff.
  extended, 200
Deutsche Bank (West Germany), 68, 73
devaluation, 23, 145–6, 153
disinflation, 32
Dobrynin, A., 40
dollar see under USA, economic policy (finance and money)
domesticism, 32, 143
Dornbusch, R., 135, 155
Dresdner Bank (West Germany), 68
Drexel Burnham Lambert (USA), 71–3
droit du seigneur (of USA over allies), 21
dual use technologies, 181 ff.
Dukakis, M., 153
  protectionism, 154
Dulles, J. Foster, 20

E. F. Hutton Inc. (USA), 74
Eagleburger, L., 110
East–West relations, 107
  trade and economic warfare, 92
  see also Cold War; detente; USA–USSR
Easton, N., 86

EC (European Community), 1, 37, 89, 104–5, 113–14, 120, 123–4, 128, 153
  agriculture, 132
  breaks taboo on questioning US leadership, 50
  budget cuts for 'framework programmes', 191
  EC–US–Japanese joint ventures in high technology, 191
  Economic and Social Committee, 184, 187
  food surpluses, 122
  liberalism vs. protectionism, 37
  Luxemburg compromise, 49
  Single European Act, xiii, 37, 132 ff.
    and internationalisation of capital, 133
  telecommunications, 128, 185
  Tindemans Report, 49
  Venice Declaration, 99, 100, 105
ecological discourse, 10, 192, 207
economists, and lack of theoretical consensus, 154
EDI (European Defence Initiative), 54
education, 38–9, 185
Edwards, G., 110
Ellison, J. J., 58
embedded liberalism, 150
EMS (European Monetary System), 144, 147–8
  lessons for Atlantic co-operation, 151
  and monetarist policies, 150
  and a possible European currency, 152–3
  and UK membership, 152
Engels, F., 85
Enlightenment, 3
environmentalism, 208
  see also ecological discourse
EPC (European Political Co-operation), 1, 90–1, 96, 105 ff.
  and monetary co-operation, 152
Ericsson–General Electric (Sweden–UK) (joint venture), 137
ERIS (Exoatmospheric Re-entry Vehicle Interception System), 169
ERP (European Recovery Plan), 203
Eskenazi, G., 73
ESPRIT (European Strategic Programme for Research and Development in Information Technologies), 128, 187
  funding, 189
  military potential, 192
  and standardisation, 189
ET (emerging technologies), 96, 173–4
Etzold, T. H., 211
EUREKA (European Research Co-ordinating Agency), 9, 51, 53, 54, 55, 82, 129, 187–8
  European Parliament Report, 188
  funding, 187
  and productivity, 188
  and R&D, 188
Euro–Arab dialogue, 99
Euro-mercantilism, 39
Eurocentrism, 4
Eurocurrency markets, 62–4, 83
  see also banks; markets; money; neo-liberalism
Europe, 3
  central balance, 98
  denuclearisation of, 173
  as 'dialectical crossroads of mankind', 3
  dilemma of 'entrapment' or 'abandonment', 94
  diplomacy, 104
  economic climacteric of, 3
  'fall-out' from Reykjavik summit, 98
  and idea of human race, 4
  identity, 88, 90–1, 94, 106
    and East–West relations, 91, 94
    in embryo, 106
    and expansion of consciousness, 107
  identity crises, 89
  as museum curator, 51
  political co-operation, 90
  new financial raiders, 74
  relative long-term weakness vis à vis USA, 50
  R&D, 187
European Defence Initiative (EDI), 54
European Integrated Broadband Communications Network (IBCN), 190
European tariff bloc, 116
European union, 203
European unity and Soviet objectives, 55–8
European Monetary System see EMS
European Political Co-operation see EPC
Europeanisation
  and globalisation of firms in EC, 190
  globalisation and military structures, 191
Europessimism, 51 ff.
Euroschlerosis, xiii, 3, 185
extraterritoriality, 22
Exxon Corporation, 73

Fabuis, L., 78
Fairchild Corporation (France–USA), 73
Falklands/Malvinas War, 30, 77, 104–5
  and European solidarity, 104
Federal Reserve Bank (USA), 25, 70, 118–19
Feldman, J., 193
Femia, J., 135
feminist discourse, 207–8
Fennema, M., 70, 85–6
Fenske, J., 109, 194
Ferguson, T., 86, 134
Ferruzzi Group (Italy), 73

Feulner, E., 84
FIAT Corporation (Italy), 67, 73, 84
fifth-generation computers, 181
Fitoussi, J. P., 135
Fleming, S., 193
Flexible Response, 176
FOFA (follow-on-forces attack), 77, 173–4, 186
Fondation Saint-Simon, 78
Fong, G., 194
Forbes 400, 72
Ford, Gerald, 16, 24, 64, 195
Ford, Glyn, 194
Ford Motor Company (USA), joint ventures with Japanese firms, 79
Fordism, 18, 38, 113, 129, 205
Foreign Affairs, 16, 20
Foreign Policy, 16
fortress America, 30, 80
fortress Europe, 132–3
Fortune, 72
Forward Defence, 174, 176
Foucault, M., 209
foundations, philanthropic, 16–17, 39, 66, 69, 84
France, 50, 73, 121
  abandons Keynesianism, 78
  agriculture, 131
  new types of financier, 73
  shift towards neo-liberalism, 68
  telecommunications, 127
Franco–German Friendship (Elysée) Treaty, 50, 77
Frank, A. G., 134
Frankfurter Allgemeine Zeitung, 181
Freedman, L., 108, 110
Frère, A., 73
Frost, E., 109
Fujitsu-Funac Inc. (Japan), 79

Gaddis, J. Lewis, 211
Gallia, P., 193
Gardini, R., 73
Gardner, R., 38
GATT (General Agreement on Tariffs and Trade), 111, 120, 123, 126, 128–9, 131, 201
  articles relating to agriculture, 124
  Dillon Round, 124
  Kennedy Round, 124
  Tokyo Round, 119, 124
  Uruguay Round, 124–5, 129, 130, 133
  stalemate, 132
Gaulle, General de, 19, 46
Gaullist Party (France), 68
GD (General Dynamics, USA), 80, 81
GE (General Electric, USA), 80
Gelli, L., 67
General Motors (GM) (USA), 79

Genscher–Colombo Plan (for Single European Act), 95
Genscher, H.-D., 57, 181, 193
Georgetown Center for Strategic and International Studies, 17, 38, 200
German Marshall Fund of the USA, 16
Germany, West, 50, 73, 114, 119, 121, 150
  austerity policy, 77
  Bundesbank, 68
  Bundespost, 128
  cost of COCOM controls, 182
  detente with East, 24
  fear of inflation, 144
  as main opponent of CAP reform, 151
  nuclear exports to Brazil, 24
  SDP–FDP coalition breaks down, 69, 76–7
  shift towards neo-liberalism, 68–9
  small farmers, 131
  terrorism and political violence, 68
Gesauvon, F. A. M., 134
GET–Siemens (USA–West Germany) (joint venture), 137
Gill, S. R., 12, 39, 84, 90, 108, 135, 154–5, 193, 196, 209–10
Gilpin, R., 134, 152, 154, 155, 193, 210
Giscard d'Estaing, V., 68
Glasnost, 11
Glickham, C., 58
global crises, 206
global economy,
  common principles, capitalism and communism, 47
  globalisation of production and exchange, 7
  imbalances and policy options, 140
  see also centrality *under* USA, economic policy (general); deregulation; finance; markets; production; regulation
Godson, J., 38
Goethe, Johann Wolfgang von, 3
gold standard, 117–18
Goldblatt, J., 178
Goldstein, W., 178
Goldthorpe, J., 154
Gorbachev, M., xi, 9, 11, 31, 40, 43, 57, 58, 61, 97, 186
Goria, G., 67
Gottfried, K., 178
Graeco–Roman world, 3
Gramsci, A., 14, 38, 111, 114–15, 135, 199, 204, 210
Graubard, S., 12
Great Depression, 8, 121
Greece, 202
Green Parties, 10
  see also ecological discourse
Greenspan, A., 83

Greiner, B., 84
Grenada, xi, 30, 105, 166
Griffiths, F., 58–9
Gromyko, A., 40
Grosser, A., 13
Group of Five (G5), 144, 147, 153
Group of Seven (G7), 47–8, 50
The Guardian, xiii
Guatemala, 202
Gulf Oil Company (USA), 69
Gulf of Oman, 103
Gulf, Persian, 102, 104

Haig, A., 30, 46, 74, 76, 93–4, 172
Halliday, F., 209
Hanreider, W., 38
Harkin–Gephardt Bill, 130, 137
Harris Trust Inc. (USA), 74
Hart, J., 137
Harvard Business School (USA), 10
Harvard Nuclear Study Group (USA), 210
Hayek, F. A. von, 66
Healey, D., 67
HEDI (High Endoatmospheric Defense Interceptor), 169
Hegel, G. W. F., 3
hegemonic
 concepts of control, 63–4
 periods, 115
 power, 114
 projects, 62
 stability, theory of, 5
hegemony, 111
 American *see* USA, hegemony
 and civilisations, 2–6, 201–6
 class, 63 ff.
 contested concept of, 199
 erosion of Western, 208
 of Europe, 3
 minimal, 118
 normalising function of, 199
 realist concept, 198
 reconstitution of USA's, 36
 see also classes; Gramsci; power
Helsinki Accords, 55–6
Heritage Foundation (USA), 17, 66, 69, 84
Hewlett-Packard Inc. (USA), 81
High Frontier Group (of US defence industries), 82
Hilferding, R., 64
Hill, C., 109
Hill, T. P., 136
Hitachi Corporation (Japan), 79
Hoare, Q., 38, 135, 210
Hobbes, T., *Leviathan,* 5, 198
Hoffmann, E. P., 59
Hoffman, S., 38
Hold, H.-H., 178
Holland *see* Netherlands
Holsti, O., 15–17, 37–8

Honeywell Inc. (USA), 81
Hoover Institution (USA), 17
Hopkins, R., 135
Hough, J., 56, 58, 61
Hoven, H. F. van den, 84
Howe, Sir Geoffrey, 105, 180, 193
Hoyos, F., 73
Hughes, T. L., 39
Hull, C., 17, 113

IBCN (European Integrated Broadband Communications Network), 190
IBF (international banking facilities), 83
IBM Inc. (USA), 48, 73, 81, 181, 190
ICC (International Chamber of Commerce), 84
Iklé, F., 74
IMEMO (Soviet Institute of World Economy and International Relations), 43, 47, 49–50, 53, 56
IMF (International Monetary Fund), 67, 116–17, 143, 201
 conditionality, 145
 fund for sub-Saharan Africa, 149
 medicine, 33
Indo-China, 202
INF (Intermediate Nuclear Forces), 35, 41, 94–6, 98, 151, 158, 162–3, 172, 186
 double zero agreement, 171–3
 zero option, 172
informatics, 128
information processing, 189
information technology, and jobs, 186
Insel, B., 136
Institute for Defense Analyses (USA), 200
International Institute of Strategic Studies (UK), 200
international relations
 as field of study, origins, 200
 Hobbesian condition in, 44
 social democratisation of, 64
 as superstructural phenomenon, 45
International Studies Association (USA), xiv
Iran, 92, 104, 202
 hostage crisis, and mood in USA, 26
 Revolution, 22
Iran–Contra scandal (Irangate), 31, 82, 102
Iran–Iraq War, 102–4
Ireland, 104
Islam, 4
isolationism, 16–35 *passim,* 113
Isuzu Corporation (Japan), 79
Italy, 104
 Historic Compromise, 67
 new types of financier, 73
 peasants, 209
 Red Brigades terrorism, 67
 and SDI, 82

ITT Corporation (USA), 84
ITT–CGE (Cie. Générale d'Electricité de France) (France–USA joint venture), 137

Jackson, H. S., 74
Japan, 2, 8, 14, 23–6, 29, 33–4, 42, 49–51, 60, 64, 79–80, 114, 116, 119, 140–54 *passim*, 182–91 *passim*
  anxious for Bush victory, 154
  economic internationalism, 153
  elite, 8
  joint ventures with Japanese firms, 79
  MITI (Ministry of International Trade and Industry), 80
  technological challenge to Europe, 51
  telecommunications, 127
Javits, J. K., 84
Jilberto, A. F., 84
Joffe, J., 109
Johnston, J. Bennett, 170, 178
Jonquieres, G. de, 194
Julien, C., 86
junk bonds, 71
Jünne, G., 80, 86, 193–4

Kahler, M., 109
Kaiser, K., 13
Kakabadse, M. A., 137
Kaldor, M., 108–9, 134, 211
Kanter, A., 109
Karaliev, E., 87
Karelov, Y., 60, 61
Kautsky, K., 113
Kelleher, C. McArdle, 21, 38
Kende, I., 211
Kennan, George F., 20, 38, 203, 211
Kennedy, J. F., 20, 112, 202
  clashes with de Gaulle, 89
Keohane, R. O., 39, 108, 109, 154, 210
Keynesianism, 11, 14, 20, 25, 36, 47, 119, 140–1, 154
  international, 47
  international monetary paradigm, 126
  military, 20
  planning, 64
  politics, decline of, 151
  in USA, 25
  see also Fordism; liberalisation; neo-liberalism; New Deal
Khomeini, Ayatollah, 103
Kiel Institute (West Germany), 150
Kimbel, D., 193
Kindleberger, C. P., 5, 12, 134
kinetic weapons, 179
Kirby, J. S., xiv
Kirichenko, E., 59, 60
Kirkpatrick, J., 28, 30, 76
Kissinger, H. A., 13, 22, 30, 105, 110

Klein, B. S., 210, 211
Kniatzhinsky, V., 59, 60
knowledge-power, 200
Kohl, H., 77, 168, 180, 193
Kongsberg Vappenfabbrik (West Germany), 182
Korea, South, 206
Korean War, 22
Korner, P., 155
Kovalev, A., 56
Krippendorff, E., 210
Kristol, I., 27, 28
Kudryavtsev, A., 60–1
Kühnl, R., 85
Kuwait, reflagging of oil tankers by USA, 102

Labour, on the defensive, 8–9, 31–5 *passim*
Labour Party (UK), 201
Laird, R. F., 59
Landes, D. S., 13
Lavrenev, V., 60
Latin America, 105 ff.
Law, D. A., 33, 39, 139, 155
Lawrence Livermore Laboratory (USA), 170
Lebanon, 101, 166
  and European multinational force, 101
Legvold, R., 30, 39
Lehman, J., 74
Lemaitre, P., 194
Lenin, V. I., 43, 58, 62
Leninism, 45
Levin, Y., 60
Lewis, F., 109
liberalisation, 112 ff.
  of agriculture, 124 ff.
  economic, 145
  of financial markets, 151 ff.
  and protectionism, 130
  of services, 125 ff.
  of trade, 126
  and uneven development, 134
  see also markets; money; neo-liberalism
Libya, 27, 30, 101, 166, 168
Lin, H., 177
Lincoln Laboratory (USA), 200
Lipietz, A., 65, 84
Lockheed Inc., 80
Lodgaard, S., 178
Lombra, R., 134
London Gold Pool, 116–17
Louvre Agreement, 146–8, 153
Lowenthal, M., 193
LTV Corporation, 81
Lucas, M., 30, 35, 194
Luddism, 209
Lukin, V., 44, 47, 50–1, 58, 60–1
  Power Centres: Conceptions and Reality, 44

INDEX   221

Lunn, S., 178
Lyotard, J.-F., 210
Lytton Industries (USA), 80

Machiavelli, N., 5
  The Prince, 198
Machtpolitik, 5
MAD (Mutually assured destruction), 179
Madonna, 72
Maier, C. S., 19
Maistre, J. de, 3
Maksimova, M., 59
Malaysia, 202
Malcolm, N., 58, 59
Mandel, E., 84, 134
Mandelbaum, M., 94, 109
Mansfieldism, 20–1
  see also Nunn Amendment
Marcum, J., 193
markets
  bandwagon effects in exchange markets, 140, 143
  Eurocurrency, 62, 64, 83
  globally integrated, unstable, 7
  international financial, 70
  melt-down of stock markets, 148
  pervasiveness of, 12
    see also Wall Street Crash
  US Presidential election and short-termism, 154
Marshall Plan, 92, 113
MARV (American manouevrable warheads system), 170
Marx, K., 4, 85
  The Eastern Question, 4
Marxist–Leninism, 45
Masonry, 67
Matuschka, Count Albrecht, 73
May, S., 109
Mazda, Inc. (Japan), 79
McCarthyism, 202
McDonnell Douglas Corporation (USA), 80
McGeehan, R., 109
McGuire, M., 178
McKinsey Inc. (USA), 79
McNamara, R. S., 20
MCTL (Military Critical Technologies List of AEAA), 182
MDFIs (Multilateral Development Financial Institutions), 145
Meese, Ed., 75
Meisel, K., 73
Mellon, Inc., 69
Melman, S., *Pentagon Capitalism*, 80
Mendlovitz, S., 211
Merrill-Lynch Inc. (USA), 73–4, 83
Mexico, 143, 145, 149
micro-electronics, 185, 188

Middle East, 105–6
  Atlantic relations, 99–102
Miller, J., 193
Minc, A., 73, 78
Minter, W., 38
MIT (Massachusetts Institute of Technology, USA), 200
MITI (Japan Ministry of International Trade and Industry), 80
MITRE Corporation (USA), 200
Mitsubishi Corporation (Japan), 79
Mitterand, F., 73, 77, 78
Miyazaki, I., 39
MLF (NATO's Multilateral Force), 160
Mobil Oil Corporation (USA), 69
modernism, 197
  of West, and otherness, 209
Mommen, A., 85
Mondale, W. F., 143, 154
monetarism, 25, 65–9 *passim*, 150
  and new Cold War, 74
  initial adoption in Chile, 66
  trimmed back, 81
  world economic stability, 138 ff.
money, international, 74–77 *passim*, 115–18 *passim*, 146–52 *passim*
  automaticity and international money, 147, 153
  balance of payments adjustment and capital flows, 141
  capital, as liquidator of corporate liberalism, 65
  currency convertibility, 116
  liquidity problem, 116
    see also classes; EMS; neo-liberalism; Triffin paradox
Mongol barbarism, 4
Mont Pelerin Society, 66, 84
Moreton, E., 55, 61
Morgan Stanley Inc., 80
Moro, A., assassination of, 67
Morozov, G., 58
multinational companies *see* TNCs
Murdoch, R., 71

NASA (US National Aeronautics and Space Agency), 81
NATO (North Atlantic Treaty Organisation), xii–xiii, 2, 7, 15–16, 18, 21, 25–8, 30, 38, 44, 48, 50–1, 53, 55, 77, 89, 93–4, 156, 158–9, 162–4, 170, 174, 177, 179–80, 184, 188, 191–2, 194–5, 201, 205
  arms build up, 186
  bipartisanship and alliance consensus, 18, 161
    its breakdown, 162–3, 176
  coherence, 9
  Europeanisation of, 30

INDEX

NATO (North Atlantic Treaty Organisation) *(continued)*
  Flexible Response Doctrine, 161
  Forward Defence Doctrine, 161
  guidance on strategy, 160–1
  importance of geography, 157
  Lisbon Force Goals, 160, 172
  'litmus test' of Allied unity, 21
  and Soviet perceptions, 157
  Special Consultative Group, 95
  structural *problématique*, 175 ff.
  and Western political identity, 204 ff.
  see also ABM; Cold War; INF; SALT
Nau, H., 32–3, 39, 118, 135, 143, 155
Nayyar, D., 137
NEC Ltd. (Japan), 79
neo-classical economics, 5
neo-conservatism in USA, 28
neo-Gaullism, 8
neo-liberalism, 10–11, 14, 25, 34, 36, 63, 72 ff., 151
  and economic strategy, 25
  and egocentrism, 72
  hegemony of, 77
  and internationally mobile capital, 11
  and morality, 70
  and parallel economy, 72
  and real capital accumulation, 72
  rise of, 66
  and social landscape, 74
  two trajectories of, 75
  see also capital; classes; liberalisation; Trilateralism
neo-realism, 5–6, 12
  see also realism
Netherlands, 70, 73, 77, 137
neutron bomb, 25, 94, 162
New Deal, 120, 121
  banking reforms, 126
  internationalisation of, 6, 113
  decline of New Deal system, 131
New International Economic Order *see* NIEO
new right in USA, 69
New World Economic Order, 44
Newhouse, J., 193
Nguyen, G. D., 137
Nicaragua, xi, 105, 166
  Contras, 30
  Sandinistas, as Reagan's obsession, 31
Nichols, W. P., 136
NICs (newly industrialising countries), 144
NIEO, 48, 64, 66, 74
Nixon, R. M., 22–4, 27–8, 46, 56, 74, 117
  Doctrine, 24
  nationalism, 46
  'shocks', 22–3
Nixon Administration
  abandons Atlantic multilateralism, 64

New Economic Policy, 23
Noel, A., 135
North Atlantic Treaty, 157
Norway, 182
Nowell Smith, G., 135, 210
nuclear threshold, 173, 174
nuclear weapons, 9, 15, 20, 24–7, 31, 35, 41, 50, 171 ff., 179–80, 184, 193, 197 ff.
  freeze, 95
  NFU ('no-first-use' of nuclear weapons doctrine), 173
  non-proliferation, 24
  as political symbols, 158–9
  and public opinion in Europe, 175
  see also ABM; INF; NATO; neutron bomb; SALT
Nunn Amendment, 96
  see also Mansfieldism

Odell, P., 58
OECD (Organisation for Economic Co-operation and Development), 47, 77, 89, 93, 129, 148, 150, 184, 186, 194
  foreign investment and domestic savings, 147
office systems, 189
Ogaden, 165
Ognev, A., 86
Ohmae, K., 80, 86
  Triad Power, 79
oil
  Arab embargo, 23, 64
  oil companies, 23–4
  price fall in, and North–South relations, 84
Olivetti Corporation (Italy), 73
Olympic Games, 26
OPEC (Organisation of Petroleum Exporting Countries), 66, 74
Orientalism, 209
Ostpolitik, 24, 160
Ottawa Summit, 76, 92
Oye, K., 109

Paarlberg, D., 135
Paarlberg, R., 136
Pacific Basin, 2, 36
Pacific Region, 4, 51, 113
pacifism, 207–8
Packard, D., 81
Palestinian factor, 99–100
Palmer, J., 39, 110
  Europe Without America, xiii, 107–8
Parboni, R., 13, 84, 134
Pargesa, Inc. (Belgium), 73
Paribas bank (France), 71
Parkansky, A. B., 60
Parkhalina, T., 59

Parkinson, C., 67
Parrott, B., 59
peace
  movements, Europe, 10, 95, 207
  'through strength', 31
Pentagon
  capitalism, 15, 32, 80–2
  mismanagement, 81
  see also USA, military policy
Percy, C., 76
Perestroika, 11, 41
Perle, R., 28, 74, 76
Perry, G. L., 135
Pershing 1A missiles, 174
Pershing II missiles, 25, 35, 156, 158, 162, 171, 175
Persian Gulf, 102–3, 106, 166
  cease-fire, 103
  US naval presence, and miscalculation, 102–3
Petersen, N., 178
Petit, R., 137
Petrov, N., 59
Pevzner, Y., 59
Phelps, E. S., 135
Philippines, 202
Phillips, S., 193
Pickens, T. Boone Jr., 71
Pierre, A., 38
Pijl, K. van der, 8, 10, 13, 23, 58, 84, 85, 86, 108, 134, 135, 196
Pijpers, A., 110
Pinder, J., 13, 108
Piore, M., 85
Pipes, R., 69
Plato, 203
Plaza Agreement, 144–6
Plessey–Stromberg–Carlson (UK–US) (joint venture), 137
Podhoretz, N., 27–8, 38
Poland, 22, 72
  crisis, 76
  martial law, 22, 92
Pompidou, G., 23
Ponomareva, I., 60
post-Atlanticism, 207 ff.
post-Cold War Internationalism (post-CWI), 16
post-colonial dependency of Third World, 205
post-war consensus, 202
power
  discourse of, 199–200
  and identity, 209
  of internationally mobile capital, 33
  /knowledge, 200
  of markets, 33
  as preponderance, 114
  projection and Western strategy, 197 ff.

  see also hegemony
power centre theory, 6, 44–5
Pratt and Whitney Inc. (USA), 80
Pridham, K., 61
product cycle theory, 79
production, 7, 12, 18–19, 37, 41, 46–50, 52, 152, 184–5, 187, 190
  and class fractions, 63
  international deployment of productive capital, 79
  internationalisation of, 49
  and markets, now fail to coincide, 65
  socialisation of, 47
productivity, 19, 22, 38, 188 ff.
  and EUREKA, 188
  politics of productivity, 19
  tendency to even out across nations, 45
profit-distribution process, 66, 70–2
  and new forms of enrichment, 72
Propaganda Due (P2), 67
Proudhon, Pierre Joseph, 3
Proxmire, W., 170, 178
PTTs (Post Telegraph and Telephone Corporations/Ministries), 127 ff.
Pryce, R., 13
public goods, 5, 138

R&D see research and development
RACE (Research and Development in Advanced Communications Technologies for Europe Programme), 128, 187, 189–90
racial conflict, 206
Rambo, 72
Rambouillet Summit, 64
RAND Corporation (USA), 74, 200
Rapacki Plan, 205
Rapid Deployment Force, 205
Reagan Administration, xi, 1, 75 ff., 99 ff., 104, 168, 171, 173
  agriculture, 123, 124
  arms build up, 76, 167
  bellicosity towards USSR, 9
  communist regimes, 28
  covert networks, 82
  debt crisis, 75
  economic liberalism, contradictions, 151
  and European technology policy, 55
  and New Right bloc, 75–7
  R&D, 80
  Reagan 'shocks', 159
  shift in economic policy, 33
  shift towards post-CWI, 35
  'strategic consensus' in Middle East, 100
  strategic legacy of, 176–7
  and telecommunications, 126
  as threat, 164
  Trilateral faction, 78
Reagan boom, 33

224 INDEX

Reagan Doctrine, 99
Reagan Plan, for Middle East, 100
Reagan, Ronald, 1, 8–9, 14–17, 22–3, 26–35 *passim*, 39–42 *passim*, 55–6, 60–1, 132, 141–3, 148, 151, 154, 163, 166, 168, 169, 172, 179–82, 190, 193, 195
  manicheanism, 27
  policy perspective, 16–17
  rejection of thesis of liberal internationalists, 32
  strategic vision, 28 ff.
  world view, 166
  vigilantism, 27
Reaganism, 8, 23, 26 ff., 74, 90, 99, 106, 108
  as anachronism, 15
  and Atlanticism, 26
  and collapse of post-war consensus, 34
  and Europe, 106
  old hegemonic habits revive, 142
Reaganomics, 31 ff.
realism, 45, 196 ff.
  see also neo-realism
Realpolitik, 5, 11, 22
Red Army Faction (West Germany), 68
Regan, D., 74, 83
regulation, 47–9, 59
  of banking, 126
  intensive regime of accumulation, 115
  international, 49
  see also deregulation
regulation school, 115
Rehfeldt, U., 86
Reilly, J. E., 38
rentier interests, 63, 67, 70–1, 74, 79
Republican Party (Italy), 67
Republican Party (USA), 26–7, 149
  1988 Platform, 154
  see also Nixon; Ford, G.; Reagan
research and development (R&D), 28, 48, 51–5, 179 ff.
  civilian versus military distinction, 191
  European Parliament's socio-economic criteria, 192
  Europeanisation of, diminishing, 191
  infrastructure, 187
  international co-operation in, 48
  as 'nerve of inter-imperialist rivalry', 52
  see also EUREKA; ESPRIT; RACE; SDI
Revel, A., 136
reverse linkage, 166
Reviglio, E., 84
Reykjavik Summit, 9, 167, 173, 201
Richie, M., 136
Rimboud, C., 136
Ristau, K., 136
Roberts, P. Craig, 155
robotisation, and slavery, 72
Rockefeller, David, 16, 64
Rockwell Inc. (USA), 80
Rocky, 72
Rogers, J., 86
Rogers, P., 110
Roman empire, 3–4
Roobeck, A., 193
Roper, J., 195
Rosenau, J., 15, 16–17, 37–8
Rostow, W. W., 202, 211
Rothschild, E., 136
Rougemont, D. de, 3, 12
Rowthorn, B., 134
Roy, A., 85
Royal Belge Insurance (Belgium), 73
Royal Institute of International Affairs (UK), 200
Ruggie, J. G., 38, 150, 155
Ruquist, R., 177
Russett, B., 135
Russia, 3–4, 22, 28, 61
  see also USSR

Sabel, C. F., 85
SACEUR (NATO Supreme Allied Command for Europe), 173
Saint-Gobain Company (France), 78
SAIS (Johns Hopkins University, School of Advanced International Studies, USA), 194
SALT I (first Strategic Arms Limitation Treaty, 1972), 160
SALT II (second, unratified Strategic Arms Limitation Treaty, 1978), 69, 160, 168
  rejected by Reagan, 94
  rejected by US Senate, 25
Sampson, A., 77–8
Sandinistas, 15, 31
Sartori, L., 109
Sauvant, K., 137
Sawyer, G., 82
SBKKVs (Space-Based Kinetic Kill Vehicles), 169
Scaife, R., 69
Schaetzel, J. R., 13
Scheer, R., 85
Schleyer, H.-M., 68
Schlotter, P., 194
Schlumberger, G., 73
Schlumberger Group (France–USA), 78
  support for French Socialist Party, 73
Schmidt, H., 76, 77, 203, 211
Schmidt government (West Germany), falls, 69
Schnieder Inc. (France), 73
Schumacher, E., 110
Schwartz, D., 177

INDEX 225

Schwartz, M., 58
scientific and technological revolution, 47 ff.
Scottish Highlanders, 209
SDI (Strategic Defense Initiative or Star Wars), xii, 9, 27–8, 30–1, 35, 53–5, 82, 96–7, 129, 156, 168, 205, 179, 180–4, 186–8, 191–4
  agreements signed with allies, 182
  leaks, 183
  changes in form since inception, 169
  effectiveness of, 170
  and European defence identity, 97
  'four points' of Mrs Thatcher concerning SDI, 179–80
  and Germany, 171
  impact on US assessment of its alliances, 171
  and military R&D, 181
  military spin-offs, 184
  research contracts, 170, 182
  and technological revolution, 184
  and UK, 171
SDIO (Strategic Defense Initiative Organisation), 169, 180–2, 187, 192
SDP (Social Democratic Party (West Germany)), 205
SDRs (special drawing rights of IMF), 117
Securities and Exchange Commission (SEC) of USA, 82
Segal, G., 55, 61
Seitz, K., 181, 193
Senegal, 205
Serfaty, S., 109
Servan-Schrieber, J.-J., 134
services, 111
  definition of, 125
  and economic development, 125 ff.
  and foreign direct investment, 126
  and international trade, 126 ff.
  and world GNP, 130
Seydoux, R., 73
Shad, J., 74
Shapiro, A., 59
Shapiro, M., 210
Sharp, J., 110
Sharp, M., 193–4
Shaw, A., xiv
Shearman, C., 193–4
Shearman, P., 110
Shell–BP (Netherlands–UK), 24
Sheridan Smith, A. M., 209–10
Shevardnadze, E., 40, 57, 61
Shiryaev, Y., 59
Shiskov, Y., 49, 51, 59–61
Shmelev, N., 59–60
Shonfield, Sir Andrew, 13
Shoup, L., 38
Shultz, G., 30, 77, 81

Siberian gas pipeline, 22, 30, 76
Siegfried, A., 3
Sigal, L., 177, 178
Simes, D., 28, 39
Single European Act see EC
Sivard, R. L., 211
sixth generation computers, 188
Smirnova, N., 60
Smith, G. C., 20
Smith, M., xiv, 30, 39, 88, 108–10, 193
Smith, Steve, xiv, 9, 30, 35, 177, 178, 193, 209
Smith, W. French, 75
social democratic form of legitimation, 119
socialist parties, and new tycoons of Southern Europe, 73
Socialist Party (France), 76–7
  Rocardist Wing, 78
  support from Schlumberger Group, 73
Socialist Party (Spain), 201
Sodaro, R., 44, 58
Sorel, G., 3
Sorenson, T., 26, 38, 134
South America, and Western Europe, 104
Soviet–American dialogue
  as problem for Europe, 97
  see also Cold War; INF; SALT; USA–USSR
Soviet intervention, Afghanistan, 25
Soviet threat, perception of, 21, 165–6, 209
Soviet Union see USSR
Spath, L., 69
Spencer, E., 81
Spengler, Oswald, 3, 4
Spinardi, G., 177
Sprinkel, B., 74, 83
SS20 missiles, 163, 171
START (Strategic Arms Reduction Talks), 167
Stanford University (USA), 17
State
  -civil society as 'organic whole', 64
  inter-state regulation, 49
  nightwatchman, 63
  sovereignty, 6, 147
Statz, A., 194
Sté Croix, G. E. M. de, 5, 12
Steltzer, I., 155
Stent, A., 109
Stern, J., 58
Strange, S., 12, 134, 135, 152, 155
strategy
  and bipolarity, 156
  a critique of, 197 ff.
  structural forces in, 156
Strauss, F.-J., 69
Suez crisis, 19
supply-side economics, xii, 32, 141

supply-side economics *(continued)*
  see also markets; liberalisation; neo-liberalism; Reagan Administration; USA: economic policy, general
Suzuki Corporation (Japan), 79
Syria, 101
Switzerland, 145

Taiwan, 206
Talbot-Poissy (France) rationalisation, 78
Talbott, S., 177
Taylor, T., 109
TC (Trilateral Commission), 8, 16, 36, 39, 48, 64, 81, 112, 119, 163
  meeting in Madrid, 83
  see also trilateralism
technocracy and global civilisation, 196–7
technoculture, of power projection, 205
technological revolution
  and jobs, 185
  Soviet views on, 51–9 *passim*
telecommunications, 111, 126–7
  and digital computers, 127
  infrastructures in Europe, 191
Teller, E., 82
terrorism, 68, 209
  different definitions, 101
Thatcher, M., 8, 11, 35, 67, 77, 151–2, 166, 168, 179–80
  'four points' concerning SDI, 180
  meeting with Reagan, 179
  see also UK
Thayer, P., 81–2
The Times, 42
Third World
  agricultural producers, 125
  and extended deterrence, 205
Thompson, E. P., 193
Thucydides, 5, 198
Thurow, L., 47, 59
Tirman, J., 177
TNCs (transnational companies), 44–6, 54, 116
  European, 50
  as progressive force, 48
  takeovers, joint ventures, 51
  Third World, 142
  transfer-pricing, 140
  see also capital; classes; money; production
Toqueville, A. de, 3
Toronto Summit, 132
Toshiba Corporation (Japan), export of computers and machine tools to USSR, 182
Toynbee, A., 3–4, 12
Toyota Corporation (Japan), 79
Tracy, M., 135, 136

trade, 7, 19, 24, 28–30, 33–4, 39–41, 47, 50, 52, 120–30 *passim*, 139–48 *passim*, 152–5, 181–3, 185, 194
transatlantic economic internationalism, 149–50
transatlantic hegemony, 115–16
transnational corporations see TNCs
transnationalisation, 151
  and foreign investment, 142
triad power, 79
Triffin, R., 135
Triffin paradox, 117
trilateralism, 63 ff.
  class alignment disintegrates, 65
  demise of, 64 ff.
  resurrected and readjusted, 79–81
  and unilateralism, 78
  see also TC
Tripoli, bombing of, 31, 101
Truman Administration, 20
Truman Doctrine, 202
TRW Inc. (USA), 74
Tsoukalis, L., 155
Tucker, R., 29–30
Tulder, R. van, 193
Turner, Ted, 71

UAW (United Auto Workers of USA), 70
UK, 70, 120, 140, 183, 190, 194, 203
  EMS after Thatcher, 152
  and Germany, 183
  imperial preference system, 17, 18
  Labour Party's defence policy, 164
  privatisation, 70
  US relations under strain, 30
  see also Thatcher
Ulam, A., 55, 61
ultra-imperialism, 113
UNCTAD (United Nations Conference on Trade and Development), 137
Unger, F., 209, 211
unilateralism, 3–4, 64 ff., 78 ff., 166 ff.
Unilever PLC (Netherlands–UK), 84
unions
  defensiveness of, 34
  power reduced, 151
United Nations, 16, 66, 103, 104
United Technologies Inc., 74
Uruguay, 152
USA
  asymmetry of power *vis-à-vis* Europe, 112
  and Canada, 36
  Communications Act, 127
  confrontationism, 166
  Department of Commerce, 126
  economic policy, finance and money

USA *(continued)*
  dollar: 'benign neglect' of, 118; devaluation, 146; international role, 146; leadership and primacy of dollar, 145; 'malign neglect' of, 152; overhang, 117; strengthens, 153; yen–dollar pact, 147
  and EC protection, 133
  foreign investment and domestic savings, 147
  Glass–Steagall Act, 133
  Mexico debt retirement plan, 149
  monetary policies, 118, 141
  pyramid of credit and debt, xii
  tactics, 52
  towards WTO, 52
  economic policy, general
    as alchemy, xii
    balance of payments, 117
    bilateralism, tendency towards, in trade, 36
    boom, Reagan years, xiii, 33–4, 141, 185
    budget deficit, 35, 83, 143, 146, 148: debt servicing, 153
    centrality (in world political economy) as double-edged sword, 107: reasserted, 34, 78
    and co-operation, 145 ff.
    'domesticism', 118, 143
    extra-territorial imposition of own laws, 2
    industrial competitiveness, 119
    macro-economic, xii, 120
    mercantilism, 17
    stake in international financial markets, 70
    sucks in capital, 33, 52, 76
    time horizons, 7
    US–German conflicts, 24
  economic policy, trade
    high-technology trade balances, 80
    protectionism, 33, 143
    Special Trade Representative, 126
    Trade Act, 126
    Trade Agreements Act, 126
    Trade and Tariff Act, 126
  economy, general
    advantages of, 14, 52–3, 141–2
    agriculture policy, 130: Farm Bill, 124, 125; farmers export incomes, 130; grain embargo, 123; 'green power', 123, 132
    decline of 'rustbelt', 25
    internationalisation of economy, 34
    as locomotive for European export interests, 7
    productivity, 119
    market shares in Europe, 117
  relative self-sufficiency in oil, 24
  hegemony, 114–17
    changing face of, 114
    consensual form, 19
    decadence, 14
    decline, 45, 116–17
    on the cheap, 24
    as key problem of world politics, 198
    and loss of Alliance leadership, 199
    military, fear of loss, 163
    and NATO, 156
    reasserted, 53
  images of Europe, 21 ff.
  isolationism, 20 ff.
  Japan *see* Japan
  liberal internationalists, 16–17
    internationalism now fading, 138
    see also trilateralism
  military policy
    arms control, 168
    bases in Europe and public opinion, 172
    build up under Reagan, 32
    commitments to Europe, 9
    debate over policy towards USSR, 29–30
    and extended deterrence, 162
    ICBMs (Inter-Continental Ballistic Missiles), 165
    interventionism, xi–xii, 202
    military–industrial complex, 74, 203
    MX missile, 167
    nuclear monopoly now lost, 160
    nuclear war-fighting capability, 167
    nuclear warheads – number in Europe, 160
    'peace through strength', 17
    reining back of, 81, 151
    see also ABM; INF; SALT; SDI
  nationalism, 118
  perceptions
    bedrock of, 15
    and political crisis, 17
    'politics of contraction', 17
    of relative decline, 14
    of USSR as illegitimate power, 165
  power
    contradictory nature of, 118
    remobilisation of global power, 15
    resurgent, 166
    see also under USA, hegemony
  telecommunications, 127
  unilateralism, 118, 138
  and USSR, 165
    as 'evil empire', 158
  US–USSR relations
    Geneva summit, 31, 97
    Reykjavik summit, xii, 9, 57, 97–8, 167, 173, 201

US–USSR relations *(continued)*
  tensions diminish, 35
  see also Cold War; INF; nuclear weapons; SALT
US Information Agency, 28
US National Academy of Sciences Report on COCOM, 182
US Office of Innovative Science and Technology, 180
US Shadow Open Market Committee, 66, 70
USSR, 2, 10, 11, 31 ff., 66, 167 ff., 201
  concern at west European defence co-operation, 56
  in crisis, 10–12
  cultivation of West Germany, 42
  Europe, views on
    integration, 49
    new emphasis on Europe, 41 ff.
  Europeanist tendency in Soviet leadership, 56–7
  ICBMs, 167
  'new thinking', 11, 40–1, 57
  opponents of readjustment away from US–USSR bilateralism, 57
  restructures foreign policy apparatus, 40
  and SDI, 53 ff.
  SS20s, 162, 167
  technology, 41
  theories of Atlantic relations, 42 ff.
  as threat to NATO, 158
UTA Corporation (France), 73

Valéry, P., 3
  The Crisis of the Mind, xiii
Varga, E., 46
Venice Declaration of EC, 105
Venvander, H., 137
Versailles Summit, 76, 93
VHSIC (very high-speed integrated circuits), 181, 184
  and DARPA programme, 192
Vietnam, 22
VLSI (very large-scale integrated circuits), 184
Vogel, H.-J., 68
Volcker, P. A., 18, 70, 83
Vorontsov, G. A., 59, 61
Vtorov, A., 60–1

Walker, R. B. J., 210–11
Wall Street Crash (October 1987), xii, 16, 34, 35, 139
Wallerstein, I., 108–9, 134
Walter, D., 177
Waltz, K., 5, 12
Warburgs Bank, 73
Warnke, P., 69
Warsaw Pact (WTO), 11, 174, 206
  as counter-modernism, 208
Watson, T., 81
Watt, D., 109
Weber, M., 198, 210
Wehrtechnik, 183–4
Weimar Republic, 150
Weinberger, C., 39, 46, 82, 180, 193
Weiner, N., 72
Welfarism, 11, 18–19, 37, 141, 150
West European Union (WEU) 50, 96, 98
Wick, C., 28
Wilkinson, P., 110
Willets, P., 108
Williams, P., 58, 110
Witte, W., 134
Wolf, M., 13
Wolfe, A., 38
Wolfe, E. R., 211
Woolcock, S., 109, 137
World Bank, 16, 145, 148–9, 201
World systems theory, 4
Wright Jr., G. V., 85
WTO *see* Warsaw Pact

Xenophobia, 23, 206

Yakovlev, A., 56, 59–61
Year of Europe, 89
Yochelson, J. N., 134
Yom Kippur War, 23, 139, 165
Young, A., 69
Yudanov, Y., 60, 61
yuppies, 10

Zimenkov, R. I., 60
Zimmerman, W., 59